D1557967

Inauthentic Culture and Its Philosophical Critics

Despite the pervasive feeling that much of the culture of Western democracies has increasingly become inauthentic or phoney, contemporary cultural critics and observers have paid little attention to the traditional philosophical criticism of inauthentic culture that began with Socrates. Aristophanes, and Plato and was applied, reworked, and extended by such philosophical cultural critics as St Augustine, Erasmus, Voltaire, Nietzsche, and Thorstein Veblen. This new study in the philosophy of culture and the history of ideas illuminates the problem of inauthentic culture and draws on the insights of major figures from the Western intellectual tradition to show that our contemporary problem is actually an old and enduring one.

Jay Newman puts the contemporary problem of inauthentic culture into philosophical and historical context. He then goes on to show how traditional philosophical criticism of inauthentic culture can help us understand many disturbing aspects of such contemporary cultural phenomena as television and public relations, as well as contemporary forms of craftsmanship, democracy, and the academy.

Inauthentic Culture and Its Philosophical Critics will be of great interest to all those concerned with philosophy, cultural theory, and the enduring problem of cultural decline.

JAY NEWMAN is professor of philosophy, University of Guelph.

INAUTHENTIC CULTURE AND
ITS PHILOSOPHICAL CRITICS

JAY NEWMAN

McGill-Queen's University Press
Montreal & Kingston • London • Buffalo

ISBN 0-7735-1676-x (cloth)
ISBN 0-7735-1691-3 (paper)

Legal deposit fourth quarter 1997
Bibliothèque nationale du Québec

Printed in Canada on acid-free paper

This book has been published with the help
of a grant from the Humanities and Social
Sciences Federation of Canada, using funds
provided by the Social Sciences and
Humanities Research Council of Canada.

McGill-Queen's University Press
acknowledges the support received for its
publishing program from the Canada
Council's Block Grants program.

Canadian Cataloguing in Publication Data
Newman, Jay, 1948–
Inauthentic culture and
its philosophical critics
Includes bibliographical references and index.
ISBN 0-7735-1676-x (bound). –
ISBN 0-7735-1691-3 (pbk.)
1. Culture – Philosophy – History.
2. Civilization, Western – Philosophy. I. Title.
CB151.N48 1997   306'.01   C97-900717-8

Typeset in Minion 10.5/13 by Caractéra inc.,
Quebec City.

To the memory of Kitty

a good soul and almost
the best mother a son could have

CONTENTS

ACKNOWLEDGMENTS

I am grateful to the Social Sciences and Humanities Research Council of Canada for facilitating my research and writing with a research grant for the period 1991–94. I am also grateful to Philip Cercone, Joan McGilvray, and John Parry of McGill-Queen's University Press for their generous attention to the manuscript and their kindness to the author.

My mother, Kate Rothbaum Newman, passed away on 17 August 1996. She taught me, among many other fine things, to seek out the reality behind deceptive appearances, to try to derive more satisfaction from being helpful to others, and to be unafraid to speak up for what I believe in.

Inauthentic Culture and Its Philosophical Critics

1

INAUTHENTIC CULTURE AS
A SOCIAL AND PHILOSOPHICAL PROBLEM

Inauthentic culture is a problem of which many reflective people have been at least vaguely aware, though they have not agreed on a name for it. They have sensed that there is something "phoney" about certain cultural products, about some of the many things that human beings, individually and in groups, create or promote with the intention that those things may be appropriated by their fellow human beings. The problem of inauthentic culture is generally not as well understood as such other social issues as violence, poverty, and bigotry and in that sense is harder to deal with. Substantial harm has resulted from the general failure of reflective people to attain an adequate understanding of the inauthenticity of culture and a full appreciation of its pervasive influence.

In this inquiry, I seek to clarify the problem, and drawing on the insights of various thinkers in the Western intellectual tradition, I try to show that the problem is actually an old and enduring one that troubled even the ancients, from whom we can learn a great deal about it. Inauthentic culture does not admit of a complete remedy, but it can probably be managed with as much success as can most other enduring social problems.

This study is intended as a contribution to the philosophy of culture. What is said in the pages that follow is essentially philosophical and thus should not be interpreted or judged by the standards appropriate to social-scientific or non-philosophical humanistic inquiry. Sometimes I draw here on relevant insights of social scientists, theologians, and other writers who illuminate the philosophical issues being addressed, but we are concerned with their work only as it relates to a philosophical understanding of the matters at hand.

The expression "philosophy of culture" may strike some readers as a bit strange, for in the English-speaking world this discipline has rarely been the major field of inquiry that it has long been in continental Europe. Though there has been growing interest in "cultural theory" among philosophers in the English-speaking world, most anglophone philosophers are not as familiar as most of their continental European counterparts with the work of such thinkers as Vico, Herder, Nietzsche, Dilthey, Spengler, Huizinga, Cassirer, and Ortega y Gasset.[1] Two of this century's most important philosophers of culture – Santayana and Collingwood – wrote in English and have maintained since their deaths a loyal following among small groups of English-language philosophers. Yet we may note, by way of example, that it was possible after the Second World War for a broad-minded American scholar such as John Wild to believe that he himself was coining the expression "philosophy of culture" and describing this possible branch of philosophy for the first time.[2] One only rarely finds a course entitled "philosophy of culture" listed in the catalogue of an English-Canadian, British, American, or Australian university.

However, even in the anglophone world, there has been a developing interest in what can be properly described as philosophy of culture. As the authors of a recent volume on such writers as Foucault and Habermas have observed, "Over the past century, four approaches to the study of culture have been pursued with growing interest and with some success ... Each is rooted in deeper philosophical traditions themselves quite distinct and in significant ways alien to the so-called 'positivist' tradition of contemporary social sciences. The first, and perhaps most familiar of these, is phenomenology; the second, cultural anthropology; the third, structuralism; and the fourth, critical theory."[3] There has yet to emerge a substantial body of literature in analytical philosophy of culture to complement the important work of analytical philosophers in such fields as philosophy of art, philosophy of science, and political philosophy, but recent events suggest that even in that domain some progress has been made.

It is a risky enterprise to try to define the scope of the philosophy of culture, for not only are philosophers notorious for disagreeing with one another about precisely what it is that they do, but the term *culture* is extraordinarily ambiguous.[4] Moreover, scholars who define "culture" often are not just trying to be helpful but are promoting some specific goals. In their detailed study of concepts and definitions of culture, the anthropologists Kroeber and Kluckhohn cited 164 definitions of culture; and the list could go on and on.[5] I hope that I make it clear below in what sense the philosophers whose work we are considering qualify as philosophers of culture. Moreover, as circumstances would have it, the greatest of all philosophers of culture happens to be also the greatest of all philosophers, and his most significant contribution to the philosophy of culture is to be found in his most influential work – a work familiar to most people seriously interested in Western philosophy. I refer to Plato's *Republic*, and it is indeed there that we find the classical analysis of inauthentic culture.

This inquiry begins with an informal consideration in this chapter of the problem of inauthentic culture as we encounter it in our own society and contemporary societies very much like our own. There follows a more precise analysis of inauthentic culture. I examine relevant issues concerning the nature of culture in chapters 2 and 3 and then consider at some length, in chapter 4, Plato's analysis of inauthentic culture. In chapters 5 and 6 we look at some later analyses of inauthentic culture that, though somewhat different from Plato's and from each other, still represent variations on the Platonic themes. I conclude the inquiry – chapter 7 – with another look at inauthenticity as it manifests itself in some important cultural products of our own age; and, applying some of the insights that we have gained from our examination of various texts, we finally consider practical measures that can be taken by individuals and groups to deal with the social problem of inauthentic culture.

For anyone interested in the philosophy of culture, the question inevitably arises as to how it is that the progressive culture of societies such as our own – with their highly developed and accessible religious, educational, artistic, political, and scientific institutions – could have allowed for the survival and even the growth of spiritual corruption. How is it that cultures that have been able to produce medical miracles, computer chips, and higher education for the poor have also brought with them so much anti-cultural rubbish that thoughtful people sometimes have been inclined to conclude that in many ways we people in "advanced" societies are living in dark times? There is no simple answer to such a question, and we may reasonably surmise that numerous factors are involved. In this inquiry we focus on one factor – what can be characterized, for the sake of convenience, as the "inauthenticity" of many cultural products.

"AUTHENTICITY" AND "INAUTHENTICITY" AS QUALITIES OF "CULTURAL PRODUCTS"

The terms *authenticity* and *inauthenticity* are not employed much in everyday conversation. They are used by certain critics of works of fine art, and they are favoured by certain devotees of existential philosophy; usually they seem to have a semi-technical significance. Still, anyone familiar with the not-very-technical adjectives "authentic" and "inauthentic" can grasp the non-technical significance of the related nouns. In everyday discourse, however, people normally choose less imposing terms to express their judgment that something is inauthentic. I have pointed to the term *phoney* as a fairly reliable substitute, and an inauthentic object, action, or institution might also be identified as "sham," "counterfeit," "fraudulent," "pretentious," "fake," "contrived," "feigned," "deceptive," or "artificial."

We would be neglecting interesting nuances if we regarded these terms as designating precisely the same quality, and each of them is also used in a variety of ways. But dictionary definitions confirm what our intuitions tell us – that these terms, in at least one major sense, all belong to the same family. A person or group of people involved in the creation or promotion of inauthentic objects, actions, or institutions might be described as "manipulative," "insincere," "dishonest," or "deceitful." These adjectives too belong to the same family as, in at least one of their senses, such nouns as "manipulator," "operator," "schemer," "con artist," "seducer," and "promoter."

None of my three lists is complete, but when I talk about the "inauthenticity" of certain cultural products and the moral failings of some of the people who participate in their creation and promotion, I have in mind these families of terms – and one large, extended family – and the closely related qualities that they often designate.

When we characterize a cultural product as inauthentic, we ordinarily associate its inauthenticity with some questionable motive or attitude of the individual or group that is promoting it. We may even want to regard the creators or promoters as themselves inauthentic. In any case, we would not ordinarily ascribe inauthenticity to a cultural product if we did not want to make some point about the questionable character and motivation of the principal producers or exploiters of the product. Cultural products, unlike natural phenomena as such, are human creations, and we usually regard them as inauthentic or authentic in relation to a judgment that we form about the human agents who have created or promoted them. The term *authentic* is sometimes used in a purely descriptive way, but when one scrutinizes closely the various members of the extended family of terms indicated above, including *authentic*, one sees that ordinarily the kind of falseness or unreality designated by them is closely related somehow to moral concerns.

Consider a few simple examples. Take first the case in which someone distinguishes an authentic Rembrandt painting from an inauthentic one. The point being made is not that one of the two paintings is literally unreal (in the sense of not existing); nor is it likely that the person distinguishing the two works is challenging Rembrandt's integrity at the time that he created one of the works. What is more probably happening is that the factual judgment is being made that one of the paintings was painted by Rembrandt, while the other was not. However, more may be happening here than initially meets the eye. The factual judgment may be being combined with a questioning of the integrity or motives of those who, for one reason or other (probably involving money or prestige), stand to benefit from convincing others that the painting in question was created by Rembrandt.

If someone were to announce to us at a meeting of some group to which we belong: "This is a phoney organization," she would not be asserting that the society is unreal in the sense of not existing. The organization truly exists, and it is what it is – nothing more and nothing less. But by characterizing it as "phoney," she is letting us know that in her view it is not what the people who control it, or perhaps even the people who founded it, would like us to believe that it is. Rather, in her view, these people, out of any of a number of questionable motives, have deceived people inside and outside of the organization into believing that the organization is something that it really is not. They have deceived and manipulated people in order to promote their own narrow personal interests or their own secret social aims.

If someone asserts that a certain politician's rhetoric at last night's political debate was inauthentic, phoney, or contrived, he probably means that the speech that the politician produced, while ostensibly lofty in spirit, was not what it was disguised as by this clever, somewhat unscrupulous fellow. Rather, it was a device by which the politician could manipulate his listeners so as to promote his own political and personal interests.

People do sometimes use the term *authentic* to describe a natural phenomenon, so that a professor of palaeontology would not be torturing ordinary language if he were to announce to his students on a field trip: "Here we find an authentic trilobite." By using the term here, he would mean that though students often mistake other things for trilobites, the object to which he is pointing is the real thing. There is a corresponding use of the term *authentic* with reference to cultural products, so that an art historian might appropriately describe a certain painting of Rembrandt's as authentic simply because she was aware that people often innocently mistake many works for those of Rembrandt. However, this essentially descriptive use of the term *authentic* is not meant to indicate the kind of authenticity that is ordinarily contrasted with the quality of being inauthentic. When we are concerned with the relative authenticity and inauthenticity of cultural products, we nearly always have in mind the relative integrity of the producers or promoters of the products, and we are concerned with why and how those people see it as in their interest (as well as perhaps ours) to accept the products in precisely the spirit in which they would like (or would have liked) us to accept them.

When I refer here to "cultural products," I am thinking not only of such products of high culture as paintings and operas but of all things, including non-material, that people create or promote that are in some way appropriated or taken up, or meant to be appropriated or taken up, by other human beings. In this sense, cultural products are to be contrasted both with natural phenomena as such and with those human products that are not shared or meant to be shared by other people. The class of cultural products is to be seen here as including not only works of fine art but creations in the spheres of industrial art and technology, philosophical and historical explanation, religion, science, social work, politics, economics and business, and education. Though the term *products* may immediately bring to mind material objects, it is appropriate to regard as cultural products ideas and theories, modes of perception and action, techniques and methods, services, rites and customs, and institutions. These things are all "produced" in some sense by human beings and can be appropriated or taken up by others in some manner. This way of characterizing cultural products is imprecise and unscientific, but it does seem to me to capture the spirit of an important popular usage of the terms *culture* and *cultural*, and it is helpful for explaining the social problem that concerns us. Still, in chapters 2 and 3 I take a closer look at the category of culture, for certain philosophical and scientific disputes about the nature of culture are relevant to our investigation.

Whether one has in mind a cultural product that has come to mark the way of life of a large community or simply one produced by an obscure, isolated individual that is not entirely forgotten or inaccessible, one will ordinarily not have much trouble distinguishing a cultural phenomenon from a natural phenomenon as such. Of course, human beings themselves constitute a part of nature, as do the things that they produce, promote, and take up in some way; and we live in an age in which it has been fashionable in some circles to give reductionistic, naturalistic explanations of human phenomena. One of the main objectives of traditional humanistic philosophy of culture has been to establish the special distinctiveness of human beings and their creations and to explain the inappropriateness of treating human phenomena as if they were nothing more than natural phenomena. But even without the aid of some humanistic philosophy of culture, most of us find it simple and useful to distinguish on some level between such natural phenomena as rocks and bananas and such human creations as statues and banana splits. A natural phenomenon as such cannot be inauthentic or phoney, and it cannot have the kind of authenticity that we contrast with inauthenticity.

A useful feature of most scientific definitions of culture is that they draw our attention to the significance of a cultural product as something that is shared or meant to be shared by human beings. An individual can create something exclusively for herself and without any intention to share the product with anyone else; though a human creation, that product would not come to be regarded as a cultural product unless it came in time to be shared in some way by other people. Most people do want others to appropriate or take up in some way some of the things that they have created or adopted; to contribute in some way to the various groups and communities to which they belong gives people an enhanced sense of dignity and importance.

It is not always illuminating to think of the human person as a social animal, but human beings are born into families, tribes, religious communities, political communities, and other groups; and they choose to be members of certain groups into which they were not born, and appropriately come to be regarded as members of certain groups to which they belong neither by birth nor by choice. All students of cultural theory see these facts as constituting one of the starting-points of their inquiry, though most place special emphasis on membership in firmly established groups. In the words of the anthropologist Malinowski, "The essential fact of culture as we live it and experience it, as we can observe it scientifically, is the organization of human beings into permanent groups. Such groups are related by some agreement, some traditional law or custom, something which corresponds to Rousseau's *contrat social*."[6] In determining their own worth and role, people consider their achievements in relation to the achievements, needs, and aspirations of their fellows in the various groups to which they belong, including humanity as a whole.

The terms *culture* and *cultured* sometimes offend certain people, who have correctly observed that such terms are often used for the drawing of cruel, invidious distinctions. Thus, when in the nineteenth century the celebrated aesthete Matthew Arnold set out to defend culture from its enemies, he recognized the necessity of declaring: "The culture which is supposed to plume itself on a smattering of Greek and Latin is a culture which is begotten by nothing so intellectual as curiosity; it is valued either out of sheer vanity and ignorance or else as an engine of social and class distinction, separating its holder, like a badge or title, from other people who have not got it. No serious man would call this *culture*, or attach any value to it, as culture, at all."[7] What Arnold has given us in these lines is a concise description of a certain paradigm of inauthentic or phoney culture, created by people who put on airs and cultivate mannerisms or skills solely as a way of establishing their superior refinement. These people have given the terms *culture* and *cultured* a regrettable association with snobbery, pretence, and ostentation.

Yet one should not have to feel ashamed to be regarded as cultured, nor should one have to apologize for pursuing culture as an end. There is a sense in which everyone is "cultured": we are all enculturated as a result of being born into, and raised in, various social groups or communities. Even the personality of the most radical individualist is substantially shaped by some of the cultural products of the groups into which she has been born. But in any given group, some people are more cultured than others, and not only in being more influenced by cultural products, or in the sense of having mastered the art of putting on airs. Some people are so by way of being more refined than others with respect to virtue or civility. When we consider the etymology of the term *culture*, we are reminded of its association with cultivation or tending. A cultured person is, in a positive sense, one who has tended to his personal improvement; he has worked hard at cultivating not airs but virtues. Others too, such as his parents, teachers, and religious leaders, have helped to cultivate in him sound values and dispositions, and this tending process, closely related to education, is carried on not only for his sake but for the good of various communities to which he will eventually be expected to make positive contributions.

Thus the term *culture* need not convey a notion of what snobs do to distinguish themselves from the common throng; it is all the more serviceable as designating that which distinguishes the person who has substantially cultivated good qualities. Now, no matter how hard one tries, one may not be able to get very far in the way of self-improvement, self-realization, or self-perfection if one is not gifted with able, high-minded teachers, yet sometimes the most disadvantaged people (and peoples) have managed to summon up the intelligence, compassion, and integrity necessary for attaining degrees of nobility and civility unmatched by the greatest that the more fortunate have managed to attain.

INAUTHENTICITY AS PERVASIVE

Typically, when describing a particular painting, political speech, sermon, or ritual as "phoney," "sham," or "pretentious," we mean to distinguish it from the common run of things of its kind, yet every so often one may be struck by the extent to which a large part of the dominant culture of one's community is riddled with inauthenticity. It is common nowadays to hear high-minded people complain that deception, pretence, ostentation, and all the other shades of inauthenticity have come to constitute the rule rather than the exception in social institutions. Many people now believe that hype and manipulation have become so dominant that they have replaced other institutions as marks of the cultures of advanced societies. Exasperated, some people make extreme generalizations, such as, "Everything nowadays is a matter of public relations," "There's a hidden agenda everywhere, and the almighty dollar is at the heart of it," and, "These days it's not what one knows but who one knows that really counts." While these maxims often apply, to embrace them without due consideration of the nobility in one's society is to have travelled too far along the road to cynicism and nihilism.

Nevertheless, when we move to the level of social criticism, we see that in an advanced society such as our own, we are not merely confronted with isolated cases of inauthenticity in aesthetic, intellectual, religious, and political fashion. We can detect patterns that indicate that the manipulativeness of those who see promotion of cultural products as little more than a matter of marketing has become so pervasive that the student of culture is now obliged to regard it as a key topic for investigation. Some of the most powerful criticisms of inauthentic culture in recent years have come from writers who are not ordinarily regarded as philosophers and seem in fact to be rather uninterested in the programs of philosophers. Many of these critics have focused their attention on U.S. culture, though what they have said about American culture substantially applies to the institutionalized cultural products of other advanced societies.

Christopher Lasch, in his study of the culture of narcissism in the United States, laments how, by the early part of this century, "The management of interpersonal relations came to be seen as the essence of self-advancement. The captain of industry gave way to the confidence man, the master of impressions. Young men were told that they had to sell themselves in order to succeed … Now success appeared as an end in its own right, the victory over your competitors that alone retained the capacity to instill a sense of self-approval."[8] The result is regrettable: "Plagued by anxiety, depression, vague discontents, a sense of inner emptiness, the 'psychological man' of the twentieth century seeks neither individual self-aggrandizement nor spiritual transcendence but peace of mind, under conditions that increasingly militate against it."[9] The literary scholar Henri Peyre also gives us a stark portrait of "a world that is more and more in danger of being surrendered to the half-lies of publicity, to the distortions of journalism, to a social pressure that curses the unhappy few who oppose atomic weapons, concentration camps, mass hysterics, the degeneration of religion into orthodoxy and into respect for money and for material and mental comfort; where artistic taste tends to be molded by a woeful underestimate of the so-called masses."[10] And F.G. Bailey observes: "It is astonishing how much patent falsehood there is in public life. This is an expression not of regret that people are dishonest but of surprise that politicians appear to get away with dishonesty so easily and so often. Is there not something strange about a culture such as ours which condemns lies but at the same time condones them with such categories as 'campaign promises' and 'mere rhetoric'?"[11]

In a similar spirit, Marshall McLuhan states in one of his early works: "Ours is the first age in which many thousands of the best-trained individual minds have made it a full-time business to get inside the collective public mind. To get inside in order to manipulate, exploit, control is the object now. And to generate heat not light is the intention. To keep everybody in the helpless state engendered by prolonged mental rutting is the effect of many ads and much entertainment alike."[12] "It is observable that the more illusion and falsehood needed to maintain any given state of affairs, the more tyranny is needed to maintain the illusion and falsehood. Today the tyrant rules not by club or fist, but, disguised as a market researcher, he shepherds his flocks in the way of utility and comfort."[13] Not long after McLuhan wrote these words, the earnest popular writer Vance Packard warned fellow citizens about "the large-scale efforts being made, often with impressive success, to channel our unthinking habits, our purchasing decisions, and our thought processes by the use of insights gleaned from psychiatry and the social sciences ... The result is that many of us are being influenced and manipulated, far more than we realize, in the patterns of our everyday lives."[14] The "professional persuaders" who constantly seek "more effective ways to sell us their wares – whether products, ideas, attitudes, candidates, goals, or states of mind"[15] – are involved in an effort to "manipulate our habits and choices in their favor."[16]

Much criticism of inauthentic culture in advanced societies has come from critics of the ideological materialism underlying those nations' political and economic institutions. Herbert I. Schiller complains: "Where manipulation is the principal means of social control, as it is in the United States, the articulation and refinement of manipulative techniques take precedence over intellectual activities. In accordance with market principles, therefore, manipulative work attracts the keenest talent because it offers the system's richest incentives."[17] Schiller focuses on control of the informational and ideational apparatus at all levels:[18] "The content and form of American communications – the myths and the means of transmitting them – are devoted to manipulation. When successfully employed, as they invariably are, the result is individual passivity, a state of inertia that precludes action ... Passivity feeds upon itself, destroying the capacity for social action that might change the conditions that presently limit human fulfillment."[19] Arnold Itwaru makes a related point: "The obsession with being entertained, being placated, is the panic of the diminished self within the devouring immensity of exploitative control. It is a retreat, a seemingly safe detour which falsifies escape in ruses of distraction."[20]

A theme underlying much of this criticism of inauthentic culture is that people need to be made aware of the cultural rubbish being served up to them and often imposed on them by clever, self-serving schemers. As Packard has written, "We cannot be too seriously manipulated if we know what is going on."[21] But there is another, quite different theme in much recent criticism – that people are often all *too* aware of their vulnerability to constant manipulation and that this awareness has led to forms of cynicism that are in their own way as dangerous as the more direct influences of cultural manipulation. C. Wright Mills observes in *The Power Elite*: "All this is sensed by enough people below the higher circles to lead to cynical views of the lack of connection between merit and nobility, between virtue and success. It is a sense of the immorality of accomplishment, and it is revealed in the prevalence of such views as: 'it's all just another racket,' and 'it's not what you know but who you know.' Considerable numbers of people now accept the immorality of accomplishment as a going fact."[22] Arthur Asa Berger, a student of popular culture, tells us: "It has been reported that many people in America, at the age of nine or ten, discover that the commercials which they had trusted previously are full of lies. This leads to cynicism and a strong sense of betrayal. The children then transfer this cynicism from the television commercials to the institutions of society at large, their parents, adults in general, and so on. Cynicism, which the dictionary defines as '[being] contemptuously distrustful of human nature and motives' is a corrosive element which poisons individuals and societies. The children learn, often from experience, to develop defenses which they believe will protect them from being manipulated and exploited."[23]

Paul Blumberg, who reports that recent opinion research reveals "a widespread climate of public distrust and even cynicism toward major institutions in American life,"[24] acknowledges that some of this distrust may be "a form of 'ritualized cynicism,' a response based on the feelings that cynicism is a more sophisticated attitude than exuberant faith or trust,"[25] but he adds that "if it were no more than that, cynicism would be expressed toward all institutions equally across the board. But this is not so; the public clearly expresses more confidence in some institutions than in others."[26]

Blumberg offers the striking example of how, in June 1970, the Knight newspaper chain in the United States conducted an informal survey which revealed that a large minority of persons actually believed that the U.S. moon landing had been faked to deceive the Russians or the Chinese, or to justify the space agency's budget, or simply to make people forget their troubles.[27] Blumberg concludes: "This is a rather extreme form of cynicism, but it actually reveals the strong predisposition of Americans to believe that much of what happens in the public arena is rigged, faked, exaggerated, passed off for what it isn't – whether in the marketplace, on T.V., in the White House, in Congress, or on the Campaign trail. It is no accident, as Marxists are wont to say, that two recent and now widely used additions to the American vocabulary are the words 'hype' and 'scam.'"[28]

There is, to be sure, a certain amount of overstatement to be found in some of the comments of the social critics just surveyed; and perhaps to some extent we have been exposed here to the unseemly whining of self-righteous ideologues. Still, if one feels inclined to make a negative assessment of the general culture of contemporary Western and Western-style democracies, there is plenty of grist for the mill, and it is in passing judgment on the cultural products themselves that we come to appreciate fully the price to be paid for allowing manipulators, schemers, and operators to have their way. Thus, even those who have managed to "understand" contemporary painting may well be given to wondering what happened to the craftsmanship, discipline, and sensitivity of the great masters of the past. For many people it is barely possible to pass by the sculptures in the lobbies of public and commercial buildings without reflecting on how shoddy they are in comparison with the sculptures created by the ancients. Most of us long ago abandoned hope of witnessing the emergence of another dramatist of the stature of Aeschylus, Shakespeare, or Molière. The airwaves are filled now less with the products of genuine composers than with the often-deafening noise created by less disciplined creators and promoted by recording studio executives. The vision and craftsmanship that sometimes gave rise to the great public and religious buildings of the ancient and medieval worlds have largely been replaced by a sensibility that has given rise to many cold and ugly edifices of concrete, glass, and steel, from which so many of us are ever eager to escape.

We also see how industrialists have been allowed to destroy serene places of natural and cultural beauty and to pollute much of the air we breathe and the water we drink. Politicians have come to be casually accepted as professional liars, thieves, and demagogues, so that even revelations of widespread corruption in the highest offices of state no longer shock most of us. And the religious leaders to whom our ancestors almost instinctively turned for guidance and inspiration seem to an alarming extent to have lost their faith and to have been reduced to the utterance of maxims and incantations that have no meaning to them. Worse yet, many so-called religious leaders are outright imposters and "con artists," and recognition of their hypocrisy has sometimes driven confused idealists into cults led by charlatans and crackpots.

Instead of making available philosophy, theology, and genuine belles-lettres, some of the most powerful publishing houses now turn out reams of pop psychology, fiction, journalism, and scandalous material purporting to reveal the intimate details of the private lives of celebrities. And as for these celebrities, who and what are they but motion picture and television "stars," business tycoons, "professional" athletes, and other so-called personalities largely invented by public relations specialists? Truly creative and progressive minds are for the most part ignored, when not held in contempt; and teachers, scholars, nurses, social workers, and kindred professionals are daily reminded that in the eyes of their fellows they are worth only a small fraction of what an investment banker, corporation lawyer, major-league baseball player, or movie star is. Consequently, the front-line troops of civilization have been left ineffective and somewhat demoralized.

Furthermore, the young are too often glorified at the expense of their elders, and the elders humiliate themselves by vainly trying to be like the young. Some scientists put their skills and knowledge to the service of crass businessmen, international adventurers, and interest groups. Mechanical recitation of dogmatic ideological formulas has replaced reasoned argument and imaginative vision in much academic discussion. Television has all but reduced some people to vegetables. Money "talks," and many people whom we once mistook for idealists seem all too eager to "sell out." Crime and random violence seem rife to the many citizens who are afraid to walk in the centres of major cities at night or even in broad daylight. Wealthy and other "trend-setting" types generally dictate what is fashionable, having been promoted to their positions of "authority" by journalists and broadcasters, while genuinely idealistic, visionary, and incorruptible individuals are on occasion dismissed as cranks, dreamers, and parasites. Most people have managed somehow to come to terms with the "way of the world," so that fewer and fewer are capable of expressing moral indignation when confronted with the fact that schemers have most of our society's material wealth and social power while many honest, hard-working, talented human beings struggle to make ends meet.

This picture is not a pretty one, and of course, neither is it a complete one. I have already indicated some of the admirable features of the culture of the advanced societies that only the ignorant or depraved cynic could neglect. Ancient and medieval societies, even the most glorious and creative among them, were marked less by wisdom and generosity than by superstition and cruelty, and only in recent years have human beings started to address forms of exploitation and corruption that have gone unchecked and sometimes even unacknowledged through the centuries. But in a sense it is the genuine and obvious superiority of advanced societies like our own that renders the inferiority of so many of our cultural institutions and other cultural products so anomalous. How is it that the real advances in civilization have not protected advanced societies from the growth of certain forms of inauthenticity of culture?

There undoubtedly are several appropriate answers, but I indicate here only what I take to be the most important. Just as advances in civilization have brought with them advances in technology that can also be used by mass murderers, they have also introduced forms of technology that can serve the purposes of propagandists and kindred manipulators and promoters. So it is not necessarily just resentment or a romantic attachment to the past that has led many social critics to the intuition that inauthenticity has come to be institutionalized and condoned to an unprecedented extent. Increased sophistication of any form always yields as a by-product a certain amount of sophistry, and that holds true for civilization as much as for less important forms of sophistication; and never before have sophists had available to them such sophisticated tools for promoting the association of sophistication with the particular brand of sophistry that they see it as in their interest to cultivate. All forms of sophistication bring with them insights and devices that can further the ambitions of sinners as well as saints.

While one must not be seduced by the rhetoric of those who would have us believe that there is no real difference between good and evil, right and wrong, civility and barbarity, it is also dangerous for one to place too much emphasis on locating the people to blame for the degraded state of many of our society's cultural products. Self-righteousness is not true righteousness; and an obsession with disapprobation almost invariably leads to the persecution of scapegoats in the form of vulnerable and often innocent minorities. Even blaming those in our community who are genuinely corrupt and destructive is not entirely helpful, for it can reinforce in us the disinclination to acknowledge the contribution that we ourselves and those close to us have made to the degradation of cultural products.

Only when we have come to the recognition that in our own way "we" are a source of the problem just as "they" are (if not necessarily to the same extent) can we see "them" for what they are. We should not allow ourselves to be paralysed by guilt and self-contempt or to blame the victims of exploitation and infer that they deserve what they get from their exploiters; but no social critic is to be trusted who is incapable of profound self-criticism or of placing the desire for constructive reform ahead of the desire to see the mighty brought down, humiliated, and chastised.

When we encounter authenticity and inauthenticity in cultural institutions and other cultural products, we rarely find them in the form of "black and white." As authenticity and inauthenticity admit of countless degrees, we find ourselves confronted with innumerable shades of grey. Just as some people are very good and some people are very bad, some cultural products are highly authentic and some highly inauthentic. But for the most part the contributions that people make to a community's culture are partly authentic and partly inauthentic; in this way, they reflect the complexity of the motives and attitudes that enter into the judgment – both highly conscious and less so – of the people who make them. Ideally, all people would strive to create and promote what is as authentic as possible, and they would follow the leadership of those who stand committed to the promotion of authenticity in culture. But it is too much to demand or expect that those to whom we look up will consistently produce purely authentic cultural products; even the greatest saints have not been angels, nor have the worst sinners been devils.

FACTORS IN APPRAISING INAUTHENTICITY

In explaining my use of the expression "inauthentic culture," I began by citing a large, extended family of terms that indicate a specific kind of dissatisfaction with both particular cultural products and at least some of the people who have created or promoted them. Offering a few examples from everyday discourse, I showed that dissatisfaction with the cultural products is based at least partly on the judgment that they have been produced or promoted by people whose fundamental objective is to manipulate others for narrow, self-serving purposes. I then cited the views of social critics who see this form of exploitation as pervasive, and to some extent institutionalized, in advanced societies such as our own. I concluded the preliminary analysis by showing how there is indeed often something inferior, unsatisfactory, unsound, and even *unreal* about the objects, ideas, modes of perception, and other products that the manipulative agent wants other human beings to appropriate.

Dishonesty

Since certain terms that ascribe inauthenticity are sometimes applied descriptively, we need to remember that we are concerned here only with a particular use of such terms. If a friend tells us that she bought some fake pearls, she is not necessarily informing us that she was conned by a schemer; she was probably buying inexpensive imitation pearls, and the sales clerk undoubtedly made clear to her that the "pearls" she was purchasing were not genuine. The term *phoney* rarely has this descriptive use, which is one reason why it is superior to most other words used to ascribe inauthenticity. It has historical and etymological associations with American "underworld lingo,"[29] and it probably originally meant that something has been dishonestly presented as what it is not. But even "phoney" is sometimes used descriptively, which is a reason for preferring the semi-technical use of the far-less popular term *inauthentic* to designate the quality that concerns us.

People are inclined to ascribe a degree of inauthenticity to products if they believe that the creators or promoters (including vendors) themselves regard the products as having been somewhat deceptively or dishonestly put forward for appropriation. As disappointed as we may be when we invest in a bad toaster, a bad novel, bad dental work, or bad education, we ordinarily do not feel that we have been conned or manipulated as long as we believe that the people who provided the product in question thought that they were being fair with us in placing it before us in the way they did. And we would not ordinarily characterize as inauthentic a religious, political, or economic institution that, despite its flaws and inadequacies, was imposed on us or offered to us by people we believe to have been, for the most part, honest with us. Our assessment of relative inauthenticity usually involves an assessment of the relative honesty of various agents who participated in the production and promotion of the product. Thus we would normally regard a drama or theory as partly authentic and partly inauthentic if we felt that some of the people promoting its appropriation had been honest with us while others had not. Our assessment is reasonably sound when it is based on a reasonably comprehensive and balanced consideration of whose effort went into the creation and promotion of the product and on reasonably accurate appraisals of the relative honesty of those people.

If appraisal of a cultural product's authenticity is to be reasonably sound and fair, it may require some complicated judgments. Say that one reasonably suspects that the author of a highly advertised novel that one is reading allowed it to be published and promoted with much hype and razzle-dazzle, even though she believed it rather inferior to what she normally produces and could have produced had she been less concerned about making a quick buck. One may well be inclined to ascribe a high degree of inauthenticity to the work. But additional factors may be relevant. Was the reader substantially influenced by the hype, or would she perhaps have purchased the novel anyway, on the basis of respect for the author's earlier novels? Did the advertisers not believe that the new novel was a work of the first rank? Could the novel be of sufficiently high quality to warrant one's purchasing it even though it fell short of the author's highest standard and of the publisher's exaggerated claims for it? Is it not possible that the author's estimation of her own work is unreasonably severe and that, despite her misgivings, her new novel is actually much better than she realizes? It is clear that such judgments can be highly complex or rather casual, just as they can be very fair or very unfair.

Considerably more is at stake when one is assessing the authenticity of a communal institution, such as hierarchical authority in one's religious community, property rights in one's political community, or sexual fidelity in one's marriage. There are paradigms of inauthentic culture, such as the blatantly manipulative and dishonest political campaign speech, the hugely overpriced restaurant meal or designer dress, and the fourth-rate movie that has received "rave" reviews from influential newspaper critics who are friends of the producer and the studio boss. But many people are quick to draw the conclusion that most things that they do not like or understand are "phoney." Ascribing inauthenticity is a common defence mechanism when people feel threatened by something alien to them, particularly when their lack of familiarity with the product undermines their self-confidence, self-respect, or perception of their status within a group. There are people prepared to dismiss all classical music, ballet, religion, and charitable work, and there are others ready to describe all spectator sports, country music, and patriotism as phoney. But while inauthenticity does characterize many products in all of these domains, it is not as pervasive as certain insecure people would have us believe.

Lack of Commitment and Respect

What more does a sensible, fair-minded person consider when assessing the authenticity of a cultural product? What clues help her to arrive at a reasonable judgment? Much depends on the product; one does not consider an item one buys in a store in exactly the way one appraises a professional service, government policy, ecclesiastical ritual, or local custom. But since our aim is to understand broadly the inauthenticity of cultural products as such, we consider the most general of possible clues.

One thing for which people look is signs that the creators and promoters of a cultural product take their product "seriously." Whether dealing with a politician, dentist, carpenter, appliance dealer, or priest, one usually looks for indications that the person respects his product and takes pride in his association with it. One scrutinizes the agent's behaviour, talk, and facial expressions in order to get a sense of whether he believes in the value and quality of the product. One may detect that the person is concerned solely with making a sale or getting on with a transaction or encounter that improves his material situation or enhances his status. We rarely expect the people with whom we deal in the realm of cultural products to have taken a vow of poverty or to have lost sight of their personal economic interests, but we regularly look for signs of "professionalism," "craftsmanship," or whatever form of commitment to one's work is appropriate to the vocation or social role. We try to determine whether that person "believes in" what he is doing when he involves us with the product. It is too much to expect a teacher, repairman, banker, or architect to be in a perpetual state of inspired enthusiasm, and such an agent can have an unrealistically high or low opinion of the worth of his product and his work, but we are apt to regard the product as somewhat inauthentic if we see his association with it being for him little more than a way of getting on in the world.

The product that we appropriate may be excellent by many standards even if the agent has little concern for its value and quality, and the product that we take up from the most inspired, dedicated agent may be very bad by many standards. But we generally believe that the more respect a person has for the product that he is sharing with us, all other things being equal, the greater the likelihood that it will be superior by the standards that concern us. In assessing the product, we often need to remind ourselves that the effort of many people may be involved in its creation and promotion, and it is usually not only the commitment of the particular agent with whom we are dealing that is to be taken into account. Moreover, a corrupt politician does not render a complex political institution inauthentic, and a clergyman who has lost his faith does not render a complex ecclesiastical rite inauthentic, just as one crooked automobile salesman who sold us a lemon does not make Chevrolet or Toyota as such an inauthentic product. We need to distinguish the inauthenticity of one particular object from that of a class of objects, and we must separate the inauthenticity of that class of objects from that of more general classes of objects.

In assessing inauthenticity, we also value claims that have been made for a product. Is it really what its promoters claim that it is? Can it benefit me in the way that they tell me it can? Even if the agent with whom we are dealing has not endorsed the claims that have been made for the product by colleagues, superiors, advertisers, critics, apologists, predecessors, experts, and the like, we expect that agent to be aware to some extent of what we have been led to believe about the worth of the product. And if the most persuasive claims made for it are extravagant, we often expect the agent to indicate that to us somehow. We do not usually wish him to enumerate for us in detail all the criticisms that have been directed over the years against the product; but we anticipate that he will be "fair" in not hiding serious imperfections and in keeping his praise for the product within realistic bounds.

When we conclude that there is something phoney about a cultural product that we have appropriated or been encouraged to appropriate, we often do so largely on the basis of judgments that we have formed about how its creators or promoters see us. We rarely expect them to love us or to treat us better than they treat most other people. But we do want them to look on us not simply as means to their personal ends or as instruments for the promotion of some elaborate communal agenda, but as flesh-and-blood human beings who, like themselves, have ideas, ideals, aspirations, commitments, emotional needs, rational capacities, and other things that we associate with human dignity. If we feel that they are treating us merely as objects or instruments, and if we feel that they have not summoned up the will to empathize with us to some extent as their fellows, we may well view their products with suspicion.

Sometimes one sees a sign in a store that reads, "Our customers are our most important concern," and though one may be inclined to regard the sign itself as phoney, manipulative, or inauthentic, it reminds us that customers do want to be regarded as being important in some sense to a shopkeeper. People generally want to feel esteemed not only as customers of a shopkeeper, but as clients of a professional, patients of a medical practitioner, pupils of an educator, congregants in a religious leader's community, citizens in a politician-statesman's jurisdiction, aesthetes being shown a fine artist's work, readers of a philosophical or scientific treatise, and so forth. If we feel that for the most part we do not "matter" to the creators and promoters of cultural products as much as we should, then all other things being equal, it will not be difficult for us to judge the products as somewhat inauthentic. Again, it is not only the attitude of the immediate agent or representative that will enter into our assessment. One may regard a political institution as highly inauthentic even when dealing with functionaries one regards as honest, fair, and sympathetic; alternatively, one may consider an ecclesiastical institution fundamentally authentic even though the ecclesiastic with whom one is dealing seems a scheming hypocrite. Even so, in such cases, we are apt to regard that political institution as more authentic than it would have been were it not for the honest politician, and to think of that church as rather less authentic than it would be were it not for the participation in it of schemers.

When we see ourselves as having been "conned," we are normally troubled for two distinct reasons: we think that we have probably been led to appropriate a somewhat inferior cultural product, and we feel that we have suffered an affront to our dignity. Thus when we ascribe inauthenticity to a cultural product, we often feel that "insult has been added to injury." When we conclude that we were duped by a drama critic who abused his position by luring us into buying expensive tickets to see his pal's appalling play, we feel that we have not only had our pockets picked and been forced to waste precious hours of our life but been used and humiliated as well. Even when we see through hype or deception before being victimized by it, we still are offended by it. We resent the manipulator's insufficient respect for our intelligence; and if she actually considered the cultural product to be of respectable quality, why did she not try to persuade us so by appealing to our reason?

Irresponsibility

We generally believe that anyone who is participating in a process by which we are being called on to appropriate a cultural product should have a sense of responsibility. When we are unhappy with certain goods, services, or experiences, it may be unfair to blame those who are responsible for our involvement with them; but at times we feel that it is fitting to bring our dissatisfaction to the attention of the agents and (indirectly) the creators and promoters that they represent, and we expect the agents to be troubled by our complaint. We may not expect them to make amends to us, but we think that they should at least reflect on the possibility that the product they offer to their fellows, or impose on their fellows, is in need of improvement on some level. (Even if the product as such is satisfactory, the means of encouraging its appropriation may need to be improved.) If a salesperson, professional, institutional functionary, or craftsman responds to criticism by suggesting that he bears no responsibility for the cultural product with which he is associated, we will ordinarily think of his product as rather inauthentic, and we may feel that he too is phoney, for we may ascribe a certain inauthenticity to the people who produce or promote phoney products and may even feel that it is an inauthentic element in their character or personality that leads them to produce or promote such products.

Talk about "authenticity" and "inauthenticity" is popular among existential philosophers; and, though each uses this terminology in a personal way, "existentialists" generally focus on the authenticity and inauthenticity of human beings and their commitments rather than on the quality of what they produce and promote. In concentrating on the authenticity and inauthenticity of cultural products themselves, I depart from the usual primary focus of existential philosophy, but it is not hard to recognize ways in which the "inauthenticity" of a person can be related to the "inauthenticity" of the products that the person presents to her fellow human beings for appropriation.

One significant connection involves responsibility. If one is to contribute some degree of authenticity to the cultural products that one creates or promotes, one must see oneself as sufficiently free to choose to share them in some way with other human beings, and this sense of freedom normally carries with it a sense of responsibility to those who have appropriated the product at least partly on the basis of one's involvement with it. When people appropriate a cultural product on the basis of what they regard as impersonal contacts or forces, they have trouble regarding the product in question as fully authentic, not least because they feel that their own personal freedom has been undervalued in the process.

Numerous determining factors enter into the processes by which people contribute to the culture of their fellows and take up for themselves what has been contributed to a community's culture by their fellows. Our ideas and actions are shaped to a great extent by such factors as our genetic inheritance, the upbringing that our parents and other early teachers gave us, peer-group pressures, and institutional pressures. Sometimes we can see that people are only slightly if at all responsible for certain of their actions, and often reflection leads us to conclude that certain people in certain situations have been rather less responsible for their ideas and actions than their naive critics would have us believe.

But despite the popularity in recent years of various philosophical, quasi-philosophical, and pseudo-philosophical determinist theories, most of us feel that in most situations we are able to make a reasonable determination of when someone is trying to evade responsibility for what she has done or made. Sometimes people who are trying to evade responsibility are being dishonest and pretending that they believe that they had little if any choice but to do what they did or make what they made, but even if a person earnestly believes that she had little or no control over the behaviour involved in her creation or promotion of some cultural product, we might still regard the product as highly inauthentic. In doing so, we would be guided by the belief that this agent failed to bring to her activity an adequate degree of awareness of what she as a free agent could have done. A person cannot bring authenticity to cultural products if she lacks a concept of personal autonomy that enables her to believe that she is somehow able, through self-definition and self-direction, to transmute to some extent, in a personal and creative way, the material given to her as a result of determining factors.

A related point is that a thoughtful person recognizes that the inauthenticity of a cultural product often is partly a function of his having to some extent freely appropriated it. Manipulation robs us to some extent of our freedom, which is one reason why it offends us. Sometimes when we are deceived, we take solace in the fact that we really could not have done much, if anything, to prevent the deception; but a thoughtful person takes into account what he might have done to avoid a particular deception and the ways in which he and his fellows meekly and unintelligently respond to manipulative techniques in general. So when a thoughtful person reflects on how phoney something is, he may be being self-critical as well as critical of his exploiters.

Dehumanization

We also associate inauthenticity of cultural products with dehumanization and depersonalization. This is a central theme of existential philosophy and has been elaborately developed by such writers as Berdyaev, who insists: "We are witnessing the process of dehumanization in all phases of culture and of social life."[30] The dehumanization and depersonalization of cultural products are largely a result of naturalistic and mechanistic conceptions of the human person and human life; if one regards the human person as essentially a physical object or a complex machine, then one cannot consider the things that people produce as being more spiritual than that. With respect to naturalism, promoters of such fashionable forms of positivistic determinism as psychoanalytical theory, behaviourism, sociobiology, and cultural-relativist determinism undermine our confidence in the traditional conceptual framework necessary for our appreciation of what is involved in free and responsible participation in cultural and social life. As for mechanism, we know how in moments of existential insight we can look at our fellow human beings, and sooner or later at ourselves, and be struck by the degree to which human activities, including creation, promotion, and appropriation of cultural products, have become mechanized routines.

The problem is not simply that the machine dehumanizes human life; more important, the human being has increasingly become, in Berdyaev's words, "the image of the machine."[31] Albert Camus has offered some poignant descriptions of those moments in which we sense that human beings "secrete the inhuman." "At certain moments of lucidity, the mechanical aspect of their gestures, their meaningless pantomime makes silly everything that surrounds them. A man is talking on the telephone behind a glass partition; you cannot hear him, but you see his incomprehensible dumb show: you wonder why he is alive."[32] The more human content there is in the processes of producing, promoting, and appropriating cultural products, the more authenticity we are likely to associate with the products involved. They actually may seem to be more real to us in a sense, since for a human being human reality is not only the principal paradigm of reality but a standard in relation to which all other forms of reality are judged. Evidence of this is our common preference for things that are hand-made over things that are machine-made, or our preference for original products over copies, imitations, and likenesses. When we characterize the hand-made or original as "the real thing," it is not because we think of the machine-made products and the copies as absolutely unreal, but because they, in being more removed from certain human elements, partake less of the essence of a human or cultural product. Though Thorstein Veblen was right to argue that preference for hand-made and original products is often related to invidious distinctions of the kind commonly associated with "snob appeal,"[33] that is rarely the whole story.

A cultural product is, by definition and nature, a human product. When one considers two objects that for all practical purposes are physically the same, but one knows that one is a purely natural object and the other a human product meant by its creators to be shared in some way with others, then one reasonably regards the two as significantly different and knows that to understand the cultural product fully and properly one must analyse it from more than a natural-scientific standpoint. This simple metaphysical insight, which has been the starting-point for philosophers of culture who have emphasized the distinctiveness of the "human sciences," has struck some tough-minded positivistic thinkers as rather mystical. It is not mystical, though it is certainly metaphysical. The thinking of the human beings that has entered into cultural products' being what they are (and having the significance that they have) can, for certain special purposes, be separated from the resulting products; but usually it is fitting to regard the human element as intrinsic to them. The product takes on its character as a particular cultural product as a result of the layers of human judgment that have gone into its conception, realization, exploitation, refinement, promotion, and appropriation. Many cultural products have outlasted not only those who created them but many generations of users, promoters, corrupters, and restorers; and the humanity of all of these people has become incorporated in a sense into them. Authenticity and inauthenticity are among the human elements that enter into cultural products, which is why it is as appropriate to consider the authenticity of culture as the authenticity of people themselves.

We generally realize that what makes a human action different from any other natural event has something to do with the thought of the agent;[34] and we can usually see that what largely, if not entirely,[35] makes a work of fine art what it is is the thought that has gone into it on various levels. But it is crucial for our purposes here that we recognize that what renders a cultural product inauthentic is not some purely "objective" feature that can be grasped apart from consideration of the human judgment that went into the creation, reworking, or employment of it. The very same product, whether it be a book, sermon, code, or political manœuvre, can accordingly be highly authentic as appropriated in one context and highly inauthentic in another. Two physically indistinguishable paintings or scientific proposals can be at opposite ends of the scale of authenticity. The same political institution can be highly authentic at one point in time or place and highly inauthentic at another. That is, in fact, what happens most of the time when cultural activity is reduced to a mechanized routine.

Consider a political tradition that was largely conceived in a spirit of good will and generosity by its founders but has come over time to be used mainly as a device for the exploitation of an oppressed class. While it may seem unfair to its founders to regard the thing as now largely inauthentic in itself, it is clearly not what it once was, though it still retains a certain degree of authenticity partly as a result of the constructive and generous spirit in which it was conceived. It will not do to say that the tradition is permanently authentic; it is, in at least one major sense, what those who have promoted it and taken it up have made of it.

Appealing to what some now largely corrupt theory or institution once was, or was at least once idealized as being, is a standard device by which manipulative people preserve and extend their influence. In religious life, a once deeply significant religious rite, prayer, or code may have degenerated into a spiritually empty phenomenon that functions mainly as a means of promoting the narrow interests of an elite class. Sometimes political or religious institutions that have been corrupted in this way can be restored to a condition approximating their original level of authenticity, but this is not always possible. Perhaps the most obvious example of the phenomenon is in the realm of high fashion, refined taste, and connoisseurship, where objects that were perhaps sincerely deemed beautiful or profound by their creators and earliest admirers have lost most of their authenticity became of self-aggrandizing promoters and operators, who have made beauty or profundity secondary to fashionableness. When we are struck by the mechanized routine into which a particular form of cultural activity has deteriorated, we are generally aware that at one time it had a degree of authenticity that it now lacks.

Devaluation of Individuality

Related to the dehumanization of cultural products brought by mechanized routine is the depersonalization of cultural products associated with the predominance of the "mass idea."[36] Kierkegaard, who realized how much his own age had become one of "advertisement and publicity,"[37] has had an enormous impact on subsequent existential reflection with his powerful advocacy of deeply felt personal commitment in the face of cultural activity limited by acquiescence to the pressures of the "crowd." Most people, even as part of the "crowd," at least occasionally sense inauthenticity in cultural products produced, promoted, and appropriated almost exclusively because it is conventional, customary, or otherwise socially accepted to do so.

When a man puts on his necktie in the morning, he may be struck by the inauthenticity of the product, but because he recognizes the prudence and convenience of being "sociable," he is prepared to go along with the fashion, however grudgingly. But in moments of existential insight, one may be haunted by the extent to which one's life has become dominated by such "sociability." The value placed on individualism in certain quarters of modern advanced societies is much higher than that which has been put on it elsewhere and certainly in most earlier societies; but we should not underestimate the importance of individualist tendencies in highly developed ancient societies or even in primitive communities.

There are connections between the dehumanization and depersonalization of cultural activity and cultural products and the self-serving intentions of manipulative communal elites. Mechanized routine and discouragement of personal commitment are standard manœuvres of those who would rather exploit their fellows than cooperate and fairly compete with them in the promotion of superior cultural products and a higher quality of life for all. Certain radical-critical theorists who have little interest in spirituality as such, and see existential reflection as somewhat self-indulgent in a world in which most people are victimized by violent oppression or economic deprivation, have provided potent descriptions of the inauthenticity of cultural products associated with dehumanization and depersonalization.

If their analysis is rather narrow because of their ideological preoccupations, it is useful on a certain level. Herbert Marcuse, for example, is not all that far from Christian existentialists such as Kierkegaard and Berdyaev when he proclaims:

The world of human freedom cannot be built by the established societies, no matter how much they may streamline and rationalize their dominion. Their class structure, and the perfected controls required to sustain it, generate needs, satisfactions, and values which reproduce the servitude of the human existence. This "voluntary" servitude (voluntary inasmuch as it is introjected into the individuals), which justifies the benevolent masters, can be broken only through a political practice which reaches the roots of containment and contentment in the infrastructure of man, a political practice of methodical disengagement from and refusal of the Establishment, aiming at a radical transvaluation of values. Such a practice involves a break with the familiar, the routine ways of seeing, hearing, feeling, understanding things so that the organism may become receptive to the potential forms of a nonaggressive, nonexploitative world.[38]

Where Marcuse differs from Kierkegaard and Berdyaev is in his conception of what kind of revolution is necessary to establish the conditions of authentic culture.

When we are able to rise above resentment, we can see how much manipulators themselves are victims of their inauthentic cultural products. Smug though they may be when they reflect on their material success, social status, and power, they are still surrounded with the inauthentic cultural products that people like them have promoted. The "crowd" has its revenge: it feeds inauthentic culture back to its exploiters, who, lacking spiritual ideas, derive their sense of their own importance, and even their values, from the "crowd." Undoubtedly many a manipulator has eventually come to see that he has been snared in his own trap and that spiritual fulfilment is not to be attained through custodianship of cultural rubbish. As for those manipulators who do not rise to this level of insight, we may be brought by some combination of moralism, sentimentalism, and resentment to see them as prone to a self-deception not unlike the deception that they practise against their fellows.

The Significance of Authenticity

Participation in social life brings with it involvement with cultural products. Born into various groups or communities, we are initially enculturated by cultural products that we take for granted. However, our appropriation of certain of them also enables us in time to pass personal judgment on the value and quality of cultural products. When we have reached the stage of intellectual development at which we are capable of making careful, reasonable judgments about the motivation and character of our fellow human beings, and of understanding the ways in which people appropriate cultural products, we are usually in a position to detect something phoney in certain of those products, and our ability to distinguish between relatively authentic and relatively inauthentic products helps us make practical decisions in accordance with our world-view.

Taking a wide view of the problem of inauthentic culture, we may remind ourselves of the opinion of those social critics who believe that inauthenticity of cultural products has become more and more entrenched, institutionalized, and accepted in advanced societies such as our own. Some of these people see inauthenticity as vitiating almost every major aspect of social life. Even without their encouragement, most of us occasionally entertain grave doubts about cultural products that we once respected greatly. Hardly a week goes by in which we are not forced to confront some dramatic exposé in the mass media, and while most of us try hard to avoid cynicism, we also know that naiveté can be immoral as well as imprudent. It is no wonder then that most reflective people are sometimes prepared to entertain the possibility that our society has come to be completely dominated by the attitudes and methods of hucksters and operators and that if we do not learn to play the game of life by their rules we will not be able to fulfil our most cherished aspirations or to provide for the security of our loved ones. But we can usually banish these dark thoughts from our mind.

However, when prepared to move to the level of social criticism, we may well want to focus on culture. Cultural products make an individual's life meaningful in several ways. Not only are one's world-view and behaviour influenced (and to some degree determined) by the cultural products to which one is exposed, but the things that one does with those products – from creating and promoting them to appropriating and rejecting them – constitute a substantial part of living. Thus no effort to understand or evaluate the quality of life of an individual or community should ignore the extent to which that person or group has been systematically exposed to inferior cultural products and perhaps become disposed to producing and being actively involved with such inferior products. In a healthy society, people come into contact, by and large, with good or sound cultural products. There are various moral, aesthetic, and otherwise practical criteria of goodness that figure into our evaluation of human products, and one of these is authenticity.

How important is authenticity in relation to the other standards of goodness? Imagine, say, how you might react if some craftsman with whom you had contracted said to you, "I admit that I did not take this job very seriously, and that I did to some degree take advantage of you, but so what? The work that I did for you was still better than what any of my competitors could have done for you." Or say an advertiser were to say to you, "My advertisement did make extravagant claims for the product, but so what? You admit that you are basically satisfied with the product." While you might be placated by such replies in certain situations – either because you are inclined to be permissive or because the worth of the products in other ways did indeed compensate for their inauthenticity – you would probably still feel exploited, and would take exception to the fact that, even by their own admission, these people had failed to live up to their responsibility to you.

As we saw above, people regard cultural products as inauthentic partly because they feel that those who have produced or promoted them have not lived up to some at least implicit understanding. By tolerating such irresponsibility, we increase the likelihood that manipulators will continue to produce and promote inauthentic products, or do so more consistently and more brazenly. And while our resentment of inauthenticity may lead us to work harder at producing, promoting, appropriating, and generally involving ourselves with authentic products, we may wonder after a while why we allow ourselves to be martyrs to an ideal that as time passes has less and less meaning for our fellows.

Since inauthentic products tend to be inferior to authentic ones by most other standards of goodness – simply because of the spirit in which they have been conceived and put forward – permissiveness with respect to inauthenticity contributes indirectly to permissiveness with respect to those other standards of goodness. If, for example, we do not speak out against the corruption of the cinema by producers and "artists" who insist on turning out rubbish because it is easier and more profitable to do so than to create work of high quality, then we have been disloyal not only to the ideal of authenticity but to the moral and aesthetic values that inferior cinema undermines.

The maintenance and advancement of authenticity are not solely of instrumental value, even though all sorts of utilitarian arguments could be raised on their behalf. Inauthentic culture represents a flight from morality and reality. Regardless of its consequences, it stands for the devaluation of such fundamental moral ideals as justice, responsibility, dignity, integrity, and concern for others. These are some of the most important ideals by which morality is to be defined. Moreover, inauthentic culture represents the depreciation of the genuine and thus of the real and the true.

2

SOME ASPECTS OF CULTURE RELEVANT TO
THE PROBLEM OF INAUTHENTICITY

In associating culture with products, I approach it from a specific perspective in order to clarify a particular social problem. The expression "cultural products" is rare in everyday language and is used here to explain complicated matters in a straightforward way, but it is not entirely satisfactory. I use the term *product* to stand for a wide range of human creations. Praying in a church, completing a tax form, shaking someone's hand, and having one's hair styled all involve appropriation of things "produced" by human beings. Theories, modes of perception, services, and methods are also "produced" by human beings.

But we normally restrict our use of the term *product* to certain things that human beings "produce," so that, in having relied on it to designate other things as well, I have put some strain on ordinary usage. More important, the terms *culture* and *cultural* are extremely ambiguous; and my use of those terms in chapter 1 oversimplified the concept of culture even with respect to the problem of inauthentic culture. The category of culture has been the subject of many philosophical and social-scientific disputes; and though we cannot hope here to resolve the major controversies, familiarity with them will enable us to appreciate aspects of culture that should be taken into account.

The references to culture and cultural products in chapter 1 were meant to establish the focus of our investigation on a certain class of things. These things, while "natural" in a sense, are usefully distinguished from "purely" natural phenomena; they are what they are partly because human beings assist in their conception, creation, exploitation, and transformation. Even in appropriating a "purely" natural object, people do in a way convert it into a cultural product, so that even a natural object that would, say, grow on trees even if there were no humans becomes a cultural product in a sense when it is appropriated for human consumption.

But the most interesting cultural products are those that could never exist in any form were it not for human activity. The terms *culture* and *cultural* help us see that certain human products are shared, or meant to be shared, by people other than the producers. Moreover, they remind us of how certain human products become organized in patterns that largely define the life of a group or community and of the processes by which various aspects of human personality are shaped by regular exposure to a particular pattern of human products. They also draw our attention to the fact that people become more sophisticated through increased familiarity with the organized pattern of human products that characterizes their group or community, especially with those elements in the pattern essential for playing a very active role in communal life.

These are the aspects of culture emphasized in chapter 1; by reference to them, I was able to describe with some precision a particular social problem. I also mentioned in passing that the term *culture* is associated sometimes with invidious distinctions and snobbery, more commonly with self-perfection, and still more commonly (in accordance with its etymology) with cultivation. But I did not elaborate on these other associations, and there are still others that I did not mention at all.

David L. Hall has written: "No single discipline has a monopoly on the word 'culture.' It is used in a technical sense by anthropologists, sociologists, and social psychologists, as well as by philosophers, and within each discipline, there are a variety of approaches to the topic. One may seek to define culture in its most generic sense as referring to any and all cultures, or one may consider the topic concretely and in terms of particular existing cultures. The theoretical approach tends to express certain normative considerations while an empirical or phenomenological approach emphasizes the descriptive rather than the normative dimension."[1] These observations require qualification. First, *culture* is rarely treated as a purely technical term. Philosophers and social scientists know that it is widely used by non-specialists in everyday language, and when they adopt it they do so because they see important connections between their own concept and phenomena associated with non-technical uses of the term. They have deliberately employed a term used in ordinary language and avoided the temptation to invent a piece of scientific jargon. Thus most philosophical and social-scientific uses of *culture* are at most semi-technical. Also, what anthropologists or sociologists say about culture may be of interest and of value to philosophers and social psychologists, and vice versa. And it is not always useful to distinguish a theoretical or normative approach to culture from an empirical, phenomenological, or descriptive one. Still, Hall's remarks indicate the importance of being flexible and broad-minded when considering approaches to the definition of culture.

We should not confuse the etymology or history of a term with its meaning, but the etymology and history of *culture* and related words give us insights into how the term *culture* has come to be associated with various phenomena. The word is derived from a French term that is in turn derived from the Latin *cultura*, a derivative of *cultus*, associated by the Romans with cultivation, and particularly agriculture.[2] According to Giles Gunn,

From the beginning, culture has always been associated with processes of nurture. Deriving from the Latin word *cultura* (from the root *colere*, 'to protect, cultivate, inhabit, or honor with worship') the earliest uses of culture always linked it to natural processes of tending and preservation. But by the early sixteenth century, cultural processes of natural preservation had been extended to human nurture, and before long were transferred from the particular domain of individual experience to the more abstract level of general or collective experience. Although it is extremely difficult to pinpoint just when these developments occurred, or when, still later, culture was further associated not only with a specific process but also with its more abstract product or result, it is not difficult to specify the thinker in whom they first became conscious. That individual was Giambattista Vico, whose contribution to the theory of culture actually came by way of his preoccupation with the category of history.[3]

Gunn attaches particular significance to the Enlightenment conception of culture and to Herder's negative reaction to it, for that disagreement reveals the roots of a major controversy among students of culture today: "The philosophes viewed culture as the opposite of barbarism. As contrasted with barbarism and the related concepts of savagery and primitivism, culture constituted for the Enlightenment not only an achieved condition but also a standard of refinement that members of the age were more than willing to use as a measure for all civilizational forms. Herder found the arrogance and historical bias of this practice intolerable and proposed his concept of civilization as an alternative. By civilization he meant essentially a way of life rather than a standard or a process, and one that is commonly formed among all peoples even though it is individually expressed by each. Herder therefore conceived of civilization as pluralistic rather than monolithic."[4]

The anthropologists Kroeber and Kluckhohn have observed that even the "scientific" concept of culture, or something close to it, was anticipated by the ancients: "The broad underlying idea is not new, of course. The Bible, Homer, Hippocrates, Herodotus, Chinese scholars of the Han dynasty – to take some of the more obvious examples – showed an interest in the distinctive life-ways of different peoples."[5] With respect to the term *culture* itself, Kroeber and Kluckhohn have noted: "The most generic sense of the word 'culture' – in Latin and in all the languages which have borrowed the Latin root – retains the primary notion of cultivation or becoming cultured. This was also the older meaning of 'civilization'. The basic idea was first applied to individuals, and this usage still persists in popular and literary English to the present time."[6] They also point out that the modern "technical or anthropological" application was established in English by the influential social scientist Edward B. Tylor, in 1871, and that Tylor appropriated this term, as an equivalent of the German *Kultur*, just two years after it had become widely popularized by the aesthete Matthew Arnold in his *Culture and Anarchy.*[7] But even the German term was associated in Tylor's day with the "distinctive 'higher' values or enlightenment of a society."[8] Its application to human societies and history dates only from the late eighteenth century, and this appropriation of *cultura* was initially confined to the German language.[9] Kroeber and Kluckhohn acknowledge that the terms *culture* and *civilization* "began by definitely containing the idea of betterment, of improvement toward perfection" and "still retain this meaning today, in many usages, both popular and intellectual."[10] The "specifically anthropological" concept, which crystallized first around the idea of "custom," departs from this usage[11] and has for this reason been criticized by many humanists, perhaps most notably by the classicist Werner Jaeger.[12]

DESCRIPTIVE AND NORMATIVE CONCEPTIONS OF CULTURE

As a classical scholar, Jaeger is bothered by what he regards as failure to appreciate the role of the ancient Greeks in having "created the idea of culture."[13] But he is concerned with more than this historical point: "We are accustomed to use the word culture, not to describe the ideal which only the Hellenocentric world possesses, but in a much more trivial and general sense, to denote something in every nation of the world, even the most primitive. We use it for the entire complex of all the ways and expressions of life which characterize any one nation. Thus the word has sunk to mean a simple anthropological concept, not a concept of value, a consciously pursued *ideal.*"[14] "This 'ideal of culture' (in Greek, *areté* and *paideia*) is a specific creation of the Greek mind. The anthropological concept of culture is a modern extension of this original concept; but it has made out of a concept of value a mere descriptive category which can be applied to any nation, even to the 'culture of the primitive,' because it has entirely lost its true obligatory sense."[15]

We may question Jaeger's arbitrary association of the term *culture* with the Greek concept of *paideia*, especially since he is equally arbitrary in denying that pre-Hellenic societies possessed an ideal of culture. What he dismisses as merely the "educational systems" of other societies has in certain ways as much to do with traditional Western conceptions of culture as do the institutions of the ancient Greeks that so fascinate Jaeger.[16] He says, rightly: "Without Greek cultural ideals ... the culture of the western world would never have existed,"[17] but a stronger case could be made for the cultural ideals of the pre-Hellenic Hebrews, whose culture Jaeger generally misunderstands. In any case, one can appreciate classical Greek ideals and their historical influence without accepting Jaeger's claims that the Greeks invented the ideal of culture and that the term *culture* should be perpetually tied to ancient Greek conceptions and institutions. Moreover, an anthropologist or philosopher could easily look at Jaeger and his disciples in much the same way as Herder looked at the philosophers of the Enlightenment, with their arrogance and historical bias. One of the traditional incentives to pursuing studies in anthropology and the philosophy of culture has been a desire to counter the destructive influences of ethnocentrism.

Yet while we can admire the broad-mindedness of those who are troubled by certain traditional normative conceptions of culture, and while we can see why they consider it proper to have appropriated the term *culture* for a more descriptive use, we can still appreciate the complaint of scholars who see dangerous ambiguity therein and believe that a useful, traditional, normative conception of culture has lost much of its serviceability. From the start, the term *culture* was associated with processes of nurture, even before it was linked with human nurture. It has long served well, along with the related term *civilization* (seen by many scholars as essentially synonymous with *culture*),[18] to designate something to be contrasted with barbarism, barbarity, savagery, and primitivism. Even the German *Kultur*, which so greatly influenced nineteenth-century social scientists, was traditionally associated with higher values and enlightenment. Humanists and moralists of many orientations have had more than merely prudential interest in preserving the normative force of traditional uses of the term in at least its primary contemporary application.

In speaking earlier of "cultural products," I did not intend to deprive the terms *culture* and *cultural* of that normative force. In writing of the "sharing" of cultural products, I had in mind how these products are related to a process involving cultivation and nurture. When we consciously appropriate those things that we regard as cultural products, we ordinarily do so because we see them as having a meliorative influence on our lives. (An English dictionary of 1791 actually defines "culture" as "the art of improvement and melioration.")[19] We see them as making our lives better and ultimately enabling us to be better human beings by the criteria of human goodness that matter most to us. Thus culture, in the sense of being or becoming cultured by appropriating products that have been created, refined, and promoted by one's fellow human beings, is an ideal akin to, but broader than, being or becoming educated. Those who seek to share the products that they have created, or are involved in promoting them, are, when behaving in accordance with sound moral standards, trying to make the lives of their fellow human beings better, and ultimately to enable them to be better people. They are on both levels concerned with meliorating the condition of their fellows. Most humanists and moralists would find it strange to hear someone characterized as having been made worse in the process of having been led to be more cultured, just as they would find it strange to hear someone characterized as having been "educated" to be a barbarian or a savage. Products that are promoted without the intention of making people genuinely better off, and ultimately better, are thus in a sense not genuine cultural products at all, though they are regularly passed off by manipulators as being such. In this sense then, it is fitting to describe them as "inauthentic" or "phoney."

The terms *culture* and *cultural* do not carry all this normative conceptual weight when used by certain anthropologists and others, and we cannot fairly say that those who do not apply these terms in a traditional way are simply doing so improperly. In fact, most of us can appreciate the positive value of a largely or exclusively descriptive use of these terms and can understand the dissatisfaction of many thoughtful writers with the ethnocentrism, arrogance, and historical bias reflected in, and promoted by, certain of their traditional uses. But we should bear in mind the ambiguity that has resulted in part from the conflicting concerns, and we ought to recognize the positive value of traditional normative conceptions of culture. Moreover, even when the terms have a normative significance, they also have some descriptive role, for they serve not merely to express approval of things but also to indicate that those things are good because they have certain detectable and describable qualities.

The desire to preserve the normative significance of the term *culture* is made evident in the definitions and characterizations given to it by many humanists who have worked harder than Jaeger to appreciate the contribution made by anthropologists and other social scientists. F.R. Cowell, for example, suggests: "Culture is that which, being transmitted orally by tradition and objectively through writing and other means of expression, enhances the quality of life with meaning and value by making possible the formulation, progressive realization, appreciation and the achievement of truth, beauty, and moral worth."[20] B.S. Sanyal expresses a similar view: "'Culture' is one word for 'realization of values in theory and practice.'"[21] The poet T.S. Eliot, while insisting that by the term *culture* he means "first of all" what the anthropologists mean – "the way of life of a particular people living together in one place"[22] – indicates, in a mode of expression to be expected from a poet, that culture is ultimately better described "simply as that which makes life worth living."[23] And the philosopher C.A. Van Peursen, while acknowledging that earlier conceptions of culture have been "discarded" partly as a result of social-scientific theory,[24] expresses respectful interest in the Kantian conception of culture as an activity that "presses on with the quest for improvement, change, reformation."[25]

When we turn to the definitions given by certain anthropologists, we can see why humanists are troubled. In an introductory text in cultural theory, the anthropologists Kaplan and Manners, in a strange attempt to steer clear of controversy, state: "We are not going to attempt another definition of *culture* here. Let us just say that *culture* is a class of phenomena conceptualized by anthropologists in order to deal with questions they are trying to answer."[26] Arensberg and Niehoff tell us: "Culture is the sum total of what human beings learn in common with other members of the group to which they belong"[27]; further, "Culture is man's unique way of adapting to environment."[28] Kroeber and Kluckhohn, while aware of the dozens of different meanings that the term *culture* has been used to convey, provide their own "scientific" definition of it as "a set of attributes and products of human societies, and therewith of mankind, which are extrasomatic and transmissible by mechanisms other than biological heredity, and are as essentially lacking in sub-human species as they are characteristic of the human species as it is aggregated in its societies."[29] While it would be improper to dismiss these various definitions as positivistic in spirit, they clearly do not specifically associate culture with ideals or even values.

The limits of such essentially descriptive definitions are easily recognized in the opening lines of Tylor's classic anthropological text, *Primitive Culture*: "Culture or Civilization, taken in its wide ethnographic sense, is that complex whole which includes knowledge, belief, art, morals, law, custom, and any other capabilities and habits acquired by man as a member of society."[30]

Tylor acknowledges that he is concerned only with the ethnographic sense of the term; he is, after all, at the very least aware of the popularity in his day of Matthew Arnold's use of the term. He then offers what looks like a definition by denotation, but he finally associates culture with socially acquired capabilities and habits. For Tylor, it is not a matter of consciously creating, promoting, and appropriating products that have a meliorative influence; indeed, for him, it is not even related to a process by which human beings have consciously created, promoted, and appropriated products. By using the term in the way he does, Tylor has cut it off from its traditional association with cultivation and melioration and, for that matter, with motives on the part of the agents who in one way or other participate in cultural processes. Tylor helped to free social science from its subservience to, and dependence on, humanistic modes of inquiry, but he appropriated a term that traditionally carried much normative conceptual weight for humanists, not least among them Arnold's disciples and critics.

Later anthropologists have gone some way towards a reconciliation with humanists concerning culture. For example, an introductory text in anthropology states that culture is "a body of common understandings"[31] and: "It is our culture that enables us to get through the day because both we and the other people we encounter attach somewhat the same meanings to the same things."[32] We can see in the emphasis there on understandings, meanings, and judgments about utility awareness that culture has traditionally been seen as related to processes of human reflection and evaluation that have resulted in cultural products being what they are. The influential anthropologist Malinowski's "functionalist" theory of culture has not always given humanists something to cheer about, but he is particularly sensitive to humanists' role in laying the groundwork for scientific studies of culture,[33] and he stresses that the organization of every cultural system of activities "implies the acceptance of certain values and laws. It is always the organization of people for a given purpose, accepted by themselves, and recognized by the community. Even were we to consider a gang of criminals, we would see that they also have their own charter defining their aims and purposes."[34]

Traditional normative considerations are central to one of the functions of the United Nations Economic and Social Council (UNESCO), which is mandated to "give fresh impulse ... to the spread of culture."[35] A working party convened some years ago by the Canadian Commission for UNESCO addressed the meaning of "*culture*" in this context and, while well aware of the ambiguity of the term,[36] provided a "working definition": "Culture is a dynamic value system of learned elements, with assumptions, conventions, beliefs and rules permitting members of a group to relate to each other and to the world, to communicate and to develop their creative potential."[37] Whatever its weaknesses, this definition, with its emphasis on values and creative potential, reminds us that when reflective people set out to confront global social problems, the "ideal of culture" may well matter to them a great deal.

À propos of our concern here with inauthenticity, cultural products, and other elements involved in processes related to culture, have traditionally been thought to be capable of being understood (at least in part) and assessed by reference to ideals that are somewhat independent of, and even transcend, cultural products themselves. The idea of authenticity, in itself or as derived from such ideals as justice and freedom, would appear to qualify as such an ideal. However, if certain social scientists and philosophers are right, then such ideals, and even the traditional Western "ideal of culture" itself, may themselves be nothing more than cultural products. That is a possibility that we have to consider, as must anyone who is seriously concerned with the relation of culture to values.

"HIGH" AND "POPULAR" CULTURE

In taking note of Jaeger's attack on "scientific" definitions of "culture," Kroeber and Kluckhohn comment on the "dissatisfaction of most Western humanists with the anthropological habit of extending 'culture' to encompass the material, humble, and even trivial."[38] Most people, including those with little interest in "high" culture, still tend, despite the influence of social scientists, to associate "culture" more with ballet and classical music than with cooking and automobile repair and, for that matter, more than with night-club dancing and popular music.

A person preparing to accompany his grandson to the opera may comment to his friends that he is "getting a bit of culture"; it would not ordinarily occur to him that he gets plenty of culture when he reads a tabloid, sees a hockey game, or carries out his duties at the office or factory. For reasons he cannot easily state, he believes that there is something ennobling about sitting through a performance in which plump foreigners sing incomprehensible words in a strange voice. He may believe that his dignity is enhanced when he can turn to his grandson after the performance and say, "I enjoyed that more than I thought I would, and the final scene was very moving."

Most of us tend to associate culture more with fine arts than with industrial arts, more with "serious" art than "popular" or "commercial" art, more with religion than science and politics, and so forth, though we may be prepared to grant, after having heard an anthropology student explain what he means by "culture," that all sorts of things qualify as "culture" when looked at in a certain way. Even an aesthete like T.S. Eliot accepts the idea that the term *culture* can be usefully seen as embracing the dart board and Wensleydale cheese as much as nineteenth-century Gothic churches and the music of Elgar.[39] Yet most people not engaged in social-scientific research still feel more comfortable associating culture with things that they regard as "higher" than the mundane products and activities of everyday life. Paradoxically, the things they regard as higher may simultaneously be regarded by them as matters of frippery. That indicates, among other things, that people recognize that high cultural products do not satisfy their most basic needs, but it also suggests that while they accept that such a product is of great value to the community and to individuals, they see high cultural activity as a rich field for the cultivation of inauthenticity.

The ancients were aware of high culture's utility as a device for promoting invidious distinctions – that was a major theme of classical comedy and satire and continues to be one in contemporary literature. Many social scientists and humanists have debunked much that has been associated with high culture or even shown that high culture as such is really not significantly higher than "mass" or "popular" culture.

The sociologist Herbert J. Gans has written: "In America, as in all Western societies, the longest and perhaps most important cultural struggle has pitted the educated practitioners of high culture against most of the rest of society, rich and poor, which prefers the mass or popular culture provided by the mass media and the consumer goods industries. Intellectually, that struggle has actually been a one-sided debate. The advocates of high culture criticize popular culture as a mass culture which has harmful effects on both individuals consuming it and on society as a whole, while the users of popular culture ignore the critique, reject high culture, and continue to patronize the sellers of media fare and consumer goods." In Gans's view, "The so-called mass culture critique is important because it is concerned with far more than media fare and consumer goods. It is really about the nature of the good life, and thus about the purpose of life in general, particularly outside the work role. It is also about which culture and whose culture should dominate in society."[40] Gans defends popular culture from the attack of cultural aristocrats, whose arguments he finds unsound, and he argues that the very distinction between "high" and "popular" culture is arbitrary and often manipulative.[41]

Gans's response mirrors Herder's to the philosophes of the Enlightenment and, in an oblique way, the social scientist's "response" to aristocratic humanists such as Jaeger. Gans sees himself as defending "cultural pluralism," much as Herder saw himself as promoting a pluralistic rather than a monolithic conception of civilization and as broad-minded anthropologists think of themselves as struggling against ethnocentrism. These people have served us well in countering destructive, invidious distinctions, but uncritical pluralism has a way of degenerating into relativism and determinism.

The basic thesis of those who seek to distinguish high culture from mere frippery is that it is in fact more meliorative, both for individuals and communities, than "popular" culture. A person or community, they claim, is ultimately better off, and better, for listening to an opera by Bizet than hearing a rock band's latest creation, or for reading a philosophy book rather than a comic book or a racy novel. Much depends on how one determines whether, or to what extent, something makes people "better off" and "better." The question of how we should make such determinations (if they can be made at all) is challenging, and we cannot do justice to it here. However, with respect to the criterion of authenticity, a stronger case can be made against most "popular" culture than against most "high" culture.

Gans recognizes that humanistic critics of popular culture believe that "[p]opular culture is undesirable because, unlike high culture, it is mass-produced by profit-minded entrepreneurs solely for the gratification of a paying audience."[42] While he rejects this argument, as a general rule more reflective, more educated, and more "cultured" people are harder to manipulate than less reflective, less educated, and less "cultured" ones. Highly reflective people are not always difficult to manipulate, and being highly reflective and highly "cultured" does make one especially vulnerable to certain forms of manipulation. But reflection, education, and culture in general make people better off and better by enabling them to see through and resist the crudest and most dangerous forms of manipulation. People such as Gans may well have closely scrutinized the arguments of humanists and remained unconvinced and unmoved by efforts to establish that it is ultimately better to be exposed to Plato, Shakespeare, and Max Weber than to television soap opera, rock music, and newspaper advertisements for designer apparel. Similarly, some cultural anthropologists may be unconvinced by the arguments given by such humanistic scholars as Jaeger to show that the greatest cultural products of ancient Greece and Renaissance Italy are superior by some transcultural standard to the greatest cultural products of most other societies. But perhaps the debunkers of high culture should study the arguments of the humanists more closely, for the relativism towards which these debunkers are moving can have a very destructive impact on the minds of people who are encouraged to appropriate it.

Distrust of those who defend aristocratic cultural ideals is rooted not only in resentment of hauteur but in recognition of evils that have been perpetrated against the lowly and oppressed of the world by the high and the mighty, who have used high cultural products as a means of exploiting their fellows. It is rarely enough for humanists to observe that cultural products that have been promoted for such evil purposes are inauthentic. Humanists must also be aware that in defending a certain aristocratic tradition, they risk becoming apologists for people who would replace democratic institutions with the instruments of tyranny. Radical-critical theorists have drawn our attention both to a certain historical pattern in which culture has been intimately connected to domination and to the extent to which myopic humanists have ignored or condoned that pattern. For example, criticizing the fashionable hermeneutics of Hans-Georg Gadamer and his disciples, John Brenkman has observed: "Gadamer ... remains impervious to the ways in which coercive and nonreciprocal relationships within a society shape its culture. Having denied a connection between culture and domination, he then asserts that the Western cultural tradition already genuinely embodies the ideal of uncoerced, reciprocal understanding. In combination those premises lend Gadamerian hermeneutics to the legitimation of domination."[43]

But many who have witnessed barbarism at close range have eloquently testified to the dangers of mass culture. People who have themselves been exploited and oppressed are routinely manipulated by despots into exploiting one another, and particularly to subjecting vulnerable minorities to barbaric treatment. The compassionate scholar's admirable sympathy for the plight of, and respect for certain ways of, the oppressed masses need to be tempered by realization that the manipulability of those who have little interest in high cultural products leaves them vulnerable to the corrupting influences of an inauthentic mass culture which, though partly rooted in pleasant and beneficent folkways, has largely been foisted on them by political adventurers, unscrupulous entrepreneurs, and corrupt intellectuals.

Closely observing the fascism, Hitlerism, and Stalinism of his day, Berdyaev was struck by the connection between the ascendancy of the mass man, the marginalization of the culturally creative thinker, the decline of the aristocratic element in cultural life, and the systematic extirpation of personal conscience and personal consciousness.[44] This theme was even more eloquently sounded by the Spanish liberal Ortega y Gasset, a disciplined student of the philosophy of culture, who in 1930 warned that the mass culture of unstable democracies was paving the way for forms of totalitarianism and barbarism of unprecedented virulence.[45] The dignified student of *Kulturgeschichte*, Huizinga, similarly bore witness to the "puerilism" of mass culture, the rampant blend of adolescence and barbarity that had begun to let loose on the civilized world evils that were hitherto unimaginable.[46]

One social-scientific student of culture who took seriously the exhortations of these philosophers of culture was Karl Mannheim, who went on to develop elaborate theories about the role of intellectual elites in culture:

Even in a mass-democracy, cultural sublimation, as for example, in art and in fashion, can take place only if small groups of connoisseurs, who create and mould taste, already exist, and slowly diffuse the content and the technique of sublimation over the rest of society. In all the spheres of cultural life, the function of such élites is to express cultural and psychological forces in a primary form and to guide collective extraversion and introversion; they are responsible for cultural initiative and tradition. If these small groups are destroyed or thwarted in their selection, the social conditions for the emergence and persistence of culture disappear. The crisis of culture in liberal-democratic society is due, in the first place, to the fact that the social processes, which previously favoured the development of the creative élites, now have the opposite effect, i.e. have become obstacles to the forming of élites because wider sections of the population still under unfavourable social conditions take an active part in cultural activities.[47]

Mannheim grimly observed how the European masses of his day had fallen under the sway of a corrupt "élite" composed of semi-cultured schemers and operators: "Whereas in the past, the normal mechanisms of selection had tended to bring the bearers of cultural values to the top, or else educated the ascending groups as they rose, at present negative selection gives a position of pre-eminence to those who were unable to live up to the standards of modern culture and were deficient in the mastery of their impulses and in self-control. As a result of their triumph, their values become the dominant ones, and an inner conflict of motives develops in the psychological life of the individual too."[48]

The forces that Mannheim described more than half a century ago are in fact still at work, and indeed were more at work in earlier societies than Mannheim realized.

CULTURE, DETERMINING FACTORS, AND CULTURAL DETERMINISM

Anthropologists are ordinarily impressed by how cultural attributes and products are, in the words of Kroeber and Kluckhohn, "extrasomatic and transmissible by mechanisms other than biological heredity" and "essentially lacking [not present] in sub-human species" and "characteristic of the human species."[49] Anthropologists' heightened awareness of the distinctiveness of human beings protects them from the fashionable forms of positivistic reductionism that have infected the other social and behavioural sciences of late, and they have rather consistently emphasized the distinction between the human and "natural" worlds. In their clear separation of "nature-concepts" and "culture-concepts," they manifest what Ernst Cassirer regarded as one of the defining characteristics of the humanistic sensibility.[50]

The natural scientist, even when not promoting the positivist program, is inclined to take a less humanistic view of culture. The historian of biology Ernst Mayr writes:

To characterize man by such criteria as consciousness, or by the possession of mind and of intelligence, is not very helpful, because there is good evidence that man differs from apes and many other animals (even the dog!) in these characteristics only quantitatively. It is language more than anything else that permits the transmission of information from generation to generation and thus the development of non-material culture. Speech, thus, is the most characteristic human feature. It is often said that culture is man's most unique characteristic. Actually, this is very much a matter of definition. If one defines culture as that which is transmitted (by example and learning) from older to younger individuals, then culture is very widespread among animals ... Thus, even in the evolution of culture there is not a sharp break between animal and man. Though culture is more important in man, perhaps by several orders of magnitude, the capacity for culture is not unique with him but a product of gradual evolution.[51]

But Mayr has had enough exposure to humanistic literature to recognize the mistake of defining culture too narrowly, and he moves on to a reflection in the spirit of philosophical wonder: "Why primitive man should have been selected for a brain of such perfection that 100,000 years later it permitted the achievements of a Descartes, Darwin, or Kant, or the invention of the computer and the visits to the moon, or the literary accomplishments of a Shakespeare or Goethe, is hard to understand. But then, of course, man will always be a puzzle to man."[52]

By the time Aristotle provided intellectuals with the standard distinction between human-made and "natural" objects,[53] he had long accepted his teacher Plato's view of the human being as a rational as well as a social animal, the difference between body and soul was generally taken for granted,[54] and the distinction between *nomos* and *physis* had been firmly established in the minds of leading Greek intellectuals.[55] Despite the periodic emergence of positivistic tendencies in philosophy and the social sciences, that classical dichotomy has had continuing utility. Even so, it still has been necessary during the last hundred and fifty years for such thinkers as Dilthey and Cassirer to remind fellow students of the "human sciences" how different cultural products are from the things that natural scientists study. Thus Cassirer, after having exposed the silliness inherent in Taine's positivistic analysis of works of fine art, points out, almost in exasperation:

The object of *nature* appears to lie immediately before our eyes. To be sure, keener epistemological analysis teaches us [to know better] whenever more numerous and more complicated concepts are required in order to define this object, in order to determine the characteristics of the 'objects' of physics, chemistry, and biology. But this determination perfects itself in a certain uniform direction: we go to and from the object, as it were, in order to learn to know it ever more exactly. But the cultural object requires a different [kind of] observation: for it lies in back of us, so to speak. Indeed, at first sight it appears to be more familiar and more accessible than any other object. For what can man comprehend sooner and more completely – as Vico has remarked – than what he himself has created? But even here there emerges a limit to knowledge which is not easy to overcome. For the *reflexive* process of conception is opposed in tendency to the *productive* process; both cannot be accomplished at one and the same time. Culture is forever creating new linguistic, artistic, and religious symbols in an uninterrupted stream. But science and philosophy must analyze this language of symbols into its elements in order to make it intelligible. They must treat analytically what was produced synthetically.[56]

That some anthropologists have listened to such talk is evidenced by these comments of Leslie A. White: "The physical category is composed of non-living phenomena or systems; the biological, of living organisms. The cultural category, or order, of phenomena is made up of events that are dependent upon a faculty peculiar to the human species, namely, the ability to use symbols. These events are the ideas, beliefs, languages, tools, utensils, customs, sentiments, and institutions that make up the civilization – or culture, to use the anthropological term – of any people, regardless of time, place, or degree of development. Culture is passed down from one generation to another, or it may be borrowed freely by one tribe from another. Its elements interact with one another in accordance with principles of their own. Culture thus constitutes a supra-biological, or extra-somatic, class of events, a process *sui generis*."[57] All that is lacking in this otherwise-fine analysis is an appreciation of the normative considerations traditionally associated with culture.

When we compare the cultural and other orders, we rarely consider only the human being's ability to do things with symbols. Ordinarily we go on to look at how this capacity, combined with other characteristics of a human being, has contributed to the development of the central features associated with "human nature." We associate some of those features with human dignity, which we see as both a quality of all (or most) human beings and an ideal to be more and more closely approximated through culture and self-improvement. Here we attach great importance to the distinctive modes of self-determination of which most human beings are capable, and we associate these with the individual's freedom, which again is both a quality of most human beings and an ideal to be increasingly realized through culture and self-perfection. As we noted in chapter 1, human dignity and freedom play a major role in our evaluations of the relative authenticity of cultural products.

According to proponents of one or another form of philosophical or social-scientific determinism, human beings are, if free at all, then not as free – and not capable of being as free – as has generally been believed by moralists and humanists. Determinists generally see non-determinists as acting on the basis of unclear concepts that retard personal and social development. Some writers, such as the behaviouralist B.F. Skinner, regard the concept of dignity as similarly problematic.[58]

According to most traditional paradigms of cultural activity, cultural products are generally produced freely and promoted for the good of the agent, for the good of those who stand to benefit by appropriating the products, and for the good of the groups and communities to which these people belong. But most of us are well aware of determining factors and know that participation in cultural processes is rather less conscious, intentional, and deliberate in some instances than in others. We indicate the limits of awareness when we observe, for example, that a certain cultural product came into being as a "largely accidental" by-product of some activity, or that a certain person was "unwittingly" a participant in a certain institution, or that a particular person "did not realize" that she had been led to see or believe something in a particular way.

Even when there is awareness of one's involvement in a cultural process, one may correctly believe that one had little if any choice but to participate. For example, one may correctly feel that one has been forced to promote or appropriate certain cultural products, particularly those related to complex, long-established institutions, or that one has been determined to appropriate certain cultural products as a result of indoctrination, conditioning, enculturation, and the like. And, of course, one may correctly believe that one has been led to do so by means of the kinds of manipulation and deception that we considered in chapter 1.

The determinist, however, sees determination by external or subconscious forces as characteristic of all or most cultural activity. He believes that careful philosophical and scientific analysis of cultural activity shows that the idea that most participation in cultural processes is a matter of self-determination is a false or confused idea – at best, in Hans Vaihinger's words, a "practical fiction." As for freedom, Vaihinger writes:

Human actions are regarded as free, and therefore as 'responsible,' and contrasted with the 'necessary' course of natural events. We need not here recapitulate the familiar antinomies found in this contradictory concept; it not only contradicts observation which shows that everything obeys unalterable laws, but is also self-contradictory, for an absolutely free, chance act, resulting from nothing, is ethically just as valueless as an absolutely necessary one. In spite of all these contradictions, however, we not only make use of this concept in ordinary life in judging moral actions, but it is also the foundation of criminal law. Without this assumption punishment inflicted for any act would, from an ethical standpoint, be unthinkable, for it would simply be a precautionary measure for protecting others against crime. Our judgment of our fellowmen is likewise so completely bound up with this ideational construct [Begriffsgebilde] that we can no longer do without it. In the course of their development, men have formed this important construct from immanent necessity, because only on this basis is a high degree of culture and morality possible. But this does not prevent our realizing that it is itself a logical monstrosity, a contradiction; in a word, only a fiction and not an hypothesis.[59]

Most determinists are prepared to go further than Vaihinger and propose that the idea of freedom, not being even a practical necessity, be eliminated as much as possible from our understanding of human behaviour.

While this is not the place to address the various ramifications of the philosophical problem of free will versus determinism, we can see that determinism is ordinarily inconsistent with the ascription of authenticity and inauthenticity to cultural products. When we ascribe some degree of authenticity to a cultural product, we normally do so on the understanding that people are not only generally responsible for their manipulativeness but to some extent obliged to counter the manipulativeness of others. Despite what Vaihinger says, if we are to take seriously the idea of freedom, and the moral ideas that rest on it or are tied up with it, then we must regard these ideas as more than useful fictions.[60] Further, if we are to deal constructively with inauthentic culture as a social problem, we must believe that it is a matter about which people, including its promoters, are in a position to do something.

Since we cannot satisfactorily deal here with all the deterministic theories applicable to the analysis of cultural processes, I consider the one most obviously relevant to our investigation – the theory of cultural determinism. Proponents might point out that the appropriation of cultural products represented in, for example, buying a vase, voting for a political candidate, or agreeing to participate with our co-religionists in a complex rite is already a highly sophisticated mode of behaviour. Such appropriation differs significantly from the ordinary mode involved in enculturation. We are subject to enculturation when, in our earliest years, we possess at most[61] a weak and rudimentary form of personal autonomy, and, despite the sophistication that we subsequently attain through development of intellectual and other skills, we can never entirely free ourselves of early influences on our character and judgment. Ruth Benedict has written: "The life-history of the individual is first and foremost an accommodation to the patterns and standards traditionally handed down in his community. From the moment of his birth the customs into which he is born shape his experience and behaviour. By the time he can talk, he is the little creature of his culture."[62] Malinowski has observed: "Every human being is born into a family, a religion, a system of knowledge, and often into a social stratification and political constitution, which, often having existed for ages beforehand, are not changed or even affected during his lifetime."[63]

Of the various groups or communities to which we belong in our earliest years, the family is in a sense the most important, even though the people who most directly raise us have themselves been subject to enculturation through the political, religious, and other communities to which they have belonged. "The primary channel of transmission of culture," Eliot thus observes, "is the family: no man wholly escapes from the kind, or wholly surpasses the degree, of culture which he acquired from his early environment."[64]

We are mightily influenced by our "social environment" at all stages of life, not just when we are very young. And of course, when we are very young, we do not possess the capacities that we normally do in later life for passing some degree of reflective, reasonable judgment on the cultural products that we encounter. We acquire the language that our parents, earliest teachers, and their fellows speak; and we gradually learn to participate in various educational, political, religious, aesthetic, and technological institutions in which those who are raising us participate. We derive from our earliest and later social environments certain ways of thinking, reasoning, and acting; even most of our basic values and ideals are derived in at least their basic form from some social environment. Why then moralize about cultural products and the people who produce and promote them? Are not our mature existential commitments, with the moral ideals that lie at the heart of them, not simply therefore the result of a highly sophisticated form of manipulation? How can we see beyond, or transcend, the cultural material that has been imposed on us from the start and reinforced and supplemented, by various groups and communities, at progressive stages of our development?

Most human beings possess capacities for personal insight and creative self-improvement that are not destroyed by enculturation and in fact are enhanced by certain of its forms. Thus, while observing that we are all "little creatures of our culture" by the time we can talk, Benedict also notes: "In reality, society and the individual are not antagonists. His culture provides the raw material of which the individual makes his life. If it is meagre, the individual suffers; if it is rich, the individual has the chance to rise to his opportunity."[65] "No individual can arrive even at the threshold of his potentialities without a culture in which he participates," but "Conversely, no civilization has in it any element which in the last analysis is not the contribution of an individual."[66] Moreover, "No anthropologist with a background of experience of other cultures has ever believed that individuals were automatons, mechanically carrying out the decrees of their civilization. No culture yet observed has been able to eradicate the differences in the temperaments of the persons who compose it. It is always a give-and-take."[67]

When a child accepts the cultural products put before him, he does not appropriate them with mature powers of reflective and reasonable judgment. (Even with those mature powers, a highly educated adult's judgments are still substantially influenced by his present and past social environments). But even a child makes important assessments in appropriating cultural products, and some involve rudimentary determination of their relative authenticity. Typically, a child looks on his mother – usually his primary contact with society and the social environment – as a source of nurture. He looks on her with trust, and, in learning to speak her language and taking up the other cultural products that she puts before him, he does so in the belief, perhaps based partly on instinct and partly on experience, that she has his interests at heart and is concerned with nurturing him rather than harming him. He believes, ordinarily correctly for the most part, that she is exposing him to cultural products in the same spirit as she attends to his most basic physical and emotional needs. He also recognizes fairly early that she wants him not only to be contented throughout life but in certain ways to be a good person, and that she and his father are equipping him with intellectual and other skills that will enable him to lead a good life long after he can no longer depend on them.

But as he gets older, the child, now equipped with powers of reason and reflection provided him largely for his own good, can make more personal and more discriminating judgments about the cultural products around him. He is able to recognize, for one thing, that some of those products, though passed on to him as elements of the nurturing process, are not necessarily good, even by the criteria transmitted to him by way of his social environment. He begins to refine and otherwise modify those criteria according to his own understanding.

In time he comes to realize that, though his parents and first teachers probably have truly loved him and been deeply concerned with his interests, even to the point of being prepared to make great sacrifices for his well-being, they also have their own personal interests and ways of understanding things. Further, their interests and modes of understanding do not necessarily coincide with those that, through his developing capacities for personal commitment and understanding, he now takes to be his own.

With that recognition, he is now ready to pass into adulthood. He also comes to recognize in time that his parents and first teachers, in putting before him certain cultural products for appropriation, have been fulfilling what they take to be a major social obligation – to prepare him to relate well to his fellows in the communities to which he belongs (and will some day belong) – and thus that they have been taking into consideration the interests of those people as well as his interest and their own. And he comes to realize more and more the extent to which his upbringing has involved elements not only of manipulation but also of force and negative reinforcement.

Consider the corresponding case of certain individuals in primitive societies. The comparative unity and solidarity of primitive societies are well known even to people who have never opened an anthropology book. But even in primitive societies, as Paul Radin has shown,[68] there are certain people of a philosophical inclination; and such people, who represent in a sense Mannheim's "intellectual élite," are given to taking a harder look than their fellows do at the quality of the society's cultural products. Since the culture of a primitive society is characteristically religious in spirit, the leaders of the society routinely justify promotion of particular cultural products by referring to the desires of gods and spirits. The intellectually adventurous members of the society, while vulnerable to social pressure and negative reinforcement, engage in creative thinking about the relevant metaphysical and ethical issues, and in that way a primitive society gradually develops into a more civilized one.

People disapprove of inauthentic culture because it fails to meet certain standards or criteria. First, inauthentic cultural products, because of the spirit in which they have been conceived, created, and promoted, tend to be inferior by the various instrumental or utilitarian criteria of goodness deemed relevant to the kind of product in question. In any number of ways, they do not satisfactorily fulfil the purposes we had in mind when we first appropriated them; they do not serve as efficiently, completely, consistently, or helpfully as otherwise comparable cultural products. They may, for example, fall apart too quickly, confuse us, fail to hold our interest, require too much of our time and energy, or disrupt our pleasant relations with our fellows. Second, in having been produced or promoted in the spirit that they have, they represent an affront to us and our fellows with respect to such standards as justice, integrity, freedom, responsibility, dignity, honesty, and compassion. Thirdly, they tend to interfere with the realization of ideals that we associate with the process of becoming better off – with our pursuit of such things as prosperity, self-respect, and peace of mind. In addition, they inhibit actualization of ideals that we link with becoming a better human being, such as wisdom, courage, temperance, tolerance, and the aforementioned justice and freedom. Finally, they fail to conform to a "metaphysical" standard, and they strike us as "unreal." In not having been conceived as genuinely meliorative, they are not truly "cultural" products. They are "imitations" of cultural products so conceived, and they have been passed off by manipulative promoters as being what they are not. They are in that sense mock-cultural products, even if they satisfy us in certain ways, and even if they turn out to have a meliorative, cultivating influence in some ways.

3

THE RELEVANCE TO AUTHENTICITY OF
WHAT IS RELATIVE AND WHAT IS NOT

CULTURE, RELATIVITY, AND CULTURAL RELATIVISM

Perhaps the standards or criteria that we apply in ascribing inauthenticity are themselves arbitrary. Perhaps they are themselves simply cultural products that were initially appropriated by us in some basic form as a result of highly sophisticated parental or communal manipulation, or as a result of other features of our early social environment that had little to do with any sort of "objective" or "absolute" truth or goodness. Perhaps then our basic standards, criteria, values, and ideals are themselves inauthentic cultural products or, worse yet, inferior to other possible standards according to some higher-order standard, of which, owing to the limitations of the social environments to which we have been exposed, is unknown to us. If our basic values and ideals, and even our modes of perception and reflection, are arbitrarily derived from the social environments to which we have been exposed, by accident or fate or "circumstances," then why should we feel entitled or obliged to moralize about the quality of cultural products?

We are faced here with variations on the traditional philosophical problem of relativism. Recognizing the relativity of certain phenomena does not make us relativists, any more than recognizing the influence of certain determining factors makes us determinists. The relativist is someone who sees relativity as much more significant than most people realize. She believes that something very important, such as reality or truth or value, cannot be "absolute" or "objective" in the way that most people think it can. Relativists come in metaphilosophical, epistemological, and all sorts of ethical variants, but those who demand our attention here are "cultural relativists," and if they are right, then we may well be being arbitrary in our preference for the authentic over the inauthentic.

Our criteria of goodness may be "culture-bound" or, worse yet, in conflict with the ethos of the community to which we principally belong. Perhaps we should even regard inauthentic culture as preferable to authentic or, alternatively, alter our conceptions of authenticity and inauthenticity to conform to the "real" values and ideals of a society that, while publicly discouraging and condemning manipulativeness, encourages it by rewarding those who have mastered and refined its techniques. Thinkers such as Callicles, Machiavelli, and Nietzsche have argued that there is something "unnatural" – or inauthentic, we might say – about the supposedly lofty ideals of compassion, tolerance, and the like that have been promoted by so many official and semi-official agents of the dominant Western religious and philosophical traditions.

Though cultural relativism can be conceptually distinguished from the cultural determinism considered in chapter 2, the two fit together, so that we may speak even of a "cultural relativist-determinist" position. Since the cultural determinist believes that all values and modes of perception are essentially derived directly from the social environment and are not influenced by personal insight into objective states of affairs, and since he also is aware of the significant differences between the value system and metaphysical framework of his own society and those of other societies, it is appropriate for him to be a cultural relativist. Again, since the cultural relativist seeks to put the conflicting value-systems of different societies on the same epistemological level, and since he denies that reason, intuition, or any other form of knowing can reveal to careful inquirers what is "absolutely" and "objectively" good, right, or true, it is convenient for him to assume that enculturation is the ultimate source of a person's basic values and ideals.

A particularly clear and influential version of the relativist-determinist position has been presented by the anthropologist Melville J. Herskovits in his popular text, *Man and His Works*. There have been other influential versions of the position, such as those of Edward Westermarck[1] and W.G. Sumner,[2] and thoughtful and balanced assessments of the position have been provided in recent years by more cautious anthropologists (such as Kluckhohn[3]) and philosophers (such as Paul Taylor[4]). But Herskovits's concise, lively, and comparatively non-technical version clarifies those aspects of it that are most relevant to an understanding of inauthentic culture.

In a chapter devoted to "the problem of cultural relativism,"[5] Herskovits says that, even though people have often made moral judgments regarding the ethical principles of different peoples, it has become increasingly evident that such evaluations depend on acceptance of the premises from which they derive. Moreover, "Many of the criteria on which judgment is based are in conflict, so that conclusions drawn from one definition of what is desirable will not agree with those based on another formulation."[6] Herskovits offers a simple example. He contrasts the polygamous family of Dahomean society with the monogamous family of our own, points out the strengths of the former, and concludes: "Thus polygamy, when looked at from the point of view of those who practise it, is seen to hold values that are not apparent from the outside. A similar case can be made for monogamy, however, when it is attacked by those who are enculturated to a different kind of family structure. And what is true of a particular phase of culture such as this, is also true of others. Evaluations are *relative* to the cultural background out of which they arise."[7]

He then gives a concise statement of what he calls "the principle of cultural relativism," which he believes "derives from a vast array of factual data, gained from the application of techniques in field study that have permitted us to penetrate the underlying value-systems of societies having diverse customs." Briefly, "Judgments are based on experience, and experience is interpreted by each individual in terms of his own enculturation." Herskovits immediately adds: "In adducing this principle we touch on many fundamental questions that philosophers have long raised."

Herskovits's defence of this principle is for the most part empirical rather than theoretical. He tells us that the principle that judgments stem from experience, which is the result of enculturation, has a sure psychological foundation,[8] and that many instances of how social norms vary are to be found in anthropological literature.[9] Even the definition of what is normal or abnormal is itself relative to the cultural frame of reference.

Of particular relevance here are Herskovits's concepts of enculturation and culture. Enculturation he perceives as "aspects of the learning experience which mark off man from other creatures, and by means of which, initially, and in later life, he achieves competence in his culture." It is thus "a process of conscious or unconscious conditioning, exercised within the limits sanctioned by a given body of custom."[10] It is the primary mechanism making for cultural stability and at the same time induces change when operative on mature people. As for culture itself, it is not simply a group to which someone belongs but rather, as conceived broadly, the human-made part of the environment,[11] though we may speak of "a culture" or "different cultures," in that people who live in different times or places are exposed to different human-made environments.

Herskovits next tells us that ethnocentrism – the point of view that one's own way of life should be preferred to all others – is the primary inspiration for the evaluation of culture.[12] Ethnocentrism characterizes all peoples, non-literate and literate. But a philosophy of cultural relativism enables us to grasp the significance of the ways of living of different peoples, to turn again to our own culture with a fresh perspective, and to develop an objectivity that can be achieved in no other manner.[13] Having himself developed this "objectivity," Herskovits criticizes the widespread beliefs that the cultures of non-literate peoples are "inferior" to our own and that we may simply contrast our own "civilized" culture with those that are "primitive." He argues that dismissing non-literate peoples as "primitive" or "savage" is pointless and childish and that anyone who has some understanding of non-literate peoples soon begins to appreciate the complexity and reasonableness of their way of life.

Herskovits realizes that the principle of cultural relativism may be seen as having dangerous implications. He pictures a potential critic as asking, "But does this not mean that all systems of moral values, all concepts of right and wrong, are founded on such shifting sands that there is no need for morality, for proper behavior, for ethical codes? Does not a relativistic philosophy, indeed, imply a negation of these?"[14] Herskovits replies that we must not assume that, because moral values are relative to time and place, they therefore do not exist or have utility within particular cultures. Cultural relativism must be sharply distinguished from other kinds of relativism that would negate all social controls over conduct.[15] "Emphasis on the worth of many ways of life, not one, is an affirmation of the values in each culture." Awareness of cultural relativity should in no way lead to belief that moral values within particular cultures are arbitrary or unimportant. To make this point clear, Herskovits introduces a distinction between absolutes and universals: "*Absolutes* are fixed, and, in so far as convention is concerned, are not admitted to have variation, to differ from culture to culture, from epoch to epoch. Universals, on the other hand, are those least common denominators to be extracted, inductively, from comprehension of the range of variation which all phenomena of the natural or cultural world manifest." When we have grasped this distinction, we realize that, "To say that there is no absolute criterion of value or morals, or even, psychologically, of time or space, does not mean that such criteria, in differing *forms*, do not comprise universals in human culture."[16] And so the doctrine of cultural relativism does not support any form of nihilism. On the contrary, it is a doctrine, Herskovits says, that teaches us that though value systems differ considerably, they are all equally valid responses to human needs.

This comparatively undiluted version of the cultural relativist-determinist position has been widely and effectively criticized, and some of its most serious weaknesses should already be apparent in the light of our earlier reflections. Nevertheless, I shall consider at some length certain flaws in this model, for doing so offers deeper appreciation of the constellation of values associated with the ascription of authenticity and inauthenticity, values that are diminished and degraded by the relativist-determinist treatment of them. One of the most objectionable features of the model is that it can easily be employed to lend legitimacy to something such as manipulativeness, which, as was noted in chapter 1, has already developed in our society to the point where many people grudgingly acknowledge it as one of the major folkways of our culture.

Herskovits's cultural-relativist position is, like most versions, vitiated by two basic confusions about what it is that the cultural relativist believes. One concerns the relation of empirical data to value theory; the other the relation of descriptive theory to normative theory. First, he makes the misleading claim that the principle of cultural relativism, in Herskovits's words, "derives from a vast array of factual data." Relativism is not simply a conclusion at which people arrive by means of induction; it is a theory. The fact that people in different societies make different judgments on the basis of somewhat different criteria does not in itself establish that all the judgments are equally sound. At one time there was widespread disagreement about whether the earth is round, but the shape of the earth has never been a purely "relative" matter. Cultural relativism requires a theoretical as well as an empirical component: the cultural relativist owes us an explanation of, among other things, why it is that disagreement about values is, from the standpoint of epistemology, vastly different from disagreement about the shape of the earth. Herskovits, like most cultural relativists, does in fact have plenty of theory to go along with his fundamental observation that people from different cultures disagree about various important matters. But this theory does not simply follow from anthropological data; rather, it is an interpretation and explanation of those data.

Second, he offers a baffling juxtaposition of two theses. The first thesis is descriptive – that a person's value judgments are essentially determined through enculturation. The second is normative – that a person's moral judgments ought to be brought by her into conformity with the ethical code of her people. The juxtaposition of these two theses is puzzling: if thesis 1 is true, then thesis 2 not only is unnecessary but makes no sense, for if people are necessarily enculturated to interpret experience as they do and make the value judgments that they do, then there is no point in suggesting that they are sufficiently free to choose one set of value judgments rather than another. Why should one worry about what people ought to value when enculturation supposedly determines their values?

The cultural relativist is not saying simply that enculturation helps determine a person's value judgments. Once he grants that other factors may enter into the agent's judgment, he is allowing for the possibility that rational and cognitive factors can and do enter into the process of value judgment, in which case it is not at all clear why he feels justified in regarding value judgments as essentially "relative" and "determined."

But by providing a normative as well as a descriptive theory, cultural relativists such as Herskovits indicate that they are at least sometimes aware of significant limits to the influence of enculturation. Not everyone in a community obeys its laws and follows its customs; within every community there are certain people who, for one reason or another, refuse to accept some of the most important cultural products that their ancestors, leaders, and peers have put before them for appropriation. Such people can pose a threat to the stability of their culture; but in undermining the influence of certain major institutions, they may ultimately be serving their fellows and their descendants well. Yet for someone such as Herskovits, who believes that cultural stability is primary and depends on respect for tradition and convention, it is not at all clear how someone who undermines cultural stability by rejecting tradition and convention can ultimately benefit his community. Only someone who is seriously prepared to acknowledge the possibility of value considerations that transcend a particular community's traditions and conventions can understand such a thing.

We took note in chapter 2 of Ruth Benedict's helpful observation that all elements of a civilization develop from the contributions of individuals. (Those individuals may perceive themselves as having derived their insights from higher beings, but in any case, higher beings are always seen as initially speaking to communities through individuals gifted with prophetic power.) Accepting the values of one's community involves at least indirectly accepting the judgment of particular individuals – the past and present leaders of the community. To appropriate freely the values of one's community is to accept that the judgments made by such individuals are sound. If one believes that founders, ancestors, or present leaders have been manipulating their fellows for their own narrow, self-serving purposes, then one will be inclined, even despite peer pressure, to reject, or at least entertain serious doubts about, the cultural products that they have put forward for appropriation.

Willingness to accept the basic institutions of one's community is ordinarily a function largely of one's trust in the leaders of the community – if not the present ones, then at least the founders. If one is not forced or deceived into appropriating communal traditions and conventions, then one freely accepts them, and while one may do so exclusively on the basis of personal insight into their soundness, one normally relies partly on one's confidence in those who have helped establish and maintain them. People are generally willing to live with the institutions promoted by those in authority, but only if they believe that those in such positions have been reasonably wise and just people, who have aimed at bettering the community and its members, not simply advancing themselves or their colleagues.

A thoughtful member or group can often see that certain values and institutions of the community are unsound – that they do not "work," do not contribute to the personal and communal realization of happiness, self-perfection, or some other ideal that seems worth realizing, or may even eventually lead to destruction of the community. Even a sophisticated child can see that it is not necessarily right to do something simply because most people in his community have done it for a very long time. Obviously, the judgments of those leaders who established a community's basic codes and institutions cannot simply be explained by the fact that they were enculturated in that community, or by their having respected authority, tradition, or convention in that community. Again, criticism of communal codes and institutions cannot simply be explained by enculturation.

Herskovits himself acknowledges that enculturation is a force that, when operative on mature people, induces change. Cultures often undergo radical transformations, and new cultures are sometimes born in the process; and the impetus for transformation of a way of life obviously cannot simply be enculturation itself. The birth or transformation of a culture has to be explained partly by reference to creative leadership, as must the origin of certain groups within cultures. Creative leadership can also prevent a people from being enculturated in destructive ways.

Great spiritual leaders, symbolized in the world's sacred literatures by such figures as Abraham, Moses, Buddha, and Jesus, can transcend certain basic ideas and values with which they have been enculturated and transform the world-view of the people among whom they live (and others as well). They are often able to induce even weak people to transcend certain aspects of their own enculturation, even when such people have been influenced by social environments that are very old, very complex, and highly evolved.

Great spiritual leaders, who are always primarily great teachers, appeal to something, or certain things, that lie beyond – or at least behind – the more limited ideas, values, and institutions that their less visionary and less adventurous fellows have been enculturated in or otherwise determined to accept. They can break through the walls of enculturation and ethnocentrism and stimulate the creation and promotion of a new and better cultural order. They can encourage the growth of spiritually creative intracultural groups, and they can prevent groups from being completely enculturated with the world-view and way of life of the larger and more powerful community in which they live. They can establish conditions by which, even in their absence and the absence of any powerful moral leadership, their world-view can still survive. There are also, of course, many less gifted people who can stimulate social transformations that, though not radical, still reveal the limits of enculturation. Alas, the influence of leaders is not necessarily positive. Barbarians too have their leaders, who are "creative" in their own way, though they are essentially agents of reaction and destruction.

David Riesman began his much-discussed social-scientific treatise, *The Lonely Crowd*, by observing: "Social character is the product of social forms; in that sense, man is made by society. Yet we know that social forms change; sometimes men change them; and character changes with them."[17] This basic insight led Riesman to consider at great length the role of character in the initiation of change. His research led him to be impressed by the differences between tradition-directed, inner-directed, and other-directed individuals, but his deterministic assumptions prevented him from relating this distinction to the relevant insights of existential thinkers and other humanists.

More satisfactory in this regard is Mannheim's description of the role of the intelligentsia in the creation of culture. While acknowledging the centrality of those social organizations that in the cultural sphere take the shape of institutions, his theory emphasizes, particularly in "liberal society," the "free, unregulated part of social life, which, in its spontaneous forms, moulds intellectual and cultural life."[18] Freedom is manifested not only in the creative activity and influence of members of intellectual elites but in the individual reflection that influences all thoughtful human beings in their determination of whether – or to what extent – to appropriate cultural products put before them. A significant part of that reflection involves assessing the trustworthiness of those who would have them appropriate those products, whether the products be consumer products, works of fine art, social policies, or elements of a world-view.

Herskovits speaks of the "humility reflected in the tolerance of the cultural relativistic position,"[19] but rather than teaching respect for other cultures, the cultural relativist-determinist undermines our confidence in the criteria by which cultures could reasonably be judged to be worthy of respect or disrespect. If the cultural products of a society are to be assessed exclusively by the society's own values, how is an outsider, whose values have been derived from other sources, to judge those cultural products? She cannot even be sure what it means to say that the institutions of the society "work" for that society; for perhaps they are functioning by that society's peculiar standards even when people are torturing and murdering members of minorities in concentration camps. According to the cultural-relativist model, it may not even be appropriate for us to expect consistency in that society's codes. But are we being tolerant if we accept that it may be appropriate for people in that society to torture their neighbours to death?[20]

The cultural-relativist position may seem to promote tolerance in its freeing of people from their ethnocentric attitudes. In fact, people have generally not been as ethnocentric as the cultural relativist suggests. Leaders of many ancient and modern societies have deliberately imported ideas and institutions from elsewhere. There have been societies in which large numbers of people have argued that certain values and modes of perception of the day should be abandoned in favour of those of earlier societies. Few if any communities that have advanced beyond their primitive phase have been so ethnocentric as to refuse in principle to integrate successful institutions of other communities into their own. Even in ancient times, people from different cultural backgrounds had considerable contact with one another – enough to learn from each other and to import "alien" ideas, values, and institutions.

Herskovits realizes that the world cannot be analysed precisely into cultures as it can into tribes, nations, or religious groups. For Herskovits, culture is the human-made part of the environment, and most people in the modern world do not simply belong to "a culture." Their social environment in societies such as our own is usually highly complex. One criterion by which we distinguish "primitive" peoples from "civilized" ones is relative complexity of culture, for in an advanced society, many cultural traditions intersect and blend. The Dahomeans are essentially just that, Dahomeans, though their culture allows for various class and vocational distinctions. But consider, for example, the social environment of a Canadian, who may be anglophone, francophone, or incapable of speaking either official language; Roman Catholic, Anglican, Presbyterian, Jew, Sikh, atheist, or whatever; of Anglo-Saxon, eastern European, or some other origin; a professional, a skilled worker, or an unskilled worker; and so forth. He may be a vegetarian, a socialist, or a Mason. Furthermore, three French-Canadian Roman Catholics may perceive themselves as being first and foremost French-speaking, Canadian, and Roman Catholic, respectively.

As most individuals in advanced societies belong to several communities, they are subject to a complex social environment that represents the combination of several social environments, and these may seem relatively distinct to those individuals or may blend together in influencing their judgment. This may suggest to some social scientists only that people in advanced societies are all the more subject to determining factors and manipulation, coming from many directions. But awareness of one's membership in various communities can also be an incentive to assessing the institutionalized cultural products of one group in relation to those of another. The competition itself provides the "consumer" of cultural products with a kind of freedom. People in advanced societies often find themselves having to make decisions or choices as to which of two competing cultural products, or sets of cultural products, they are going to appropriate. Most of us know what it is like to have to weigh the judgment of parents against that of peers, of that of religious teachers against that of learned secular thinkers, of that of political leaders against that of classical authors, and so on. Our judgments in these cases are influenced by determining factors from enculturation and other sources, and by manipulation as well, but rational considerations routinely enter into our judgment too, and one thing that we are ordinarily inclined to examine closely is the character or motivation of both the immediate and the traditional promoters of competing cultural products.

Most people in our society recognize that their moral judgments reflect to some extent the attitudes and beliefs of the people (and peoples) among whom we live. We know that the fact that we ought to wear certain clothes to a formal dinner party has nothing to do with the world-view of Dahomeans. The rightness of wearing formal clothes on certain occasions is something that pertains to a particular culture with which we associate ourselves, and few of us are scandalized when we see films of African tribesmen attending their most formal rites without such clothes. We also know that when we enter the home of a friend or business associate who is from a faraway land or a religious community very different from our own, we should not do all the things that we are accustomed to doing in the homes of friends from cultural backgrounds more similar to our own. Part of being a cultured or civilized person is being tolerant of certain elements in the world-views of people who have certain ways that are strange, alien, or exotic to us. Thus, if the cultural relativist is indeed saying something exciting, as he thinks he is, then he must be saying rather more than that the judgments that a person makes, and the cultural products with which he associates himself, are partly determined by his enculturation.

As we saw above, there is another reason why the cultural relativist-determinist must be making a stronger claim. When one such as Herskovits tells us that "(e)valuations are *relative* to the cultural background out of which they arise," he is denying that any other influence on the individual's value judgment can outweigh enculturation. If there are, let us say, good reasons for refraining from something such as human sacrifice that are not simply culture-bound, then certain moral evaluations are not simply relative to individuals' social environment. This is so even though perhaps the educational processes involved in his enculturation made him aware of rational considerations that transcend the traditions and conventions of the communities to which he has belonged.

For all her tolerance and open-mindedness, a reflective person tends to be less tolerant of certain attitudes and practices than less reflective people are. The "intolerance" of reflective people is a major impetus to progressive change. In our own society, for example, "cultured" people increasingly recognize that while we should work hard at being tolerant of most of the ways of minorities, we should not be indiscriminately tolerant, or "permissive," with respect to such things as sexist and racist attitudes, domestic violence, and manipulativeness. Having been enculturated to make moral and political evaluations prejudicial to women has not necessarily prevented people from coming to realize in time that sexist institutions are inauthentic and generally corrupt and that there is a need for progressive legislation to combat sexism. Moreover, the reflective person who works hard at appreciating the relativity of particular cultural products can also draw the line and refuse to be "tolerant" of sexist institutions in societies very different from his own, even when he has been told by certain self-professed experts that sexism is all right in societies with traditions very different from our own. A thoughtful person regards the rational arguments against something such as sexism as valid across cultures. Criticism of the cultural institutions of other peoples does not necessarily imply ethnocentrism, for there is no a priori reason for assuming that the criteria by which we assess our own institutions are necessarily irrelevant in other societies.

INTERCULTURAL DIALOGUE AND THE IDEAL OF CIVILIZATION

Some of us have had an opportunity to discuss moral issues with people from different cultural backgrounds, but even most people who have not are aware that intercultural dialogue not only is possible but is often useful. Through intercultural dialogue, people have managed to change the ideas and attitudes of those from different backgrounds and in turn been persuaded to change some of their own ideas and attitudes. I refer here to genuine dialogue, not rhetorical manipulation, and specifically to the kind of rational discourse that appeals to shared ideas, interests, and values. It is not always possible to draw others into dialogue; appreciation of the value of dialogue is itself something that develops with increased civility. What are the conditions of intercultural dialogue, particularly on moral issues? How is such a thing possible?

The most obvious condition of intercultural dialogue is uniformity in human nature. Thus, as Kroeber and Kluckhohn have observed, the anthropologist typically attaches as much importance to uniformities in culture as to the historicity of culture.[21] The literary scholar Lionel Trilling remarked: "Generally our awareness of the differences between the moral assumptions of one culture and those of another is so developed and active that we find it hard to believe there is any such thing as an essential human nature; but we all know moments when these differences, as literature attests to them, seem to make no difference, seem scarcely to exist. We read the *Iliad* or the plays of Sophocles or Shakespeare and they come so close to our hearts and minds that they put to rout, or into abeyance, our instructed consciousness of the moral life as it is conditioned by a particular culture."[22]

Stephen Fuchs is one of several anthropologists who has argued that his discipline has done more to undermine cultural relativism than to promote it: "The study of the origin of man and his culture has … been profitable in providing the proof that present-day social institutions and moral standards are sound and healthy; that they are basically the same as those that prevailed when mankind was young and that they will stand the wear and tear of the centuries yet to come. Mankind and human culture are subject to change and evolution, it is true, but this change and evolution is restricted and limited to unessentials. Not all human values are relative and unexchangeable; some are absolute values which cannot be touched and modified or else human society will suffer therefrom and be reduced to sterility and decay."[23]

Fuchs has overstated the point, but it is still worth stating. All human beings have certain needs, and there are specific cultural responses to those needs. In providing a brief analysis of the relation of transcultural needs to cultural responses, Malinowski draws attention to the basic needs of metabolism, reproduction, bodily comforts, safety, movement, growth, and health and to the corresponding cultural responses of commissariat, kinship, shelter, protection, activity, training, and hygiene. Beyond the basic needs are "derived" needs and their specific cultural responses: economics, social control, education, and political organization.[24]

Herskovits recognizes the existence of "universals," though he does not see their existence as counting in any way against the cultural relativist-determinist model. But in defending Dahomean polygamy, Herskovits presents a rational argument to show that it "works." Determining what works, or what is good or right by any other criterion, ordinarily requires the use of reason. One does not defend an institution such as Dahomean polygamy simply by pointing to the phenomenon of enculturation; one defends it by presenting reasons for believing it to be sound. Herskovits realizes that as different as Dahomeans may be from his readers, those readers can be brought to appreciate the reasonableness of those who have established certain Dahomean institutions. Herskovits, speaking on behalf of the Dahomeans, has in effect entered into intercultural dialogue with his readers; he knows that readers can relate to the Dahomeans because, despite their unique qualities, Dahomeans are human beings with human problems. All people have common needs, interests, weaknesses, fears, and aspirations; and when they have reached a certain level of cultural development, they can enter into rational discussion of the best ways to fulfil human aspirations and realize human ideals.

A second condition of intercultural dialogue is the human fascination with the "other." People often are irrationally antipathetic to those who differ from them in innocuous or positive ways; but even some of those very people like to travel in faraway lands, eat exotic foods, and chat occasionally with the immigrants next door. Interest in the exotic, which can be traced back to ancient times, has itself given rise to anthropological studies. People often experiment with foreign cultural products for the sake of experimentation itself and without any prudential motive; but often individuals look to other cultures to provide them with fresh ideas about how to improve their own lot and that of their fellows.

A third condition of intercultural dialogue is recognition that comparatively neutral and objective "third parties" can and do pass judgment on which of two competing cultural products (or sets of cultural products) is superior. Those who participate in intercultural dialogue on moral, political, aesthetic, and religious issues sometimes are impressed by the fact that they will be judged by "outsiders" and by posterity. Many people (and peoples) want outsiders, and their own distant descendants, to appreciate and respect the quality of their cultural products.

This is not simply a result of pride, vanity, or status; it is a matter of taking a wide view of one's place in the world and, indeed, of one's role in the development of the human order. And of course, we can and do make sensible judgments – judgments that are both reasonably sympathetic and reasonably critical – about the quality of cultures. We need to make those judgments because, among other reasons, we have to decide what cultural products of past cultures and alien cultures are worth our appropriating. Our judgments do not necessarily involve ethnocentrism. For example, T.S. Eliot wrote in 1948: "We can distinguish between higher and lower cultures;

we can distinguish between advance and retrogression. We can assert with some confidence that our own period is one of decline; that the standards of culture are lower than they were fifty years ago; and that the evidences of this decline are visible in every department of human activity."[25] Many people have made a comparable assessment of the cultural products of their own society.

An important aim for the cultural relativist, and clearly for Herskovits, is to undermine the traditional distinction between civilized and primitive peoples. However, one of the foremost students of cultural relativity, Edward Westermarck, speaks about a crucial difference between what he characterizes as "lower races" and "peoples more advanced in civilization." On the basis of his own anthropological studies, he concludes that the moral rules of different peoples are very similar.[26] Morality among "savages", however, has, "broadly speaking, only reference to members of the same community or tribe," and, "[a] stranger is in early society devoid of all rights." "When we pass from the lower races to peoples more advanced in civilization we find that the social unit has grown larger, that the nation has taken the place of the tribe, and that the circle within which the infliction of injuries is prohibited has been extended accordingly."[27]

The term *civilization* is almost as ambiguous as the term *culture*, not the least because there is widespread disagreement among its users as to whether it is properly interchangeable with the term *culture*. However, the suffix *-zation* reminds us that in at least its primary sense, the term *civilization* has been associated with a process of melioration or progressive development,[28] so that to treat it as interchangeable with the term *culture* is to draw attention, at least indirectly, to the traditional associations of culture with personal and communal development and the realization of personal and communal ideals. Those thinkers who have offered a philosophy of civilization have seen it as being a core element, if not the essence, of their philosophy of culture. Even Herskovits, despite his denial of the existence of ethical absolutes, sees *civilization* as for his own practical purposes a synonym of *culture*.[29] However, the term *civilization* has traditionally been even more widely employed than *culture* to contrast the condition of comparatively refined people with that of people who are in a state of relative savagery or barbarity.

Consider, for example, John Henry Newman's distinction between barbarous and civilized states in his 1853 lecture on "Barbarism and Civilization." "By 'barbarism', then, I suppose, in itself is meant a state of nature; and by 'civilization', a state of mental cultivation and discipline."[30] More specifically, "Brutes differ from men in this; that they cannot invent, cannot progress," whereas a human being "comes into the world with the capabilities, rather than the means and appliances, of life. He is, in his very idea, a creature of progress … Civilization is that state to which man's nature points and tends; it is the systematic use, improvement, and combination of those faculties which are his characteristic … It is the development of art out of nature."[31] "While bodily strength is the token of barbarian power, mental ability is the honourable badge of civilized states. The one is like Ajax, the other like Ulysses; civilized nations are constructive, barbarous are destructive. Civilization spreads by the ways of peace, by moral suasion, by means of literature, the arts, commerce, diplomacy, institutions; and, though material power can never be superseded, it is subordinate to the influence of mind."[32] Newman sees civilization – or culture – as a process of personal and communal self-perfection, and he associates a person's or community's becoming more civilized, more cultured, less barbarous, and less brutal with a condition of mental cultivation, discipline, and refinement inclining individuals and groups towards progressive development in four main areas: creativity and art; sociability and political stability; intellectuality; and reluctance to resort to force.

A somewhat more sophisticated version of this theory was offered almost a century later by the philosopher R.G. Collingwood, whose concern with explaining the essential cultural differences between the Allied powers and the Axis powers in 1942 was not unlike Newman's with articulating the same type of differences between Christians and Turks. Recognizing both the value and the limitations of etymological analysis,[33] Collingwood concludes that "civilization" is primarily "the name of a process whereby a community undergoes a mental change from the a condition of relative *barbarity* to one of relative *civility*."[34] That is, it designates primarily a process of "asymptotic approximation" to a certain ideal state or condition,[35] though it can also refer to the actual result of the process or to civility itself. What it means "specifically" as opposed to "generically" must be understood in terms of three factors. First, in relation to members of the same community, it means coming to obey rules of civil intercourse.[36] Second, with reference to the world of nature, it implies scientific or intelligent exploitation.[37] Third, vis-à-vis members of other communities, it means relative reluctance to use force.[38]

Collingwood elaborates on these three conditions in relation to education, wealth, law, peace, prosperity, and the ideals being realized in the meliorative process. Unlike Newman, however, he distinguishes barbarism from mere savagery – the condition of not being civilized. For Collingwood, barbarism is "hostility towards civilization; the effort, conscious or unconscious, to become less civilized than you are, either in general or in some special way, and, so far as in you lies, to promote a similar change in others."[39] This is a useful distinction, even if the terms *barbarism* and *barbarous* are more ambiguous than Collingwood indicates.

Writers such as Newman and Collingwood believe that it is very important, at least at certain times, to evaluate cultural products by reference to an ideal of civilization or culture. The criteria by which such evaluation is to be performed are not restricted to the conceptual frameworks operative in a particular community, but are implicit in the transcultural idea that people (and peoples) can become more "civilized" or more "cultured." But the cultural relativist-determinist is likely to be unimpressed and to regard this sort of theorizing as rather dogmatic. For one thing, he does not feel entirely comfortable with traditional concepts of culture rooted in the conception of *cultura* as cultivation; and to the extent that he is prepared to acknowledge that culture involves some sort of cultivation, he believes that the criteria of cultivation are relative to the particular culture. Confronted with the evidence presented by humanists and anthropologists that finds very significant uniformities in the values, rules, and institutions of different communities, the cultural relativist-determinist insists that such "universals" are for all practical purposes not "absolutes." He does not attach much importance to the fact that these uniformities, whether "absolutes" or not, make possible not only sophisticated forms of intercultural dialogue but useful and reasonable transcultural evaluations of cultural products.

If the cultural relativist insists that the Turk's concept of culture as such is essentially different from the Englishman's, then the appropriate response is to invite her to consider more precisely how different. Newman and Collingwood were not anthropologists, but they were dedicated students of the history of ideas, and, by insisting that their statements about Turks and Englishmen be understood in a broad historical context, they have invited us to consider certain historical patterns. The cultural relativist is apt to attach little significance to those patterns; but most people are likely to find them rather more interesting and familiar. According to thinkers such as Newman and Collingwood, there is a discernible pattern of historical transformation in the direction of certain transcultural ideals, and appreciation of this pattern is the key to making assessments of cultural products that are not merely expressions of emotion or indications of how much one's mind has been moulded by the arbitrary values derived from one's social environment.

But Collingwood recognizes that it may not be possible to bring certain students of culture to the point at which they interpret historical and anthropological patterns in the way that most users of terms such as *civilization* and *culture* traditionally have. Thus Collingwood writes: "We speak of 'Bronze Age civilization' as a constellation of historical facts different in character from 'Neolithic civilization'; of 'Chinese civilization' as different in character from 'Indian civilization'; and so on … In speaking thus we neither assert nor deny that the creators of one such 'civilization' are trying to do at bottom the same kind of thing as the creators of another, namely to bring a given community into a condition of 'civility'. We are free to assert this and equally free to deny it. The denial would only involve striking an admittedly obsolete work, 'civility', out of our vocabulary, and out of our thought whatever it stands for. If we deny it, we maintain that all the creators of a particular civilization aim at creating is the civilization they do in fact create."[40]

Still, how are we to explain major cultural differences? Why should people who agree on so much be so different in important ways? We must take into account at least three considerations. One is the fact of determining factors. Another is the importance of the transcultural phenomenon of undercommitment or hypocrisy, in which human beings are distracted from their world-view by subsidiary motives arising from intemperance and the vulnerability to manipulation. The consistency associated with integrity never comes easy to mortals, even the noblest of them.[41] And yet another is that people, lacking omniscience, naturally disagree a great deal about the proper means to their shared ends. The effectiveness of proposed means is something that can and must be weighed; and perhaps no task in life is nobler and more interesting than doing that weighing, not only to bring deeper meaning to one's own life, but to help one's fellows to do the same for theirs. Our ideas, attitudes, and behaviour are largely the result of determining factors, not the least of which are those that derive directly from our nature as human beings. But freedom, a freedom that is itself capable of being developed and cultivated through both personal discipline and communal educational institutions, is itself something given in human nature, and the choices left open to us are significant indeed.

If the transcultural values and ideals that some people call "absolutes" and others call "universals" represent nothing more than the greatest aspirations, at some level of awareness, of almost all human beings, then the loftiest criteria for evaluating cultural products may be based on nothing more than tradition and convention, albeit transcultural or universal tradition and convention. Cultural products, especially those highly abstract ones that have occupied our attention for the last while, have seemed to most people throughout the centuries to be related to religious life. As religious faith has been the most traditional form of commitment to a world view,[42] culture itself has been for most people a matter of religion in some sense. And most people throughout history do not seem to have had much trouble regarding the specific ideals associated with culture and civilization as in some sense "transcendent" – as transcending not only their own social environment but the human order itself. Thus they have not had to regard those ideals merely as human inventions, arbitrary traditions and conventions, or derivatives from human nature. While generally recognizing that the ideals were put before them as cultural products, with a form that is a result of human activity, they have nevertheless conceived of those ideals as somehow related to the cosmic schemes of higher forces. This religious conception, which renders them more than cultural products, merits close consideration.

CULTURE AND RELIGION

According to classical, nineteenth-century positivist theories, religion, while having some utilitarian value for certain individuals and communities, is essentially a pre-philosophical, pre-scientific form of experience and culture that, in preserving pre-rational, superstitious modes of thinking and acting, slows development of the scientific thought necessary for personal and communal growth. Philosophical and theological critics of positivism have often responded that the "positive" sciences cannot satisfactorily explain either the human order or the realm of values and ideals and that positivists do not understand the close involvement of religion with the ideal of culture and with specific transcultural ideals.

Christopher Dawson, an English Roman Catholic scholar, has observed that, even before the rise of positivism, the thinkers of the Enlightenment had established a tendency among sociologists and historians of culture to undervalue the study of the fundamental social aspects of religion. Viewing historic religion as an obscurantist force, "dragging back the human spirit in its path towards progress and enlightenment," they "hacked through the luxuriant and deep-rooted growth of traditional belief with the ruthlessness of pioneers in a tropical jungle."[43] However, not only is the entire social life of a primitive people "bound up" with its religion, but the development of a higher culture in the Middle East, along with the beginnings of agriculture, irrigation, and city life, were "profoundly religious in their conception."[44] Dawson concludes: "From the beginning the social way of life which is culture has been deliberately ordered and directed in accordance with the higher laws of life which are religion."[45] Thus, "Religion is the key to history. We cannot understand the inner form of a society unless we understand its religion."[46]

In Dawson's view, modern scientific approaches have not released us from our need to conceive of culture in terms of its special relation to religion.

Secularist thinkers, while neglecting or criticizing traditional associations of culture with religion, live off the capital of religion, unwittingly drawing their inspiration from religious sources and clothing traditional religious ideas in a new imagery.[47] More important, "The whole history of culture shows that man has a natural tendency to seek a religious foundation for his social way of life and that when culture loses its spiritual basis it becomes unstable. Nothing has occurred to alter these facts."[48] Deeply troubled by the emergence of a secularized scientific world culture that is "a body without a soul," and by the fact that religion has correspondingly become "a spirit without a body,"[49] Dawson insists: "It is necessary to recover the ground that has been lost through the progressive secularisation of modern civilisation" and to "transcend the subjectivity and relativism of nineteenth-century thought and recover an objective and realist sense of spiritual truth."[50]

Dawson does not identify religion with culture. Acknowledging that a social culture is now generally seen as essentially an organized way of life based on a common tradition and a common environment, he observes that the relation between religion and culture is two-sided: "The way of life influences the approach to religion, and the religious attitude influences the way of life."[51] He believes that it is necessary to restore to our culture its religious foundations: "It is the religious impulse which supplies the cohesive force which unifies a society and a culture. The great civilisations of the world do not produce the great religions as a kind of cultural by-product; in a very real sense, the great religions are the foundations on which the great civilizations rest. A society which has lost its religion has lost its culture."[52]

These themes have been sounded with notable frequency by leading modern religious thinkers. T.S. Eliot, who was much influenced by Dawson, shares his view that no culture can appear or develop except in relation to a religion[53] and asks whether the culture and religion of a people "are not different aspects of the same thing: the culture being, essentially, the incarnation (so to speak) of the religion of a people."[54] Though people in advanced societies usually regard religion as an aspect or dimension of life, there is a sense, Eliot suggests, in which it is appropriate to see a religion as the whole way of life of a people, a way of life that is also its culture.[55] Like Dawson, Eliot points to the reliance of even radical secularist Western thinkers on values and modes of perception derived directly from the Western religious tradition, and he speculates that Western culture could not survive the complete disappearance of its traditional religious faith.[56]

The Protestant theologian Emil Brunner, speaking about civilization in the sense in which it is not distinguished from culture,[57] tells us: "Civilisation is determined, first, by natural factors like formation of country, climate, possibilities of maintenance, within which, as a given frame, human life has to develop. Civilisation is determined, secondly, by the physical and spiritual equipment of men within a given area, by their physical and spiritual forces, their vitality, their energy and their talent. These two complexes we can put together as that which is outwardly and inwardly *given*. Apart from these given factors, which are inaccessible to human determination and freedom, there is a third, which is just as important for the formation of a certain civilisation in its specific character, namely the spiritual presuppositions of a religious and ethical nature which, not in themselves cultural, we might call the culture-transcendent presuppositions of every culture."[58] Culture, Brunner argues, is "an expression of the spirit" and "necessarily degenerates where it is made God."[59] "If culture is to become and to remain truly human, it must have a culture-transcending centre. Man is more than his culture. Culture is means and tool, but not the essence of human life. It is not culture that gives man his humanity, but it is the human man that creates a human culture."[60] Failure to recognize these facts has consistently contributed to the weakening of the ideal of human dignity.[61]

The Protestant existentialist theologian of culture Paul Tillich, while critical of the tendency of many of his fellow theologians to depreciate culture in its secular forms, insists: "Religion is not a special function of the human spirit";[62] efforts to reduce it to the status of a special sphere among others within culture have resulted in the "tragic estrangement of man's spiritual life from its own ground and depth."[63] For Tillich, "religion is the substance of culture, culture is the form of religion," and while every religious act is "culturally formed," "there is no cultural creation without an ultimate concern expressed in it."[64] With respect to Christianity Tillich states: "The Church judges culture, including the Church's own forms of life. For its forms are created by culture, as its religious substance makes culture possible. The Church and culture are within, not alongside each other. And the Kingdom of God includes both while transcending both."[65]

While recognizing that the term *culture* has meant many things to many people, the Calvinist thinker Henry R. Van Til uses it to designate "that activity of man, the image-bearer of God, by which he fulfills the creation mandate to cultivate the earth, to have dominion over it and to subdue it."[66] "Man as cultural creature is an analogue of the great Architect and Artist of the universe. Man as creature, therefore, is co-worker with God in bringing creation to its fulfillment."[67] In Van Til's view, the cultural crisis now facing the West has resulted from culture's having been "uprooted" as a consequence of the denial of God promoted by the "priests of Secularism" who now control the mass media of communication and most social institutions.[68]

The Scottish theologian J.C. Shairp, a contemporary of Matthew Arnold and E.B. Tylor, worried aloud about the ways in which their approaches to culture undervalue religion. "We had thought it had been religion which set forth the ends of life, and supplied the motives and the power for striving towards them. But now it seems that there is some rival power, called Culture, which claims for itself these architectonic functions which we had hitherto thought belonged of right to Religion."[69] Shairp insists: "Culture must embrace Religion, and end in it."[70] "In short, the transition from the objects on which culture dwells to those on which religion dwells is the passage from a region in which human thought, human effort, human self-development, are paramount, to a region in which man's own powers are entirely subordinate, in which recipiency, not self-activity, is the primary law of life, and in which the chief worker is not man, but God."[71] In being subordinated to religion, culture is "transmuted from an intellectual attainment into a spiritual grace."[72]

Despite differences in emphasis and expression, the theories considered above represent variations on a set of common themes. All treat culture as something that can be fully and properly understood only in terms of its special relation to religion and insist that attempts to divorce religion from culture, or to diminish its role in culture, are on one level futile and on another level destructive. All indicate that while religious energy manifests itself in specific cultural products, it is itself derived from awareness of, or at least belief in, a culture-transcendent spiritual reality. And all at least imply that there are criteria for evaluating cultural products that are not merely human inventions, or traditions and conventions, or even derivatives from human nature, but rather ideals that have been somehow revealed to human consciousness so that human beings can, individually and in groups and as an order, attain the kind and degree of perfection or fulfilment that is in keeping with their role in the cosmos.

This vision must be understood on several levels. With its reference to some transcendent spiritual reality that is the source of transcultural values, it is clearly a metaphysical vision, and, as articulated by theists, a theological vision. On another level it is a psychological or historical observation, concerning how in fact most people have thought about certain important matters on at least some plane of awareness. On yet another level it is a moral or pragmatic view of what one ought to believe – or at least ought to try to believe – if one's most basic conceptions are to be consistent and if one is to be able to become a substantially better person and to contribute significantly to the betterment of the communities to which one belongs. It is also a moral or pragmatic view of what one should be encouraging other people to believe, in one's effort to elevate the quality of communal life.

The different aspects of this vision may not go together very well, and numerous arguments have been offered both for and against each aspect. Philosophers, both academic and amateur, have debated the existence of a transcendent spiritual reality since the earliest days of philosophical inquiry yet have failed to come up with a metaphysical argument that effectively settles the debate once and for all. With respect to controversies between religionists of different faiths and between religionists and secularists, the best that can be said is probably that over the years more and more disputants have come to appreciate the value of politely agreeing to differ. Psychological and historical data have been more concrete, but it is not entirely clear what normative conclusions can be drawn from such "evidence." As for the moral or pragmatic considerations, they clearly involve complex and highly personal evaluations; and in any event, it is extremely difficult to believe something simply because one would like to believe it or thinks that one would be a better person if one did believe it. Nor is it easy to promote among one's fellows a world-view that one appreciates but regards as inconsistent with truth and reality.

We are left with one possible way of conceiving of culture and of cultural products, particularly those cultural products by which we evaluate all other cultural products. This conception takes one a step beyond acknowledging the existence of transcultural absolutes or universals and thus reinforces one's confidence in, and respect for, the primary criteria that one applies when one participates in cultural processes. Yet many admirable human beings get by, and lead quite productive lives, without adopting a religious conception of culture, or any other religious conception. And, of course, religious commitment has not necessarily prevented people from ruining their lives and the lives of others and in fact has often seemed to be a factor contributing to personal and social problems. People can be as hypocritical with respect to a religious commitment as a secular one; religious hypocrisy is indeed the most traditional and most obvious form of hypocrisy, just as religious commitment is the most traditional and most obvious form of commitment to a world-view. And again, cultural products associated with religious institutions can be as inauthentic and corrupt as any others when they are used by hypocrites or unbelievers as means of exploiting their fellows. Given the common association of religion with our highest ideals, we find that the inauthenticity and corruption of those products leave a particularly strong and unpleasant impression.

The person who sees no good reason for adopting a religious conception of culture need not be intimidated by the pronouncement of Dawson and kindred apologists that the secularist is a promoter of cultural decline. Such a person has a right to be sceptical about the kinds of metaphysical and theological arguments that have been advanced in defence of the existence of a transcendent spiritual reality; to wonder why traditional and conventional perspectives are still appropriate in an advanced society; and to remain unpersuaded by the speculative claim that the decline of religious commitment necessarily contributes to a loss of cultural authenticity and vitality. He has considerable justification for being concerned about the association of certain religious products with forms of exploitation and manipulation that interfere with personal and communal development.

Moreover, he is not doing violence to ordinary language by looking at "religion" as being at most a form or aspect of "culture," or a particular type of cultural activity and product, despite the religious associations of such terms as *cult* and *cultus*; religionists themselves draw a solid line between the concepts of culture and religion. (In *Christ and Culture*, H. Richard Niebuhr puts forward a useful typology to distinguish different answers to the question of the relation of Christ and culture, and he is more thorough in his analysis of the historical relations of religion and culture than apologists such as Dawson when he observes that the historian of Christianity encounters not only the Christ of culture, the Christ above culture, and Christ the transformer of culture, but also the Christ against culture and Christ and culture "in paradox.")[73] Moreover, the secularist usually knows that even in communities in which culture has been bound up with religion, it has still been appropriate to distinguish the realm of the sacred from that of the profane, the mundane, or the secular. Only a saint or a mad person is so obsessed with spirituality that it manifests itself in her daily routine as much, and in the same way, as in her moments of prayer, meditation, and moral reflection.

In declining to tie culture as closely to religious conceptions as certain religious apologists do, one is not forced to retreat to determinism or relativism. One can rightly argue that commitment to a secular world-view does not necessarily involve less conviction, devotion, passion, or personal involvement than the typical religious commitment does. The "mass man" is probably more likely to be a "conventional religious believer" than a secularist, mainly because of the traditional and conventional associations of religion and culture. Moreover, moral knowledge does not necessarily require metaphysical or theological insight; it may involve only, for example, a kind of moral intuition, or the drawing of ethical conclusions from data that one regards as relevant to values derived solely from one's understanding of human nature and the laws of logic – considerations such as utility, duty, and self-realization.

Nevertheless, many people in our society share the view of the Dawsons, Brunners, and Van Tils that there is a close connection, perhaps causal, between the decline or marginalization of traditional religious institutions and modes of perception and the increasing inauthenticity and corruption of culture. For such people, it is not enough that secular cultural activity and its products reflect indirectly and almost imperceptibly the influence of centuries of religious reflection. Most people do not belong to a creative intellectual elite and are not in a convenient position to attain much in the way of existential, philosophical, or social-scientific insight into the conditions of authentic culture. That, of course, is not only why they rely on intellectuals for clear, explicit, precise criticism of inauthentic culture, but why they are more vulnerable to crude forms of manipulative exploitation than intellectuals are.

Accordingly, regardless of what she herself is able to believe, and to encourage others to believe, the critic of religion should not take lightly the role that religion can play, and has often played, in making authentic cultural products available to those who might otherwise have to settle for the inauthentic, made all too readily available by operators concerned with exploiting them rather than bettering their condition. Many a critic of religion is, consciously or not, following in the footsteps of aristocratic cultural theorists who would rather look down on their fellows than do something to meliorate their condition. Such thinkers risk forms of alienation that only a few minds can bear, much less harness creatively. Berdyaev writes: "The masses participate in culture. That is both right and necessary: the masses must not remain in darkness. In the past the masses participated in culture by way of religion, and the culture of the broad masses was almost exclusively a religious culture. Religion was the meeting-place of the masses with the aristocratic cultural class. Only religion is capable of making such a combination: neither philosophy nor science, nor enlightenment, neither art nor literature can do this. Deprived of religious basis, any high-qualitative culture inevitably becomes separated from popular life and an isolated cultural elite is produced, which keenly feels its uselessness to the people."[74]

When misunderstood and undervalued by intellectual elites, religious cultural products all too often fall into the hands of unscrupulous schemers, who proceed to render them as inauthentic as the dogmatic secularist had assumed them to be. A humanistic moralist need not feel obligated to promote a type of world-view that he regards as unsound, but, mindful of the fact that the wise as well as the perplexed have benefited from openness to religious cultural products, he should make a whole-hearted effort to appreciate them in their authentic forms. That will not only bring deeper insight to his own world-view but will put him in a better position to contribute to social progress.

Nevertheless, one must also be on guard against those reactionary thinkers who see traditional associations of religion and culture as justifying attacks on religious pluralism. For a variety of ethical and theological reasons, religious liberty is a necessary condition of advanced civilization. Religious cultural products that are imposed by force or deception may have considerable utility, even in advanced societies; and the social unity derived from the political establishment of a particular religious denomination can be salutary on several levels. But freedom of thought, faith, and conscience is so basic to a reflective person's conception of human dignity that any attempt to undermine it must be regarded as inconsistent with the ideal of culture.[75] Imposition of religious cultural products by force promotes unsound forms of religious commitment, and imposition of them by deception renders them inauthentic in a way that inevitably leads to their degradation both in themselves and in people's perception of them.[76]

PHILOSOPHIES OF CULTURE AS CULTURAL PRODUCTS

The theories of culture that philosophers and others put before us are themselves cultural products, and in deciding whether or not to appropriate them we weigh a number of factors, including their relative authenticity. The philosopher who simply reflects upon culture and keeps her ideas to herself is not creating or promoting a cultural product; but once she proceeds to share her ideas with other people, she is participating in a cultural process. Since the people with whom she is communicating are people that she deems to be capable of understanding philosophical ideas and arguments, she expects them to be somewhat sophisticated in assessing her motives for encouraging them to appropriate her perspective. If they regard her as a genuine philosopher, and not merely a manipulative sophist, they will see her as having put forward a product that, if not sound in other respects, is at least authentic and meant to improve their condition and perhaps that of the communities to which they belong.

Philosophers seek knowledge at least partly for its own sake but are almost always also convinced of the cultural value of the fruits of their reflection. Moreover, unlike most people, philosophers have a vocational interest in the most fundamental ethical considerations, and even their most recondite metaphysical theories have an ethical dimension and are usually rooted in ethical concerns. The ethical concerns of the philosopher of culture are rarely hard to detect. Philosophers of culture are concerned with the human being as thinker and agent; as humanists, they are interested not simply in empirical description but in the complex thought processes involved in free and responsible participation in cultural processes. One of their aims is to promote among their fellows a deeper appreciation of the special distinctiveness of human action and of the individual's responsibility to bring intelligence, discipline, and integrity to his various roles in cultural activity. Thus most philosophers of culture have at least indirectly addressed the problem of inauthentic culture.

Philosophers of culture usually offer social criticism. Though their message is directed primarily at individuals, it is ordinarily communicated in such a way as to indicate to those people that they have some obligation to contribute to communal culture or civilization in its highest sense. Philosophers of culture have, since ancient times, been deeply impressed by the limits of the culture of their communities; they have seen it as one of their duties to contribute to the general improvement of cultural products and the people who share them. In the relevant ideas of such philosophers as Kierkegaard, Berdyaev, Ortega y Gasset, and Collingwood, we can see that at least some philosophers of culture are particularly troubled by cultural decline, the general deterioration of cultural products, which they see as related closely to moral decline, both as cause and as effect.

Philosophers, of course, have not been the only humanists who have had such concerns, which are apparent in the writings of theologians, historians, and literary scholars and are of course reflected in the themes of many works of drama, poetry, and fiction. Philosophers deal with cultural decline in their own fashion, but in addressing actual or perceived decline, or the vulnerability of culture to decline, they are part of a larger humanistic tradition. That tradition itself is akin to that of the prophets of all ancient faiths – men and women more sensitive than their brothers and sisters to the concrete presence of remediable human evil and corruption, who felt a special obligation to exhort their listeners to summon up the wisdom and courage to fight such horrors effectively. For every true prophet there have been countless preachers, many of whom have had questionable or mixed motives for passing loud and severe judgments on the character and works of those they perceive as rivals.[77]

There is a sermonic quality to many passages in the writings of philosophers of culture, and when we come on it we are reminded that philosophers, despite their professed respect for calm rationality and stoical dignity and their claim to be seekers of truth, are often passionate moralists, in search of disciples to promote their ideas for cultural reform. Once one has become aware of a particular philosopher's perception of himself as an earnest cultural reformer, one is better able to appreciate the moralism that underlies even some of his most abstract metaphysical and epistemological arguments.[78]

And though philosophical moralists have often been admired for their earnest criticism of cultural decline, they have sometimes themselves been criticized for what has been seen as self-righteous, self-important whining. Long before Nietzsche attacked the resentment of the philosophers, the astute analyst of vanity and self-interested motives La Rochefoucauld had written off the lamentations of philosophical moralists with the observation that philosophers' criticisms are their way of avenging themselves against fortune, "by having contempt for the very things of which she deprived them."[79] It was easy for La Rochefoucauld to regard the diatribes of reform-minded philosophers as inauthentic, given his view that the steadfastness of the wise is nothing more than their ability to lock their agitation in their hearts[80] and his belief that what passes for sincerity is usually only a clever pretence by which to gain the confidence of one's fellows.[81]

Nevertheless, the sermonizing of philosophers of culture does not usually grate on people as much as does that of most other cultural critics. First, most people are not as cynical as La Rochefoucauld and are prepared to accept some of this philosophical sermonizing as authentic, meant to better potential disciples and their communities. Second, the philosopher of culture usually seems to be appealing to the potential disciple's reason and intelligence, rarely to such motives as fear and greed, though sometimes to resentment. Third, in urging the listener or reader to join him in the noble struggle against cultural decline, the philosophical preacher is indicating his confidence in that person's ability and, furthermore, is presenting the individual with an opportunity for renewed self-respect and self-direction. The disciple of any preacher is offered a chance to perceive herself as the "chosen," the "enlightened," and the "righteous." Fourth, unlike many religious and political leaders, the typical philosophical preacher asks for little in the way of personal devotion. Though cults have developed around certain philosophers, the typical practitioner is satisfied with knowing that the listener or reader has taken her exhortation to heart and to mind. Finally, the philosopher who attacks the quality of communal cultural products often manages to shed useful light on something that had already bothered the listener or reader but which that individual did not previously understand so clearly. Thus the master's cultural criticism both confirms the student's "intuitive" judgment and provides him with constructive insight.

Not all philosophers of culture fit the paradigm outlined above. Some speak and write in such a cool, dignified, academic manner that it is necessary to dig way below the surface to uncover the hidden moralism. Then again, some have rather complicated minds and are guided by conflicting motives. For example, Nietzsche, one of the most influential philosophers of culture, attacks the very distinction between good and evil[82] and urges his readers to overcome their compassion for the masses.[83] Yet this "immoralist"[84] is as passionate a preacher as any philosophical critic of conventional culture, and he is constantly exhorting his readers to contribute to the elevation of the human "type."[85]

A philosopher of culture who more clearly appears to depart from the paradigm is Oswald Spengler, whose famous study of cultural decline, *The Decline of the West*, is so deterministic and so relativistic in places that one might be moved to regard it as "philosophical" only in an attenuated form. "A Culture," Spengler tells us, "is born in the moment when a great soul awakens out of the proto-spirituality (*dem urseelenhaften Zustande*) of everchildish humanity, and detaches itself, a form from the formless, a bounded and mortal thing from the boundless and enduring. It blooms on the soil of an exactly-definable landscape, to which plant-wise it remains bound. It dies when this soul has actualized the full sum of its possibilities in the shape of peoples, languages, dogmas, arts, states, sciences, and reverts into the proto-soul."[86]

Setting aside the problems inherent in the conception of a culture as an organism,[87] we may ask of what use to us a theory is that tells us that there is no more that we can do to prevent the decline of our culture than to prevent our own ageing and eventual death. Yet Spengler wrote a huge tome because he thought that we would be better off, or better, for knowing what he is telling us about cultural decline. Spengler, like an earlier and greater determinist, Spinoza, believes that determinism has a meliorative influence on our lives, and so, like Spinoza, he is a moralist too, in his own peculiar way. But the combination of determinism and moral exhortation is even stranger in the writings of a humanist than it is in the writings of a behavioural or social scientist such as Freud, Skinner, or Herskovits. A similar problem arises with the combination of deterministic and moralistic elements in classical Marxist theory, though it is not entirely clear to what extent Marx was offering a genuine philosophy of culture.

The philosopher of culture cannot realistically expect her exhortations to meet with the popular response that religious exhortations often meet. When one considers the emotional power of many a religious teacher's criticism of contemporary cultural products, one may be reminded of religion's pre-rational and suprarational appeal, its accessibility to those with limited education, its vivid symbolism and imagery, its long history of saints and martyrs, and so on. Some philosophers have often found it prudent to work with religious teachers in order to promote their own cultural products. But certain philosophers have been so eloquent and so well situated that they have been able to preach successfully, even despite the animosity of religious establishments. And there is one particular philosopher of culture whose work has influenced the entire course of Western humanistic cultural criticism – philosophical and religious. It is in the work of that thinker – Plato – that we encounter the classical world's greatest contribution to the normative philosophy of culture, and central to that philosophy of culture is an analysis of inauthentic culture that in every major sense of the word qualifies as the "classical" analysis of that problem.

4

PLATO AND THE CLASSICAL ANALYSIS OF

INAUTHENTIC CULTURE

Nowhere is Plato more incisive than in his elaborate descriptions of phoney cultural products and the crooked characters who trade in them. We now consider various passages in the *Republic*, which contains Plato's main contributions to the systematic philosophy of culture, and then we look at the themes raised in these passages from a broader perspective.

The first book of Plato's *Republic* is a Socratic exercise, and whereas in the later nine books the character of Socrates is used as the spokesman for Plato's own constructive views, most of which the real Socrates is not likely to have endorsed, the first book is more representative of the Socratic style of critical analysis. It introduces the basic subject matter of the entire work – the nature and value of justice. Though largely devoted to Socratic criticism, it indicates Plato's interest in character and character types, and it relates specific character types to particular conceptions of justice. Though the term *cultura* did not yet exist, we can now see that Plato regards alternative conceptions of justice as themselves being cultural products that are appropriated in various ways by different character types under specific circumstances. The elderly merchant Cephalus represents the type whose appropriation of a guiding principle in life has been largely unconscious. His son, Polemarchus, appeals to the authority of a respected figure, the poet Simonides, and, unlike his father, he demonstrates a willingness to enter into rational discussion of the reasonableness of the principle in question. In subjecting the principle to critical examination, Socrates not only encourages Polemarchus and the reader to appreciate the value of such rational analysis but emphasizes the dangers inherent in appropriating a certain kind of cultural product exclusively on the basis of respect for authority, even that represented by tradition and convention.

Thus even in the first pages of the *Republic*, Plato draws our attention to the problem of inauthentic culture: the conceptions of justice of Cephalus, Polemarchus, and the character types that they represent are inadequate, even if they partially reflect certain traditional and conventional insights into the true and real nature of justice; and they have generally been appropriated in a society like Plato's because most people fail to bring to the appropriation of a fundamental cultural product the degree of disciplined rational reflection necessary for sound commitment. The people represented by Cephalus and Polemarchus have thus left themselves vulnerable to certain forms of manipulation.

With the introduction of the type represented by the clever sophist Thrasymachus, Plato gives us a direct view of the manipulative personality. Thrasymachus has corrupted the world-view of earlier, somewhat high-minded sophists such as Protagoras, but he is nevertheless their true heir. In putting the radical subjectivistic, relativistic, and conventionalistic notions of earlier sophists to the uses that he does, he shows us some of the inevitable, negative long-term consequences of adopting and promoting these radical conceptions. When Protagoras taught his disciples that the human being is "the measure of all things," he may not have seen such instruction as providing them with a philosophical licence to exploit their fellows; but in Plato's view, reliance on techniques of exploitative manipulation ultimately follows on failure to appreciate the power of reason to provide people with some form of objective moral knowledge. For the self-serving, manipulative Thrasymachus, justice is merely what is in the "interest of the stronger." The standard of right conduct is on one level the invention of the clever, selfish fellows who recognize their ability to shape the ideas, values, and attitudes of the manipulable masses, and on another level a conception appropriated more or less unreflectively by those too unsophisticated to recognize it for what it really is.

While he himself has failed to appreciate the true value of reason in leading the genuine philosophical inquirer to moral knowledge, the sophist is at least intellectual enough to have recognized that one's conception of justice need not be derived exclusively through indoctrination and conditioning. He is imaginative enough to have conceived of a concrete idea of justice as a device that is "naturally" employed by the strong to exploit the weak, and therefore his own conception of justice is more profound than that of the mass man, who more or less unconsciously appropriates a conception of justice. Thus the manipulative sophist, or any manipulative type, knows certain things that the less reflective person does not. Because he has been willing to reflect a bit on the human condition, he is able to transcend to some extent the purely traditional and conventional notions that leave mass men vulnerable to his manipulative techniques.

In criticizing Thrasymachus's idea – that a community's ideal of justice is little more than the specific laws and values that its powerful people have manipulated their less clever fellows into believing should regulate their social activity, Socrates points to an inconsistency in Thrasymachus's discussion. If a manipulative leader is mistaken about what is in his own interest, which Thrasymachus initially allows is possible, then justice may be something that in fact is not "in the interest of the stronger." To extract himself from this difficulty, Thrasymachus argues that in a "strict" sense no communal leader can make a mistake: at the moment he misapprehends his own interest, that person is really not being a leader at all, any more than any other craftsman or professional deserves his status when he is not properly doing his job. That is, just as a physician is not, "strictly speaking," a physician when he does his job badly, or is engaged in activities outside his professional work, a leader is only "strictly speaking" a leader when he is successfully exploiting his fellows.

But by making this move, Thrasymachus acknowledges that the leader is a kind of craftsman or professional person. That being the case, Socrates points out, the leader is concerned essentially with the weaker party, with those individuals who require a cultural product that they cannot adequately provide for themselves, which is represented by the specialized skill through which the craftsman or professional serves his fellow citizens. The physician serves the patient who to some extent is unable to heal himself, the teacher educates the student who is somewhat unable to educate himself, and so forth; and similarly, the leader serves the subject who has a genuine need for the political and social skills practised by trained leaders.

Thrasymachus ridicules Socrates for failing to recognize that the craftsman or professional ultimately "serves" others only to further his own narrow personal interests: the shepherd is merely fattening up his flock for the kill, the physician is ultimately concerned with being paid handsomely for his services, and the leader ultimately plies his craft for his own good, not that of his fellows. But Socrates then reminds Thrasymachus that he himself had earlier insisted that a craftsman or professional, "strictly speaking," warrants that status only in so far as he is satisfactorily practising his craft or profession. Thus, a leader, like any craftsman or professional, deserves the name only in so far as he is providing a service to those who stand to benefit by it. All other considerations are irrelevant to leadership as such.

In thus distinguishing between the motivation of a mere manipulator and that of a genuine craftsman or professional, Socrates is laying the foundation for a distinction between authentic and inauthentic culture. The cultural products created or promoted by the manipulator are apt to be corrupt, inferior, and to some extent even "unreal." They are not what the manipulator has pretended that they are; rather, they are devices by which he can satisfy his narrow personal interests at the expense of his fellows. But the craftsman or professional brings a different attitude towards his cultural offerings; he takes pride in his ability to serve those who appropriate them and ordinarily asks for nothing more than the remuneration and respect that he deserves from those that he has truly served.

Unlike the manipulative type, he does not seek advancement through the exploitation of others; rather, he sees it as wholly compatible with the improvement of his fellows. He rightly sees himself as having something useful to offer to his fellows, something genuinely worth sharing, for which he is entitled to be rewarded and honoured by them. To the extent that he is a genuine craftsman or professional, and not an imposter or incompetent, his product is truly meliorative. As for the manipulator, even if he produces and promotes products that may sometimes turn out to be meliorative, he has done so in the context of aims that are in theory as compatible with turning out cultural rubbish as with creating genuinely meliorative and cultural products.

Plato does not regard sophists alone as responsible for the inauthenticity of so many cultural products; there are, he argues in the *Republic*, plenty of people who must share the blame with them for the degradation of culture. But Plato attaches special importance to their corrupting influence, for he sees them as rivals of the philosopher in a special way. They are pseudo-philosophers, pseudo-intellectuals, and thus they subvert the influence of genuine intellectuals in a direct and particularly destructive way. Plato saves his most powerful critical comments on sophistic manipulation for Book VI; for only after he has described the true philosopher-intellectual and explained his importance in a civilized society can he satisfactorily indicate the contrast between the philosopher and the sophist.

Yet in suggesting, in the closing sections of Book I, how the life of the just person may be richer, more rewarding, and more fulfilling than that of the unjust person, Plato emphasizes how arbitrary is the assumption of a manipulator such as Thrasymachus the sophist that happiness, success, and the conditions of a life worth living are to be attained through exploitation. While more perceptive than the mass man, the manipulative personality suffers from moral failings that are partly the result of his misuse of intellect.

In this sense he knows even less than the simple, unlettered individual who uncritically appropriates ethical and religious notions and other cultural products put before him by those who sincerely have his interests at heart. Plato wants the intellectual tempted by the trappings of worldly success to realize that those who appropriate the sophist's criteria of happiness, success, and fulfilment are victims of a cruel deception that has left them with a life built around phoney cultural products.

THE INTEGRITY OF THE CULTURAL LEADER

In Book II of the *Republic*, Plato, having left behind him the Socratic phase of his inquiry, proceeds to develop his own theory of the nature and value of justice. Plato has Socrates recommend concentrating for the time being on the justice of states or societies rather than on that of individuals. Since justice and injustice are generally regarded as dispositions of both states and individuals, he suggests, perhaps an understanding of justice on the larger scale will lead us to an understanding of personal justice.

Having adopted this method, Plato turns to political philosophy and presents his vision of an ideal state. Working from the assumption that a society in its original constitution is not corrupt in any way, and that corruption enters into communal life only as a by-product of forms of sophistication that develop within the civilizing process, Plato proceeds to indicate what kinds of institutions would enable a society to advance without suffering from the obstacles represented by corrupting influences. Plato again has Socrates emphasize the individual's developing the outlook of the genuine craftsman or professional, and he expands on this theme with reference to the social value of specialization or division of labour. The most important craftsmen or professionals in any society are its leaders or Guardians, and thus the utmost care is to be devoted to establishing a high-minded and competent leadership class.

Leadership, Plato insists, is to be entrusted only to those who from early in life have demonstrated those traits that can be developed into the noblest virtues; and young people with the highest moral potential need to be carefully educated so that they will grow properly into true Guardians. The appropriate primary education, described at some length in Books II and III, is no mere manipulation. It is to be carried out by wise and just teachers for the good of the students and of all citizens. What the true educator offers is thus quite different from what the sophist offers; instead of feeding bright and promising young people with values and attitudes that will ultimately retard their self-development and their society's, the true educator inculcates self-realization together with a sense of responsibility to fellow citizens.

Plato's program reflects his awareness of the miseducation routinely practised by those who lack the understanding, discipline, and high-mindedness to establish the special conditions that will enable students to appropriate those cultural products that are most valuable to them at their particular stage of development. The true educator is not concerned merely with enculturation or socialization; one of his basic tasks is to counter the influence of those forces in society that offer the students cultural or pseudo-cultural products that are inauthentic, or at least unhelpful.

In "censoring" or otherwise modifying certain cultural products placed before the student, the true educator is not so much showing contempt for the general cultural environment as he is enabling the student to appreciate what is best in that culture, with respect to the interests of both the student and the state and its citizens. But that which is best is so not only for utilitarian reasons but because it is related to timeless truths, realities, and values that Plato symbolizes by his famous reference at *Republic* 402c to "Forms" or "Ideas," invocation of which represents his direct repudiation of the kinds of sophistic relativism that ultimately turn bright and promising young people into destructive manipulators who believe that cultural products are simply to be devised by the clever and for whatever purposes they see fit. Immediately after invoking the timeless, immutable Forms, Plato shows how understanding of the Forms enables human beings to experience love of the purest and noblest kind.

In outlining a program of primary education for future leaders, Plato does not directly blame manipulative types for the general miseducation of the young. He realizes that most people in his society have been miseducated not by sophists but by well-meaning but unwise relatives and communal functionaries. Thus while the sophists' influence is pervasive in many ways, miseducation is not simply a matter of manipulation. Yet even at this early phase of the inquiry, Plato indicates some suspicion about the moral respectability of various educators of his society. Criticizing the theologian-poets for portraying the gods in a way that makes the gods poor role models for the young, he at least intimates that these theologian-poets have been somewhat morally deficient. Criticizing the actor who by playing many roles undermines the respect of the young for the division of labour, he does not portray him simply as an innocent fool and even suggests that such a person should not be allowed in the state. When in discussing physical training he pauses to reflect on the medical and legal professions, he implies that there is something manipulative about at least some of the people who enter these professions. Though he recognizes that people are themselves largely to blame for their reliance on these particular professionals, he is also aware of the extent to which these professionals recognize that they benefit materially from the reliance of intemperate people on their services.

Near the end of Book III of the *Republic*, Plato makes some comments that have troubled many of the work's readers, who see them as indicating that Plato is to some extent quite prepared to condone the manipulativeness that he ordinarily regards as destructive. Recognizing that many people not suited for leadership will seek entry into their society's leadership class because of their unwarrantedly generous appraisal of their own abilities, Plato encourages the founders of a new or reformed state to make use of a noble lie, a useful fiction, that will facilitate each and every citizen's acceptance of his proper role in society, the role for which he is suited by both nature and educational attainments. Plato's myth of the metals provides a foundation for a highly structured class system that sharply distinguishes between those who were born with gold or silver in their souls and those who were not, and it is not hard to see why Plato has been vilified for advocating use of such a myth.

Yet, shortly after introducing the myth of the metals, Plato insists that Guardians be deprived of the material benefits that ordinary citizens of the state enjoy. The character Adeimantus is so struck by the apparent harshness of the Guardian's life that he criticizes Socrates for having made the Guardians sacrifice so much for their fellows. It is indeed a curious sort of manipulativeness that leaves those in political power with so little of what most human beings want. But in one of the finest passages in the *Republic*, Plato has Socrates reply to Adeimantus that it is wrong to assume that the truly wise and just people who are alone to be entrusted with leadership will want those things for which the masses care. At *Republic* 421a–c, Socrates observes that while the best people should be prepared to make great sacrifices in order to promote the happiness of the community as a whole, what will bring true Guardians the happiness appropriate to people with their moral and intellectual qualities is not the pleasure for which less gifted people strive but rather the fulfilment derived from having attained the personal development that goes together with the ability to appreciate the special service that they have been able to provide to their fellows.

When Plato in Book IV completes his complex analogy between the state and the soul, and shows the correspondence between the parts and virtues of the society and of the individual, he provides an illuminating definition of justice. His definition enables us to appreciate how the highest happiness that a person can attain is not the pleasure to be derived from indulgence or acquisition of wealth or honour but rather activity in accordance with the condition of being a certain kind of person, one who has actualized his superior moral and intellectual potential and attained a spiritual vision of his situation in relation to a higher order of realities. The "manipulation" condoned is thus not selfish or exploitative but compatible, at least in theory, with the degree of justice, self-realization, and happiness to which each and every citizen can reasonably aspire.

While a severe critic such as Karl Popper condemns Plato for advocating the resort to certain lies,[1] even he allows: "Plato's declaration of his wish to make the state and its citizens happy is not merely propaganda."[2] He says that we should acknowledge the fundamental benevolence[3] of a reform-minded thinker who sincerely hated tyranny.[4] Having ourselves seen how through the ages even the most dedicated liberals have sometimes felt forced to resort to the methods of illiberalism, we must not permit Plato's lapses to blind us to the high moral tone of his philosophy as a whole.

SAGE AND SOPHIST ON THE SHIP OF STATE

In Book V of the *Republic*, Socrates' suggestion that philosophers should be the leaders of the community is greeted with scepticism and derision. Plato has Socrates illustrate in the ship parable at *Republic* 487e–489d how most people are simply unable to appreciate the philosopher's activity and capacity for knowledge. On the ship of state, the master (the general public) is constantly being pressured by crafty, self-serving operators to give them control of the ship. These operators administer intoxicants or drugs to the master in order to obtain a political power that they are incapable of putting to constructive use. Meanwhile, the philosopher who should be steering the ship of state is gazing at the skies above, endeavouring to determine how to navigate the ship through troubled waters. But to those who are unaware of the realm of the Forms and do not understand how genuine moral and political knowledge is to be obtained, the mysterious intellectual seems a useless stargazer. To make matters worse, as Plato says at *Republic* 489d–497a, the philosopher, who has not mastered the techniques of self-promotion and public relations, has left the general public with the idea that the only useful intellectual in society is the clever, manipulative sophist, whose commitment to social progress is suspect but who has managed to step into the void left by the philosopher, who has failed to explain to his fellows what he is doing, what he knows, and what he has to offer them.

Plato believes that only when philosophical leaders have taken control of the ship of state can it be properly steered. Such a leader can put forward for the appropriation of his fellows high cultural products that are sound and authentic, because he has used his own intellectual powers to attain the knowledge necessary for creating and promoting such products. Along with his intellectual capacities go certain moral dispositions, partly natural, partly developed through education and other aspects of the civilizing process. These dispositions not only enhance his ability to attain higher forms of knowledge but incline him to apply his insights to genuine melioration, with regard to himself, his fellow citizens, and the state.

Whatever we are to make of Plato's talk about transcendental Forms, his analysis rests in part on several profound propositions. Moral and political knowledge is possible. Matters of value are thus not merely "relative" and are to be resolved by the use of reason rather than through force, deception, or exploitative manipulation. Fundamentally sound and carefully cultivated moral dispositions not only help a potential leader to attain the requisite knowledge but incline him to make constructive use of it and provide him with further insights that enable him to be a still better person as well as a competent leader.

But the true philosopher has a powerful rival in the community, the phoney expert who pretends to have the skills and insights necessary for providing genuine leadership. This person not only lacks moral and political knowledge but is committed to relativistic conceptions that lead him to regard the search for wisdom as futile. For such a person, authority is ultimately to be established with manipulative techniques. Slick politicians, and the sophists of various kinds who serve them, attain the power, glory, and wealth that they seek by disorienting the public mind with "drink" and "narcotic" – false promises, propaganda, and related appeals to the lower emotions and appetites. They are unable to create and promote sound cultural products because they lack genuine understanding of what a true leader needs to know and display moral failings which, in addition to having led them to use their limited intellectual skills and insights for selfish and ignoble purposes, have prevented them from developing the world-view appropriate for genuinely cultural, meliorative processes. But since the masses find it difficult to believe that the unworldly intellectual, the stargazer, is suited for leadership, they accept the manipulator's drink and narcotic and, in doing so, strengthen the hand of the phoney expert in his competition with the true sage.

On one plane, Plato acknowledges the superiority of the clever manipulator to the mass man. He laments the waste of the talents of those who, had they been properly educated and freed from the values and attitudes that corrupt their souls, could have attained the wisdom and other virtues necessary for creating and promoting the highest cultural products. "Evil," Plato has Socrates observe, "is a greater enemy to what is good than to what is not": "There is reason in supposing that the finest natures, when under alien conditions, receive more injury than the inferior, because the contrast is greater."[5] Plato suggests that the manipulator is himself the victim of manipulation by the very crowd over which he thinks himself master. Lacking wisdom, the pseudo-intellectual or phoney expert has derived his basic values and attitudes from the crowd, even if he seems to himself and others to be so much more successful than the suckers.

It is not the individual sophistic teacher who corrupts promising young people so much as it is the public itself, the greatest of all sophists. "When they meet together, and the world sits down at an assembly, or in a court of law, or a theatre, or a camp, or in any other popular resort, and there is a great uproar, and they praise some things which are being said or done, and blame other things, equally exaggerating both, shouting and clapping their hands, and the echo of the rocks and the place in which they are assembled redoubles the sound of the praise or blame – at such a time will not a young man's heart, as they say, leap within him? Will any private training enable him to stand firm against the overwhelming flood of public opinion? or will he be carried away by the stream? Will he not have the notions of good and evil which the public in general have – he will do as they do, and as they are, such will he be?"[6] The manipulative type of individual, lacking a mature intellectuality, can be "successful" only by the standards that he has uncritically derived from those intellectually inferior to him.

SOCIAL DYNAMICS IN THE CAVE

In the cave parable or cave allegory (514a–521b), Plato uses a comprehensive, synoptic device to bring together his ethical, sociological, political, educational, epistemological, and metaphysical ideas. In this section of the *Republic*, where he returns to certain themes and issues touched on in the ship parable, he provides probably his most subtle account of inauthentic culture.

In the cave parable, we encounter three basic types: the prisoner, the puppeteer, and the liberator. The prisoners have from childhood been chained down in such a way that they cannot move but can only see the cave wall in front of them. Above and behind them are a fire and a low wall, behind which puppeteers are performing a puppet show, so that the only "reality" of which the prisoners are aware consists of shadows on the wall. If a prisoner were liberated and compelled to look at realities of a higher order, she would initially resist the liberator's efforts to educate her and make available to her a richer way of life than that to which she had become accustomed. Blinded by the light, she would at first seek to return to the mode of perception and the way of life with which she had previously been familiar and with which she had become comfortable in a certain sense.

But if the liberator were to do her job patiently, and to make due allowance for the condition of the former prisoner's mind at each stage of her intellectual development, the former prisoner would eventually come to realize that what she had formerly taken to be realities were only images of images, shadows of puppets that are themselves only copies of living creatures. Having become accustomed to the light, the former prisoner would be able to apprehend realities of a higher order; she would now understand how deprived she had formerly been of both knowledge and the capacity for a rich and fulfilling life, and she would feel sorry for those still imprisoned in the cave. She would not be envious of those prisoners in the cave who had been honoured by their fellows for being experts on shadows, and she would for a time seek to avoid having to return to the world of the cave.

But with her newly acquired moral understanding, the former prisoner could eventually be made to appreciate her moral obligation to return to the cave as a liberator and to free others as she herself had been freed. Now, if she did not allow herself to become accustomed once again to the darkness of the cave world, then when she returned to the cave she would be ridiculed and eventually hated by her former fellows, who would say that her inability to see shadows in the dark indicated the folly of seeking "liberation."

Thinking of the fate of his beloved teacher, Socrates, Plato bitterly observes how much at a disadvantage a wise and just person can be when he is compelled in law courts or elsewhere to fight about the shadows of images of justice with those who have never apprehended the essence of Justice itself, or even been aware that such a thing exists. If, however, the enlightened person allows her eyes to become accustomed once again to darkness, and is able to relate to her former fellow prisoners on their own terms as a means towards preparing them to be liberated, she will be able to avoid the fate of the naive, unworldly idealist and to fulfill the educational task that martyrs such as Socrates have initiated.

While Plato offers some explanatory comments on the cave parable, even he seems to be aware that ordinary discourse cannot convey its deeper significance. But one feature of the parable, and of Plato's explanatory remarks on it, calls for our attention – the striking symbolism that it employs to convey to us insights about inauthentic culture. The shadows on the cave wall are images with which, for one reason or other, puppeteers fill the minds of mass men and women. The puppeteers are obviously manipulators of public opinion, and it is with that fact in mind that I have elsewhere drawn on the symbolism of the cave parable in order to elucidate the social role of journalists and other influential shapers of public opinion.[7]

But the shadows on the cave wall represent more: they are in a sense the cultural products that the puppeteers promote; it is, after all, these shadows that constitute the primary material with which the prisoners in the cave organize their lives. Chained down so that they cannot make proper use of their cognitive and other faculties, they are left to organize their lives around shadows. Their ideas, values, and activities are bounded by the shadows put before them. They may bring some creativity to determining what to make of the shadows and how to organize their lives and their relations with their fellows. But they can never attain self-realization richer or nobler than attaining the honours to be derived from being "quickest to observe the passing shadows and to remark which of them went before, and which followed after, and which were together" and being "best able to draw conclusions as to the future."[8] Whatever their natural abilities, individual prisoners cannot aspire to anything more than becoming experts on the shadows put before them.

But who are these puppeteers? What are we to make of them? What is their motivation? Plato says remarkably little about them, though what he has said elsewhere in the *Republic* and in other dialogues about various types in society provides many clues. He is clearly thinking, at least in part, of those gifted but unenlightened individuals who seek power over the minds and lives of their naïve, manipulable fellows. He is thinking, at least in part, of the poets, dramatists, rhetoricians, power-hungry political demagogues, and, above all, pseudo-intellectual sophists who exert an influence on public opinion and public life, and on the values and ways of life of their less ambitious fellow citizens, of which a true philosopher-intellectual-moralist-educator can only dream.

Plato clearly means us to infer that the people running the "show" in the cave parable are the very ones who are running the "ship" in the ship parable, as it founders in troubled waters. Returning at *Republic* 519a to a favourite theme, Plato has Socrates ask, "Did you never observe the narrow intelligence flashing from the keen eye of a clever rogue – how eager he is, how clearly his paltry soul sees the way to his end; he is the reverse of the blind, but his keen eye-sight is forced into the service of evil, and he is mischievous in proportion to his cleverness?" If only, Plato sadly observes, such people had received an education that would have freed them from the materialistic appetites that have weighed down their souls and prevented them from attaining the wisdom and other virtues that would have converted them into forces for good rather than evil.

Though Plato says little about the puppeteers, their curious, largely unde-fined role invites deeper speculation. The puppeteer obviously understands much more than the prisoners do; his field of insight is not limited to shad-ows on the cave wall. He knows himself to be more than a mere shadow, and he skilfully handles his puppets to bring a certain order to the life of those before whom he places his shadows. He is more than just an appropriator or user of cultural products; he is in a sense a creator and promoter of such products. This master of the shadow play knows shadows for what they are – images of puppets – and he is aware that the puppets themselves are merely copies of creatures like himself. Yet he is no liberator.

Whether or not he has ever himself left the cave, he has declined the role of liberator and has not helped to free the prisoners from their chains so that they may at least attain whatever degree of understanding he has reached. Why has he chosen to leave the prisoners in chains and hide from them the truth about the shadows and his shadow show? Is it solely because he enjoys the power that he has over their minds and lives and is satisfied with feeling superior to such people? Or does he not know how to remove their chains? Does he underestimate their ability to make constructive use of whatever freedom he himself enjoys? Does he feel obliged to keep them occupied with shadows that will at least bring a minimal degree of interest and capacity for achievement to their otherwise empty, meaningless lives?

Plato undoubtedly sees the puppeteer class as itself composed of various personality types who, despite their mutual dedication to performing their shadow play, differ in significant ways. They clearly differ in skills, vocations, and methods: there is at least something of the puppeteer in the typical poet, actor, politician, and physician, as well as in the sophist. They differ in motiv-ation and degree of integrity as well; while all seek some form of self-realization or, at the very least, happiness and success, they attach different degrees of importance to the matter of their responsibility to their fellows. Plato recognized that even among the sophists, there was a significant differ-ence between operators such as Thrasymachus and Callicles and a man such as the great Protagoras, who, while paying too much attention to his material interests and self-promotion, was justified in seeing himself as providing valuable service to the community.

Just as the Protagoras whom we encounter in the Platonic dialogue that bears his name has been portrayed in a way that indicates that Plato was not unmindful of his admirable qualities,[9] Plato's views on certain major poets, rhetoricians, and statesmen are rather more generous than some of his sweeping condemnations, in the *Republic* and elsewhere, of unphilosophical cultural leaders might lead one to assume. Plato's appraisals of such figures as Homer, Aeschylus, Isocrates, and Pericles are, if not balanced, at least mixed.

As Plato recognizes that the former prisoner has, at any particular stage of enlightenment, been liberated to a certain degree, he could well have seen different members of the puppeteer class as being enlightened to different degrees. He could well have seen, as we can now today, that some manipulative types are more intelligent, more compassionate, and more constructive than others. He could even have regarded all puppeteers, being bright but somewhat confused, as having very mixed motives, especially as they have something of both the prisoner and the liberator in them. The puppeteer, himself so dependent on the attitudes and values of the Great Sophist, the public, may be somewhat mindful of the extent to which he is in one way or another a servant of those for whom he has spent his time performing his show, and, as he may have more or less contempt for those whose minds and lives he regards as so manipulable, he may have more or less pity for their plight, and for his own.

Despite strains of elitism throughout his writings, Plato regarded even those who had "seen the Forms" as capable of further liberation. He believed that it would be necessary to convince the "liberated" type to return to the world of the cave; and in some of his later dialogues Plato not only acutely senses the limitations of his revered teacher, Socrates, but displays profound self-criticism. There are many passages in the *Republic* and elsewhere in which Plato is clearly striving to overcome resentment and to understand the determining factors that have contributed to making prisoners and puppeteers what they are, apart from their will or choice. He is prepared to criticize philosophers such as Socrates and himself for having failed to find the right words for communicating their insights to their fellows on the foundering ship of state.[10]

Still, Plato never lets us forget that the cultural or pseudo-cultural products that are promoted by those who are insufficiently wise, just, compassionate, and responsible lie at the core of any imperfect society. These products – poems or dramas, speeches or paintings, medical practices or judicial ones, "educational" institutions or political ones – need to be recognized for what they are – inauthentic "shadows," images of images, that corrupt the minds of the clever as well as the foolish, of the potentially noble as well as the masses. They make a mockery of genuine cultural processes by distracting human beings from the human vocation of cultivating personal virtues and a proper sense of responsibility towards society and humanity. They are created and promoted by people who, while undeniably possessing certain talents and perhaps even some good will and social interest, are not disciplined and courageous enough to free themselves from narrow, selfish, materialistic desires and superficial, conventional standards of success. They are thus unable to cultivate, in themselves and others, those intellectual and moral dispositions that would lead to a higher, more spiritual view of true reality and their proper relation to it.

The manipulable masses must share some of the blame for the chains in which they are bound. They rarely attempt to summon up even the minimal effort, generosity, and imagination available to them so as to listen to those worthy, idealistic types who whole-heartedly seek to enrich their lives by replacing the shadows to which they have become accustomed with more nourishing cultural fare.

THE DECEPTIONS OF THE POETS

Plato's attack on the epic and dramatic poets in Book X of the *Republic* has elicited an enormous amount of commentary, most of it negative. But if we bear in mind the relation of his discussion of the poets to his general project as a critic of inauthentic culture, we find much in Plato's analysis that is pertinent to contemporary culture as well as insightful in itself. Jacob Burckhardt has suggested: "In a sense, philosophy and art were at daggers drawn, the latter glorifying the myths, the former striving to obliterate them from the Greek mind. Philosophic thought was hostile to the beautiful and the highly imaginative, perhaps regarding itself as competing with the arts; its silence may well have betrayed envy."[11] E.A. Havelock has even argued that Plato's fundamental project is an attack on the Homeric culture represented by the poets.[12]

Such interpretations overstate relevant points, but Plato was hardly less critical of the poets than of the sophists and political demagogues, whose phoney and corruptive cultural products had been the primary focus of his criticism in Books I–IX of the *Republic*. A striking feature of the *Republic* is its author's appreciation of the wide range of cultural products and cultural processes, and Plato recognizes that the cultural influences of the high arts, both within and beyond formal systems of education, are as much to be reckoned with by the cultural critic as are the influences of political structures, theological conceptions, moral teachings, domestic arrangements, and medical and legal traditions, all of which both influence and are shaped by the creations of poets and dramatists.

Plato resents the influence of the tragic poets. He sees that they enjoy a degree of cultural influence to which the philosopher-intellectual, with his abstract conceptions and his emphasis on the discipline of rational analysis, cannot realistically hope to aspire. But whereas the philosopher offers people truth, knowledge, and reality, the poet and dramatist offer only "appearances," and, in doing so, they not only distract people from the intellectual tasks required for self-realization but fill their minds with shadows and images. Attaining their influence at the expense of the genuine educator-liberator, they belong to the ranks of the puppeteers in the cave, and deliberately or unwittingly, depending on their character, they serve the interests of others who seek to exploit the general public and prevent the liberator from promoting culture in its most profound sense.

Plato prefaces his attack on the poets with a criticism of the painters; but it is the intellectual's rivalry with the poets that is his principal concern here. The poets' pretence to knowledge is more serious than the painters', and Plato's contemporaries saw them, despite their lack of intellectual discipline and understanding, as being among the greatest moral and spiritual teachers of ancient Athens. As influential as Plato was in his own day, he was aware that his influence on the ideas, attitudes, and values of his fellow citizens could never match that of the leading tragic and comic poets of the Greek world. He knew further that the epic and dramatic poets, by blending their moral and cultural judgments with popular entertainment, could almost effortlessly step into the cultural void left unfilled by the true intellectual, who had not yet found the right words for communicating with the prisoners in the cave world. Plato was not merely envious or resentful, and Havelock is not far from the mark when he pictures Plato as believing that poetry "is a kind of disease, for which one has to acquire an antidote. The antidote must consist of a knowledge 'of what things really are.' In short, poetry is a species of mental poison, and is the enemy of truth."[13]

Plato begins his attack on the poets by extending his argument against the painters. As the painters do, the poets, he argues, deal in images, appearances, rather than truths and realities. "Then must we not infer that all these poetical individuals, beginning with Homer, are only imitators; they copy images of virtue and the like, but the truth they never reach?" (600e). "And still will [they] go on imitating without knowing what makes a thing good or bad, and may be expected therefore to imitate only that which appears to be good to the ignorant multitude?" (602b). For Plato then, the poet's creations are metaphysically inauthentic; they are far removed from the realities that the poet, having not engaged in patient, disciplined intellectual inquiry, cannot know.

Like the sophist, the poet can at best feed back to the masses a contrived, phoney version of the world-view or value system to which the masses are already committed. At worst, he can fill the minds of innocents with dangerous falsehoods about the gods, justice, love, and the other high matters that can be properly understood only through the exercise of reason. Moreover, the poets undermine rationality and discourage its cultivation by appealing to an inferior element of the personality – emotion. By doing so, they not only promote emotionalism but soften up people's minds so that they will be passively receptive to whatever messages the poets and those whom they serve wish to see transmitted.

What Plato's criticism of poetry lacks in breadth it compensates for in depth. It was obvious even in the ancient world that Plato's conception of poetry and drama is narrow and one-dimensional; but what Plato does understand he understands very well, and he has explained it to many generations of readers with exemplary clarity. To appreciate the full force of Plato's remarks about drama, consider how those remarks apply not only to drama but to its numerous extensions and variants in the modern world, particularly to cinema and television, and generally to all mass media of communication. The litany of complaints raised by high-minded critics against the cultural products now promoted in the media is a reverberation as much of Plato's ancient indictment of the poets and dramatists as of his oft-sounded condemnation of the sophists. (Plato's attack on the poets parallels his attack on the sophists, and at *Protagoras* 316d he has the title character describe the great poets of the past as sophists working in disguise.) In fact, thinking back to the criticisms of today's cultural products considered in chapter 1, one might conclude that Plato's criticism of the poets applies more properly to contemporary mass media fare than to the admirable creations of such literary giants as Homer, Euripides, and Aristophanes.

At the core of Plato's attack on what I have characterized as the "inauthenticity" of the works of poets and sophists are two closely related themes, which appeared over and over again, in various forms, in chapter 1. The first concerns matters that may loosely be characterized as "moral": a cultural product that is essentially authentic is one that has been produced or promoted by a genuine craftsman, who has both a sincere desire to serve his fellows and the knowledge and competence to provide a genuine service. But people who generate largely inauthentic cultural products participate in a cultural or pseudo-cultural process that is of dubious value and perhaps quite destructive and have little regard for the well-being of those whom they profess to serve and too much concern for their own selfish interests.

The second theme, which we may label "metaphysical," is that inauthentic cultural products, though promoted as "real," are largely if not wholly unreal. They involve "appearances" or images that are substituted for the realities that people need to know if they are to be wise and just and capable of helping to build a sound community. The corrupt and corrupting individual typically substitutes some manipulative deception for an appropriate cultural process that genuinely serves the interests (though it does not necessarily satisfy the immediate desires) of those whom it professes and indeed is intended to serve.

Clearly the contemporary cultural critic is arguing in a Platonic spirit when she observes, for example, that most motion pictures, popular novels, and television soap operas and situation comedies represent "escapist" fare of a dangerous kind and fill people's minds with foolish notions while at the same time atrophying their cognitive faculties. And surely she is being Platonic in complaining that a distorted form of moral education or at least practical guidance for life is indirectly provided by media that are substantially controlled by people concerned primarily with making profits. Again, even if motion pictures, television programs, plays, and best sellers occasionally encourage people to think in a disciplined way about important subjects, our critic, in the spirit of Plato, could reasonably complain about how many works of popular and even high culture aim to do little more than shock, titillate, or amuse, and appeal primarily to such emotions as fear and resentment. And still again, it is wholly Platonic in spirit when she laments that most citizens of the Western democracies have less exposure to philosophy and related humanistic disciplines in a lifetime than they do to television programming or pop music in a single month.

As applicable as Plato's criticism of the poets may be today, even with respect to communications media of which Plato could not have conceived, one might still wonder how Plato could have been so critical of the work of a Homer or Euripides. It will have to suffice here to observe that Plato was so concerned with the promotion of reason that, even while respecting the cultural contributions of the greater poets, he felt it necessary to counter the influence of cultural processes and products that influence people in non-rational ways. Plato did not invent or discover rationality, but he significantly transformed the conception of it and, in the process, promoted it in a uniquely influential way. Plato lived in an age when the consistent, systematic appeal to reason was something quite extraordinary, regarded by most religious traditionalists as somewhat subversive to established cultural ideals. Modern critics of Plato have sometimes objected to what they perceive as his excessive rationalism, but Plato saw himself as struggling against reactionary forces that sought to limit rational inquiry, particularly vis-à-vis the most important matters.

UNDERSTANDING ANATROPIC CULTURE

In various passages from Plato's most comprehensive and most important contribution to the systematic philosophy of culture, we have seen how the most influential version of the classical analysis of inauthentic culture took shape. A detailed account of Plato's analysis of inauthentic culture was offered shortly after the Second World War by John Wild, who, like Popper and others, felt that recent events had made a reappraisal of Platonic thought particularly appropriate. Unlike critics who saw Plato as a forerunner of modern totalitarian ideologists, Wild regarded him as an implacable foe of nationalism, barbarism, and tyranny, and he emphasized Plato's sustained attack on cultural and other forms of relativism, on irrationalism, and on contempt for the individual human being.[14]

Central to Plato's philosophical project, Wild claims, are "his thorough-going and elaborate attempt to lay bare the hierarchical structure of human culture, including art, life, and thought, and his impassioned attack upon that primary cultural disease of *sophistry*, by which this hierarchy is inverted."[15] Plato sees that while all human beings by nature seek the good, good and evil are so closely related to each other (as opposites) that they are readily confused, and this complex, dynamic confusion in the soul's eye – *anatropé*, "inversion" – is a basic source of moral evil.[16] Wild observes that Plato is concerned with analysing not only the general structure of practical "anatropism" or inversion, but also its specific manifestations in the various anatropic arts, the "fawning" arts that are now most often characterized as "quackery."[17] The anatropism of individual life can ultimately be avoided only by education, but just as individual life, social life, and true art are all subject to inversion, education itself is inverted in the form of sophistry.[18] Thus, to Plato, the sophist Callicles is an inverted Socrates, and Socrates an inverted Callicles.[19]

Plato, Wild observes, sees true arts as deteriorating into corrupt or "fawning" arts when they are detached from their true and proper ends. For example, rhetoricians may use their cultural knowledge and command of language not for rhetoric's proper end – the instruction of an audience – but for mere pleasure. Similarly, the sophist may devote logical skill and information to producing a pleasing appearance of knowledge – a mere by-product – rather than knowledge itself.[20] While genuine arts achieve sound ends in ways that are required by the nature of those ends, spurious arts are concerned essentially with providing human beings with power over other human beings.[21] Though there are manipulative corrupters in all major creative domains, sophistry is ultimately the most dangerous of the anatropic arts, because it is on one plane the inversion of philosophy itself.[22] The sophist sways the multitude by the appearance of rational argument and for a fee enables others who will be active in communal life to do the same.[23]

The sophist is thus the most dangerous creator of inauthentic cultural products. The sophist is *"the maker of something*. His acquisitive power results from some sort of production." And what he actually produces are "distorted monstrosities, ... false, subjective idols."[24] "The sophist is *essentially* a maker or fabricator of ideal replicas, though he is also, as a result of this, a persuader of the young, a wholesale or retail dealer in intellectual wares, a retail maker of goods for retail sale, a false purifier, and a practitioner of the art of eristical dispute."[25] "Spreading out from [the] hidden root of subjective pride the disease of sophistry ... first inverts the understanding of being, then substituting higher faculties for lower, and lower for higher, turns education into its opposite, until individual life is turned upside down, social life collapses into tyranny, and the whole vast cultural structure of the arts is overturned."[26] The sophist, largely through his influence on other craftsmen and artists, thus bears within himself the seeds of all cultural inversion and decay.[27]

Plato knows that incompetence and even manipulativeness among craftsmen existed prior to the rise of the sophists. He realizes that inferior and pseudo-cultural products were being created and promoted long before the first sophists came to Athens and spread relativistic ideas and taught the art of manipulative rhetoric. But he sees the sophistic rejection of the existence of objective reality and absolute moral ideals as having promoted an almost nihilistic attitude that has somehow infected all the arts and crafts (from the religious and educational to the political and poetical) on such a grand scale that the leading promoters of true culture have been marginalized and the ideal of culture has itself been turned upside down. By undermining education itself, and the love of wisdom that nurtures and strengthens it, the sophist has deprived his fellows of access to the principal means by which the various practical arts and crafts can be restored to their proper condition – that is, dealing with reality rather than mere appearance and with the needs of the practitioner's fellow human beings as well as his own, narrower interests.

Plato has harsh words for all creators and promoters of inauthentic cultural products, particularly for the most callous and most manipulative among them, but he generally reserves his most severe criticism for the sophists. By inverting philosophy and education as such, they invert the very ideal of culture; they poison the minds of poets, politicians, and the like, all of whom need to be constantly reminded of the value of true knowledge and the need to serve rather than exploit their fellow human beings. The sophists provide craftsmen in all creative spheres with a phoney, pseudo-philosophical licence to create and promote whatever "cultural" products it suits their fancy or their narrower interests to create and promote, rather than the genuine cultural products that it is their true vocation as craftsmen to put forward for the useful appropriation of their fellows. Whatever their confused motives, the sophists thus encourage and justify manipulative exploitation as well as providing instruction in the techniques for accomplishing it.

What perhaps impresses Wild most is the relevance of Plato's analysis of phoney culture to cultural and anti-cultural tendencies in this century. But how fair was Plato's characterization and appraisal of the sophists of his own day? Even some of Plato's admirers have felt obliged to come to the defence of the sophists, who, after all, have had the misfortune of coming to be known to later generations mainly by way of Plato's powerful denunciation of them. In recent years, a number of scholars have attempted to provide us with a sounder and more balanced view of the sophists than that which Plato offers in his dialogues.[28] And the sociologist Alvin Gouldner, though very respectful of Plato's contributions to social-scientific theory, writes: "The modern empirical study of man shows more continuity with the standpoint of the Sophists than that of the Platonist."[29]

Perhaps even more striking to the open-minded modern scholar is the extent of Socrates' and Plato's own debt to the sophists. It was, after all, the sophists who transformed philosophical inquiry by concentrating more on ethical, political, and cultural subjects than abstruse cosmological ones,[30] and moreover, as Jaeger himself has observed, the sophists "were the first to conceive the conscious ideal of culture" and to give "wide publicity and influence to the claim that areté should be founded on knowledge."[31] When modern scholars suggest that Plato overemphasized the contrast between the worldly, greedy sophists and his revered teacher, Socrates,[32] we may well be reminded of the fact, perhaps most vividly evidenced by Aristophanes' great comedy, the *Clouds*,[33] that many in the ancient world directly associated Socrates with the sophists and sophistry.

And yet, with due respect to the sophists (and considerably more respect is due to them that can be conveyed in a couple of paragraphs), Plato was right to see them as promoters of inauthentic culture. For one thing, Plato was justified in raising pointed questions about their motivation and integrity. Though he was able to appreciate the noble qualities of a great sophist such as Protagoras, he was not alone in resenting the arrogance and venality of the typical sophistic hack. While regarding Plato's attack on the sophists as partly a matter of the utopian thinker's disgust with the mere "technician,"[34]

Gouldner appreciates the visionary moralist's hostility towards intellectuals who "seemingly indicate that they are not concerned with ends and that they are, in a sense, ethically neutral. It appears that, as teachers, they sometimes seek to prepare their pupils to realize any end they wish; for example, it seems to Plato that in teaching rhetoric they prepare their students to win any side of a litigation and, indeed, to make the worse side appear the better."[35] Moreover, "In taking their students' ends as given, the Sophists tend to service the pursuit of conventional political careers."[36] The sophists, Jaeger observes, "lived on their culture. It was, says Plato, 'imported' like a marketable commodity and put on sale."[37]

The point here is not that Plato objected to their receiving fair recompense for their services, but that he saw them as preoccupied with self-interest, in terms of social status and financial rewards, in a way and to a degree that someone entrusted with the intellectual and moral development of his fellows should not be allowed to be. From Protagoras on, the sophists also promoted themselves alternately as moralists and business teachers, who make their students better but perhaps more usefully make their students better off by conventional standards of wealth, status, and power.[38] Their use and promotion of manipulative rhetoric understandably offended Plato, who in the *Phaedrus* and elsewhere indicates that he disapproves not of rhetoric as such but only of the abuse of rhetoric in exploiting people and leading them away from the truth.[39] "The sophists," William Temple has observed, "undertook to instruct men in the art of success," and associated success with the conventional material and social rewards to be attained by smooth talk.[40] Plato and his followers resented the material and social success of the sophists themselves, but, more important, they deplored the influence of such people as teachers and role models on many of their community's brightest and most promising young people. They came to see the philosopher as being in part the individual who resists the sophist and attempts to develop right order in his soul through resistance to the diseased soul of the sophist.[41]

Though he could not have been unaware of Socrates' debt to sophistic teaching, Plato was nevertheless justified in resenting the widespread view, reinforced and promoted by Aristophanes, that Socrates was himself essentially a sophist.[42] How, after all, could Aristophanes and others have fairly ignored the crucial differences between the sophists and a poor man[43] who took no money for his "teachings,"[44] if they were indeed teachings at all,[45] and who consistently acted with integrity,[46] avoided political involvements,[47] placed the interests of the community ahead of his own personal and family interests,[48] sought objective truth and virtue and encouraged others to do the same,[49] and ultimately died a martyr at the hands of both privileged elites and a manipulable mob?[50]

Critics of Plato, mindful of the fact that he came from a background of wealth and privilege, are right to detect some degree of bias in his contempt for both the masses and the hard-working, fee-charging sophists. Still, the aristocratic Plato took for his greatest hero and teacher an impoverished man who acted with an integrity that he had never encountered among the conventionally privileged and successful. And as different as he was from Socrates in background, temperament, and ultimately in philosophical orientation, Plato never ceased to follow his teacher in advocating unselfishness,[51] sincerity,[52] resistance to tyranny,[53] independence of thought,[54] commitment to reason,[55] and a sense of civic responsibility,[56] all of which he found conspicuously lacking in the great majority of sophists.

There is, of course, a significant theoretical dimension to Plato's condemnation of the sophists. Plato saw that at the heart of the sophistic world view is a thoroughgoing relativism. On one level it is a cultural relativism,[57] but on a deeper level it is a metaphysical and epistemological relativism that obfuscates the difference between reality and appearance, knowledge and opinion. Plato held that there can be little if any respect for genuine moral ideals when there is no belief in objective truth and reality, and he took it on himself to restore to philosophical inquiry what the sophists had taken away from it – its proper concern for the categories of truth and reality. In the *Theaetetus*, Plato offers a brilliant if somewhat flawed critical analysis of the metaphysical and epistemological relativism of the sophists that is rooted in Protagoras's conception that "Man is the measure of all things."[58] In a "digression" that he places in the middle of that dialogue, he suggests that conflicting attitudes towards this doctrine lie at the core of the disagreement between the philosopher and the corrupt rhetorician.[59]

This analysis complements a major theme of the *Republic* (as well as the *Gorgias* and other dialogues) – that those who do not believe in objective truth and reality, and in the capacity of reason to know them, will sooner or later end up promoting force, deception, and manipulation as appropriate substitutes for a truncated form of rational discourse that cannot lead people to a wisdom that transcends mere prudence. In the *Theaetetus*, Plato has Socrates pointedly raise the question of why a sophistic teacher such as Protagoras should receive a handsome fee from his pupils when he believes he has no more objective knowledge than they do;[60] and he has Socrates answer for Protagoras that the sophist believes that he can substitute *better* "appearances" for the one's his students currently have.[61] Plato proceeds to indicate weaknesses in this line of defence; and of course, in such a model the criteria of good and better have themselves been deprived of objective significance. Still, Plato was prepared to acknowledge that despite his fondness for money and prestige, a man of Protagoras's stature and dignity must have sincerely believed, at least at times, that he was genuinely serving his clients and the community as well. However, Plato also saw clearly the road that leads straight from Protagorean subjectivism and relativism to the outlook of a Callicles or Thrasymachus; and the entire history of inauthentic culture is in large part a matter of people acting on the basis of what they take to be some sort of natural right to alter the "appearances" of their less sophisticated fellows.

PLATO ON CULTURE AND RELIGION

A related aspect of Plato's antipathy to the sophistic movement is his strong disapproval of the sophists' anti-religious tendencies. Though it was not always apparent to their contemporaries, many of whom regarded philosophy itself as a threat to religion, both Socrates and Plato were deeply religious. Both were prepared to challenge what they took to be corruptions and perversions of the religious spirit, and so they inevitably were targeted by theological reactionaries as enemies of religion. But both men were religious reformers with a substantial respect for tradition, and Plato may be usefully characterized in general as a sort of "critical traditionalist."[62]

While a sophist such as Protagoras could appreciate the practical value of religion as a form of culture and experience, his subjectivistic and relativistic orientation was incompatible with the spirit of traditional Greek religious commitment, and his public position on theological matters was agnosticism.[63] Atheism, or a position rather close to it, was taught by such sophistic thinkers as Diagoras, Prodicus, and Critias.[64] Some modern thinkers, such as Popper, have seen the sophistic rejection of supernaturalism as one of the high points of the development of science in the classical world; but we can well understand that the typical ancient found the radical theological views of prominent sophists troubling and offensive. In Aristophanes' *Clouds*, the main attack on Socrates as a practitioner of sophistry focuses on his supposed rejection of the existence of the gods. In the *Apology* and elsewhere, Plato goes to great pains to refute the charge of impiety against Socrates[65] and in places suggests that Socrates is a true believer in a way that the hypocrites who have condemned him are not.[66]

Plato's own mode of religious spirituality is complex and has been the subject of various interpretations. Popper regards Plato's attitude towards religion as fundamentally "pragmatic," in much the same way as the sophist

Critias's, and he argues that those who defend Plato for attacking the subversive conventionalism of the sophists are inconsistent when they fail to censure him for making an invention, indeed a lie, the ultimate basis of religion.[67] Popper suggests further: "Wherever Plato considers religious matters in their relation to politics, his political opportunism sweeps all other feelings aside."[68]

Scholars who, unlike Popper, are not engaged in a systematic criticism of the Platonic world-view generally grant a practical dimension to Plato's attitude towards religion, particularly as expressed in Plato's last and longest work, the *Laws*.[69] Being well acquainted with the varieties of atheism in his time, Plato appraised each according to its content and practical significance,[70] but looking back to an ancestral, imaginary age of innocence and good morality, he was consistently inclined to consider belief in the gods and observance of their cults as a source of security. For Plato, religion was a social anchor and piety a defence:[71] "The religious practices of the city state constitute a magical cement that holds its social structure together. Sophistic criticism of the way society works and of its assumptions about the practice of life – not merely about the gods – weakened the adhesive power of civic-religious bonds. Direct criticism of the gods and the mythoi concerning them, their supposed attitudes and their way of life, carried the debilitation to a dangerous further stage."[72]

Nevertheless, Plato was not merely "pragmatic" in his attitude towards religion. As Rankin observes, whereas someone such as Protagoras or Critias was an atheist according to the standards of ancient opinion,[73] Plato "gave the social contract back to the gods and nature,"[74] and, unlike the sophists who stressed custom and convention, "Plato believed that nomos [law], like everything else, should be based upon some apprehension of the true nature of reality, and he never excluded the gods from a validating role."[75] Plato never denies the existence of the "popular" gods and is adamantly opposed to those in the sophistic movement who do.[76] Jaeger stresses that despite his criticism of the theologian-poets, "Basically, Plato's philosophy is a reincarnation of the religious spirit of earlier Greek education, from Homer to the tragedians: by going behind the ideal of the sophists, he went beyond it."[77]

Writers such as Paul Elmer More and William Temple have discoursed at great length about Plato's significance as a precursor of, and influence on, Christianity.[78] Temple reminds us of aspects of the Platonic world-view that can hardly be regarded as embodying a purely pragmatic conception of religion: "At the crown of the whole system as represented in the *Republic* is the Idea of Good; whether or not Plato thought of this as something personal when writing the *Republic*, there is no doubt that later on his supreme principle is the purpose or thought of a Living God. So he exclaims in the *Sophist* (248e): 'Can we ever be made to believe that motion, and life, and soul, and mind, are not present with perfect being?' ... Perhaps the greatest height that he ever reaches is in the *Theaetetus* (176a, b), where he says that the wisdom of man is to fly away from this world to the spiritual world, and this flight consists in becoming holy and just and good."[79] With respect to theology proper, Temple observes, Plato's leading principle is that God is good and the author of good only, and in emphasizing this dogma in the system of elementary education outlined in the *Republic*, Plato attacks the poets' characterizations of the gods not only because they are a bad influence on children but because they are untrue.[80]

Plato was not merely a traditionalist but rather a purifier of religion;[81] he set for himself the imposing tasks of systematizing informal Greek religious beliefs, blending the central elements of Olympic and Orphic religion and reconciling faith and reason.[82] These tasks required him to work at cleansing conventional forms of religious commitment and practice of what he took to be corruptions. Michel Despland has recognized the complexity of the amalgam of traditionalist, radical, practical, and intellectualist elements in Plato's religious vision. "Plato ... strives to understand the Greek religious tradition; he wants to reform it. In religious matters, as elsewhere, the philosopher wants to bring back to disturbed Athens a sound insight into the true nature of its own welfare. The assumption is that religion plays a crucial role in the transmission of paradigms of culture."[83] Plato challenges the authority of the theologian-poets and repeatedly expresses contempt for certain religious ceremonies, but he also clearly upholds the authority of certain features of the Greek religious tradition.[84] However, "That Plato dares to offer imitation of God or assimilation to the deity as the imperative stemming from the highest morality indicates how completely confident he is that he has thoroughly reoriented images of the divine. He fully knows that the behaviour of the Homeric gods has been used as excuses by all kinds of immoralists ... But in the dialogues there is no doubt that assimilation to the divine will be a schooling in moral measure."[85]

There is undoubtedly a practical concern in Plato's account of the relation of religion to culture; but his is not the "pragmatism" of the sophist. He believes, of course, that religious commitment safeguards the individual's confidence in the objectivity of truth and value and that public piety can be a protection against the individual's (and the community's) inclination to appropriate inauthentic, contrived cultural products. But he is convinced that a religious world-view is intellectually as well as practically sound. His religious conceptions are not merely derived from his political and cultural concerns but complement them. In Despland's view, "Plato is a great philosopher because he ventures, openly, into the management of the inauthentic. He tries to find a *modus vivendi* between philosophy and public religion."[86]

Gouldner recognizes that Plato's emphasis on the universally valid is on one level an attempt to overcome the relativistic conceptions of the sophists, which he feels have opened the door to moral anarchy and the degradation of Athenian culture.[87] He can see that Plato does not merely appeal, as Aristophanes does, to the value of respecting religious traditions but with great sincerity puts forward for the appropriation of his readers a world-view, based on rational reflection, that he believes provides a sound account of objective, transcendent reality and the individual's and the community's relation to it.

Plato's account, according to Gouldner, makes it clear why one should not settle for the "appearances" promoted by pretenders to wisdom, why it is sensible to treat one's fellows and one's community as ends rather than as means, and why one is acting in harmony with the cosmic order when one aims for, and helps others to achieve, self-perfection rather than an inferior or illusory form of "success." Plato does not advocate promotion of religious beliefs and practices simply because they are traditional, or bring some order to society, or can help people to be honest, sociable, and diligent. He certainly knows that the corrupt aspects of conventional religion can be as inauthentic and destructive as any secular cultural product.

As any genuine philosopher does, Plato provides us with an account, based on rational reflection, of how he believes things are. His is a lofty, spiritual account, which he believes compatible with any decent, healthy-minded, thoughtful individual's intuitions about the superiority of justice to injustice and about the dignity and meaningfulness of human life in relation to a universal order that accommodates and reflects human spirituality. "He justifies his critique of conventional values by counterposing them to the goods of the soul, which he now infuses with heightened pathos and sacred potency. Indeed, he transforms the traditional Athenian concept of the sacred itself by rejecting, as he does, the conventional Homeric picture of the gods as doing evil to men."[88]

While in the *Republic* Plato acknowledges the significance of religion, in his last dialogue, the *Laws*, he attaches considerably more importance to the theological foundation of culture. In this final phase of his philosophical reflection, his repudiation of sophistic relativism and all that follows from it is couched in explicitly theological language: "Now God ought to be to us the measure of all things, and not man, as men commonly say (Protagoras):

the words are far more true of Him. And he who would be dear to God must, as far as is possible, be like Him and such as He is."[89]

Later, in Book X of the dialogue, Plato proposes various punishments for different forms of impiety, and the content and tone make it clear that he sees the decline of a certain kind of religious commitment as a particularly grave threat to the stability of the community. Popper notes: "Plato demands, in the *Laws*, the severest punishment even for honest and honourable people if their opinions concerning the gods deviate from those held by the state." Further, "If they do not recant or if they repeat the offence, the charge of impiety means death." Popper wonders aloud whether Plato had simply forgotten that Socrates himself had fallen a victim to that very charge.[90] Leo Strauss believes: "In the *Laws*, the Athenian stranger [speaking for Plato] devises a law against impiety which would have been more favourable to Socrates than the Athenian law."[91] But Plato leaves no doubt that he sees the decline of culture as substantially the result of the unchecked decline of religious faith in an objective, transcendent order.

But even in *Laws* X, Plato's analysis cannot fairly be regarded as "pragmatic," for he uses detailed rational theological argumentation in justifying it, a method that has none of the marks of manipulative rhetoric or contrived propaganda. Though his attack on religious freedom is ultimately indefensible, Plato believes that secularists and radical religious humanists not only are dangerous to their fellows but have been led by a truncated rationality to a world-view that is demonstrably unsound.

There is plenty of which to disapprove in Plato's social and cultural theory, even without considering his more recondite metaphysical speculations and adventures in mysticism. There are, as Gouldner observes, significant lacunae in Plato's model, perhaps most noticeably in his inadequate responses to war, poverty, and slavery and in his failure to allow for sufficient creativity and the generating and sustaining of valuable novelty.[92] Moreover, even sympathetic readers of the dialogues can see that Plato's inability to overcome envy and resentment sometimes interfered with his stance as a cool, rational observer. In places he shows marks of fanaticism, and we may have to concur with Havelock's suggestion that Plato's revulsion against sophistic relativism "went beyond argument and reached into the depths of his consciousness."[93] There are places in the dialogues where the author seems to be almost as manipulative as the manipulators that he is constantly denouncing.

Yet, as we noted above, even a hostile commentator can concede that the great man was fundamentally benevolent and sought to persuade by appealing to a reason or rationality in which he had, if anything, too much confidence. Though from an aristocratic background, he turned his back on most of the privileges and prerogatives of high birth and accepted the view of an impoverished Socrates that wealth, fame, and power count for little or nothing when considered in relation to virtue, love, and the things of the spirit. He exposed forms of individual and social corruption that need to be periodically uncovered – and as much in our age as in his – and he moved on from criticism to suggesting, carefully and in detail, methods for clearing away obstacles to personal and communal improvement. He examined a wide variety of human creations – intellectual, religious, political, literary, and so forth – and was able to see in their production, promotion, and appropriation certain fixed patterns that later came to be understood as "cultural." He invited his readers to consider the motives of different types of people who create, promote, and appropriate cultural products, and he vividly described for them the price that individuals and communities pay when they pay insufficient attention to the quality of those products. He affirmed the importance of the search for knowledge of truth and reality and emphasized its relation to sound values. And whether discussing the Forms, or the gods, or God, he remained a truer humanist than those who believed in man-the-measure, for he quite consistently drew attention to a universal human dignity that cuts across cultures and classes and eras.

5

THE CLASSICAL ANALYSIS REWORKED:
FOUR STUDIES IN THE TRADITION

To understand Plato's impact on Western civilization, one must consider among other things his influence on Christianity. Since much of Christian thought is imbued with Platonic inspiration, Platonic insights have been communicated, if imperfectly, to countless people with little interest in academic philosophy. Never was the Christian intellectual's appropriation of Platonic modes of thinking more striking and more influential than in the writings of Augustine of Hippo. Though Augustine defends rhetoric in the *De Doctrina Christiana*, his attack on corruptive rhetoric in the *Confessions* is, after Plato's, the most intense and most influential philosophical attack on such rhetoric.[1] Much of Augustine's work is a response to what Augustine takes to be the corrupting effect of morally deficient intellectuals; and no major figure in the history of philosophy has been more obviously or more directly engaged in a confrontation with heretics that he perceives as undermining the very foundations of civilized society. Moreover, particularly in *The City of God*, Augustine shows a profound interest in the philosophy of culture.

Etienne Gilson has provided a valuable expository summary of Augustine's relevant themes: "If we give the name 'city' to any group of men united by a common love for some object, we say that there are as many cities as there are collective loves ... [S]ince there are two loves in man, there should also be two cities to which all other groupings of men are reduced. The scores of men who lead the life of the old man, the earthly man, and who are united by their common love for temporal things, form the first city, the *earthly city*; the multitude of men who are joined together by the bond of divine love form a second city, the *City of God*. Once we have grasped the nature of these two cities, moral philosophy will expand into a philosophy of history, and beneath a multiplicity of peoples and events, will see how the two cities have persisted from the beginning of the world and will extract a law permitting us to forecast their destiny."[2]

The order of the earthly city, which is "ever bent on gaining the mastery over material things and the enjoyment of them," is "fundamentally nothing but a mockery of the true order against which it is in permanent revolt."[3] The City of God alone is founded on true order and alone enjoys true peace; and it is thus "the only abode of a people worthy of the name; in short, it is the only true city."[4] Making allowances for Augustine's medieval Christian language and cast of mind, we can see that his description of the earthly city in its relation to the properly functioning society mirrors or at least parallels Plato's analysis of the anatropic culture promoted by groups of subversive, self-interested materialists.

Augustine does not simply offer a variant of Plato's classical analysis of inauthentic culture. His views on corrupt culture were influenced by other thinkers besides Plato. More important, he was not only a philosopher but a Christian theologian; not only did he constantly have to deal with theoretical and practical theological problems, but he may perhaps be said to have opened a new era in the history of Western thought by making religious faith in some revealed truth the obligatory starting point of rational knowledge.[5] Nevertheless, as a key figure in the transmission, application, and transformation of Platonic doctrines and attitudes, he contributed to the continuity of a certain traditional philosophical way of understanding the corruption of culture.

Augustine was an intense man who saw the culture of his community of believers and of all civilized humanity as under siege. Having at one time succumbed to the Manichaean heresy, he felt that he had personal experience of how easy it is for one to be deceived into adopting a false, pernicious, anatropic world-view, despite the wise teaching and emotional support of loved ones. Though a true intellectual, he saw himself as having a special mission to confute the teachings of Manichaeans, Pelagians, Donatists, and other promoters of false ideas, evil practices, and corrupt institutions; he passionately believed that there was an urgency to exposing these purveyors of inauthentic products for the wicked deceivers that they were. Though of a different temperament than Plato, he shared with him the conviction that the intellectual must account for and respond forcefully to the cancerous growth of anti-cultural tendencies in his society.

Later medieval philosophers rarely were able to summon up anything quite like this passionate conviction of Augustine, mainly because they could not see civilization as under siege in the way or to the degree that it had been in Augustine's time. Indeed the scholastic philosophers of the thirteenth century could well be comfortable with the serene wisdom of the patient Aristotle, who, unlike his teacher, Plato, was a generation removed from the intellectual and cultural crises surrounding the moral decline leading up to and following the unjust execution of Socrates.

ERASMUS

As an increasingly arid and technical scholasticism proved incapable of countering the deterioration of cultural institutions in the final phase of medieval European life, it was almost inevitable that visionary thinkers would again seek to restore the classical analysis of inauthentic culture to the prominence that it had enjoyed in equally troubling times.

A vigorous, sustained attack on inauthentic culture typified much of the philosophical discussion of the Renaissance and accompanied a pronounced growth of interest in the works of Plato. No one better represents these tendencies than Desiderius Erasmus, and the spirit of his attack on inauthentic culture is encapsulated in these opening lines of his popular colloquy of 1522, "The Godly Feast":

EUSEBIUS. Now that the whole countryside is fresh and smiling, I marvel at people who take pleasure in smoky cities.

TIMOTHY. Some people don't enjoy the sight of flowers or verdant meadows or fountains or streams; or if they do, something else pleases them more. Thus pleasure succeeds pleasure, as nail drives out nail.

EUSEBIUS. Maybe you refer to moneylenders or greedy merchants, who are just like them.

TIMOTHY. Those, yes, but not those alone, my good friend. No, countless others besides them, including the very priests and monks themselves, who for the sake of gain usually prefer to live in cities – the most populous cities. They follow not Pythagorean or Platonic doctrine but that of a certain blind beggar who rejoiced in the jostling of a crowd because, he would say, where there were people there was profit.

EUSEBIUS. Away with the blind and their profit! We're philosophers.

TIMOTHY. Also the philosopher Socrates preferred cities to fields, because he was eager to learn and cities afforded him means of learning. In the fields, to be sure, were trees and gardens, fountains and streams, to please the eye; but they had nothing to say and therefore taught nothing.[6]

These charming, whimsical lines touch on some of the Christian humanist's favourite themes: the pervasiveness of venality and corruption; their presence even among those charged and entrusted with spiritual and cultural leadership; the contrast between the integrity of the reflective pagan and the shallowness and selfishness of the phoney "Christian"; the dignity of learning; the transience of common pleasures; and the superiority of the human sciences to the natural sciences.

Erasmus's debt to Plato may not be obvious. Many would agree with Huizinga that Erasmus did not have a "philosophic mind,"[7] and his interests were generally more theological and literary than philosophical. The simplicity that he admired seems to be of a different order than that which Plato commended, and he scoffed at Plato's confidence in the intellectual's competence to govern.[8] In temperament and style, he was often closer to Aristophanes than to Plato. Yet Plato was a great favourite of Erasmus, who admired him not so much for his speculative thought as for his moral teaching.[9] Erasmus was largely indebted to Plato for his psychology[10] and for the anthropology that underlies all of his thought on religion and moral duty;[11] and he drew most heavily on Plato and Aristotle for his program to form the perfect, ethical individual for high office.[12]

In the *Enchiridion*, Erasmus is clearly following Plato when he urges his reader to move away from earthly reality towards the truer reality of the spirit,[13] and in 1521 a Wittenberg student wrote to a friend that Erasmus was not much thought of there partly because the *Enchiridion* had made Plato rather than Christ his model.[14] Following Plato, Erasmus consistently held that the body restrains the aspirations of the human being's higher nature;[15] and the latter part of his most celebrated work, *The Praise of Folly*, endorses what is at least a diluted form of Platonism.[16] Even Erasmus's satire often has a Platonic flavour; it is, after all, as W.M. Gordon has noted, in Plato's work that "the spirit of merry seriousness" finds its fullest expression.[17] When we consider what Erasmus regarded as the dominant requirements – simplicity, naturalism, purity, and reasonableness[18] – we realize why Erasmus regarded Plato's philosophy as particularly congenial to the Christian outlook.[19]

Erasmus's criticism of inauthentic culture was not, however, based entirely on the Platonic model. "Mockery with a moral" was a form of satire characteristic of the age in which he lived; we find it, for example, in the works of Luther and Rabelais.[20] And his criticism was shaped in part by the cultural products of his age that he sought to expose as foolish, useless, and soulless. Still, it is natural that someone who thought as much as Erasmus did along Platonic lines should have been so concerned with, and so astute in his observations about, cultural corruption.

Consider *The Praise of Folly*. This remarkable "eulogy," one of the masterpieces of world literature, is, despite its breezy banter, extraordinarily complex. Not only can it be usefully approached from many perspectives, but it is filled with paradoxes, ironies, subtle allusions, and conceptual twists that force readers to work very hard for their moral instruction. But despite the playful tone, we can detect a familiar pattern to the author's pointed comments. Erasmus sees the deterioration of cultural products as a disease, or the result of a disease, that has infected all major aspects of his society's culture. He sees one cultural product after another as having been gradually deprived of almost all original value and significance, to the point at which the products have virtually become empty, illusory "appearances." He sees those who profess to be serving their fellows as manipulating and exploiting them; and he sees the quacks and imposters too as victims of their own narrow idea of "success." He sees bigotry where there should be tolerance, contempt where there should be compassion; and he sees the highest religious institutions as having been taken over by hypocritical operators who have undermined the simple, pure religious commitment of plain folk and weakened the spiritual bonds that hold society together. In short, Erasmus sees the culture of his society as gradually being turned upside down.

Many of Erasmus's barbs are as relevant today as they were in his own time; and many were appropriate in Plato's day. He describes how while intellectuals are despised or ignored, the medical doctor is in constant demand, though "the more unlearned, impudent, or unadvised he is, the more he is esteemed, even among princes."[21] Lawyers are ridiculed by the public, "yet there's scarce any business, either so great or so small, but is managed by these asses."[22] Religion itself has in large part been reduced to gross superstition, so that the merchant, soldier, or judge who parts with a small amount of money can believe that he is thereby cleansed from sin and free again to indulge in perjury, debauchery, deceit, breach of trust, and treachery;[23] along with such foolishness goes the superstitious worship of saints.[24] And yet the priests receive and cherish the superstitious "as proper instruments of profit." But if a true spiritual teacher "should step up and speak things as they are, as, to live well is the way to die well; the best way to get quit of sin is to add to the money you give the hatred of sin, tears, watchings, prayers, fastings, and amendment of life; such or such a saint will favor you, if you imitate his life – these, I say, and the like – should this wise man chat to the people, from what happiness into how great troubles would he draw them?"[25]

According to Erasmus, the academic philosophers, scientists, and theologians who claim to be seeking truth have for the most part lost themselves in increasingly trivial technical exercises and are concerned more with winning arguments and enhancing their status among their small group of colleagues than with attaining and promoting wisdom.[26] Of course, "The apostles also confuted the heathen philosophers and Jews, a people than whom none more obstinate, but rather by their good lives and miracles than syllogisms: and yet there was scarce one among them that was capable of understanding the least 'quodlibet' of the Scotists."[27] And as for "those that commonly call themselves the religious and monks, most false in both titles, when both a great part of them are farthest from religion, and no men swarm thicker in all places themselves,"[28] they are simply "stage-players" and "dissemblers."[29]

The corruption that angers and troubles Erasmus most is that at the highest levels of social, political, and cultural leadership. There are the princes who "believe that they have discharged all the duty of a prince if they hunt every day, keep a stable of fine horses, sell dignities and commanderies, and invent new ways of draining the citizens' purses and bringing it into their own exchequer; but under such dainty new-found names that though the thing be most unjust itself, it carries yet some face of equity."[30] "Nor are princes by themselves in their manner of life, since popes, cardinals, and bishops have so diligently followed their steps that they've almost got the start of them."[31] The bishops "feed themselves only, and for the care of their flock either put it over to Christ or lay it all on their suffragans, as they call them, or some poor vicars";[32] and the popes, rather than imitating Christ and his poverty, labour, doctrine, and cross, ignore their proper model, for they realize that to imitate Christ's life would lose them the earthly treasures that they have amassed – wealth, honours, riches, victories, offices, dispensations, tributes, mules, guards – and, of course, their pleasures.[33]

And so Erasmus sees his nominally "Christian" society as dominated by a gang of schemers and con artists, of manipulators and imposters, who are doing almost precisely the opposite of what they ought to be doing and the inverse of what they pretend to be doing. The increasingly complex organizational and professional machinery of the church and the state was making the exploited and exploitative alike worse rather than better, worse off rather than better off. Everywhere there is deception and illusion; and materialism and selfishness are rife.

Erasmus realizes that it will not do merely to carp and whine. Despite obvious weaknesses in his character, which have made him much more vulnerable than a Plato or even an Augustine to the ridicule of his detractors,[34] he is a genuine idealist, if, in Huizinga's famous description, a "thoroughly moderate" one,[35] and he is not content with simply showing off what a clever satirist he is. In the last part of his encomium, there is a moving appeal to his readers to appropriate for themselves, and to promote among their fellows, what Erasmus conceives of as the "philosophy of Christ." This is an entirely proper appeal on the part of someone who considers himself a defender of the faith.

But he directs his appeal to a highly literate and sophisticated audience – for what "simple" believer could understand *The Praise of Folly*?. His audience knows him to be a fellow sophisticate and someone who has hardly made a point of imitating Christ in his own personal affairs. Erasmus knows that his audience will not be content with what can be easily dismissed as a perfunctory note of Christian piety, and so in the last part of the work he moves to the level of philosophical humanism and translates his message into Platonic form. He describes the higher folly, the divine madness, that inverts and transcends the shallow folly of small minds.[36] Christian humanist that he is, he can remind his readers: "The Christians and Platonists do as good as agree in this, that the soul is plunged and fettered in the prison of the body, by the grossness of which it is so tied up and hindered that it cannot take a view of or enjoy things as they truly are."[37] And in going on to commend a true spirituality to his audience, he completes the Platonic task of revealing the higher way of life that ultimately alone can save the individual and society from anatropic culture, with its illusions and false values.

Erasmus can hardly do better than invoke the imagery of the cave parable. To put authentic and inauthentic culture, higher and lower folly, into proper perspective, he reminds his audience of

those that being cooped up in a cave stand gaping with admiration at the shadows of things; and that fugitive who, having broke from them and returning to them again, told them he had seen things truly as they were, and that they were the most mistaken in believing there was nothing but pitiful shadows. For as this wise man pitied and bewailed their palpable madness that were possessed with so gross an error, so they in return laughed at him as a doting fool and cast him out of their company. In like manner the common sort of men chiefly admire those things that are most corporeal and almost believe there is nothing beyond them. Whereas on the contrary, these devout persons, by how much the nearer anything concerns the body, by so much more they neglect it and are wholly hurried away with the contemplation of things invisible. For the one give the first place to riches, the next to their corporeal pleasures, leaving the last place to their soul, which yet most of them do scarce believe, because they can't see it with their eyes. On the contrary, the others first rely wholly on God, the most unchangeable of all things; and next him, yet on this that comes nearest him, they bestow the second on their soul.[38]

Bringing together Christian wisdom with Platonic wisdom, and eschatology with moral exhortation, Erasmus promises the truly pious that in the life hereafter they will experience the highest happiness, which "though 'tis only then perfected when souls being joined to their former bodies shall be made immortal, yet for as much as the life of holy men is nothing but a continued meditation and, as it were, shadow of that life, it so happens that at length they have some taste or relish of it."[39] And so, presumably having at least tried hard to believe what he has just taught, Desiderius Erasmus, Christian humanist and heir in his own way to the Platonic style of cultural analysis, has played out his role as philosophical liberator in the cave world of early-sixteenth-century Christendom.

Augustine, Erasmus, and their disciples might have ended up thinking about inauthenticity along Platonic lines, even if they had never heard of Plato or read one line from his dialogues. Plato has enormously influenced countless people who have never heard of him; and then again, perhaps many would have eventually come to view inauthentic culture in the "classical" way even if Plato and the ancient Greeks had never existed. But we shall never know; and in any case, what we have come to think of as the "philosophical tradition" is in many ways the "Platonic tradition."

Of course, one does not have to be a philosopher to complain about the decline of culture. Many people who know nothing about philosophy, or disapprove of it, complain about cultural corruption; and they sometimes blame philosophers for much of that corruption. Plato was at times obsessed with the bad name that the loose-thinking, loose-talking Aristophanes had given Socrates and the philosophers, and it was a masterful stroke on his part to take Aristophanes' rough version of the classical analysis of inauthentic culture and adapt it for his own purposes.

Erasmus himself entered into theological controversy with a certain unphilosophical critic of corrupt culture who would have an even greater influence than his on Christendom. Martin Luther's vituperative attack on phoney indulgences and the like was certainly not served up in a philosophical spirit, and while it had many salutary results it also gave rise to a reaction against subtle reasoning and its promoters that would thrust Europe into violence and bloodshed for generations and permanently undermine the ecclesiastical unity for which Erasmus had so long agitated.[40]

VOLTAIRE

By the late seventeenth century and the early eighteenth, so many people had had enough of religious conflict and hatred that the time was ripe for the widespread institutionalization of religious toleration in certain western

European countries.[41] Philosophers were among the most vigorous and influential promoters of tolerance in this period, and they and their literary followers consistently drew attention to how extensively European culture had been for so long corrupted by manipulative, selfish ecclesiastical bigots. It is instructive to reflect briefly on one of the most prominent spokesmen for the new spirit of liberalism, Voltaire.

When one considers Voltaire's broadsides against the Catholic hierarchy, and against institutionalized Christianity in general, one may well be reminded of Erasmus's attack on inauthentic Christianity, with its ridicule of the "religious" superstitions of the masses and its bold denunciation of clerical abuses in high and low places. Like Erasmus, Voltaire was committed, in principle if not always in practice, to the defence of reasonableness, tolerance, and integrity. With his stylish wit and wide range of interests and skills he may seem to have been Erasmus reincarnated.

But the two men had quite different goals. Voltaire's cultural criticism was much more focused than Erasmus's. Having absorbed the wisdom of progressive thinkers such as Locke, and witnessed the persecution of decent people such as Jean Calas, Voltaire felt obliged to be harsher and more explicit than Erasmus in indicating the primary source of all cultural corruption, and few rallying cries have been more famous than his: "*Écrasez l'infâme.*" He disliked *The Praise of Folly*, with its Christian piety and its metaphysical speculations,[42] and his attitude towards Plato himself was ambivalent.

That the most celebrated philosophical (or at least semi-philosophical) cultural critic of the eighteenth century should have been thus ambivalent is worth considering. Voltaire did feel a certain kinship with Plato;[43] he was, after all, a believer in "reason," and he saw in Plato's account of the martyrdom of Socrates a powerful image of the religious bigot's contempt for the wise and just people of the world. But as much as Voltaire admired Plato as a moralist and cultural critic, he could not forgive him for his metaphysical speculations. He associated Plato with all the other metaphysicians who, with their talk about "spiritual being," had spread maleficent nonsense.[44] Voltaire's view of Plato's metaphysics, which Peter Gay has aptly described as "embarrassing,"[45] is related to his identification of it with a Christianity that he despised. Whereas Erasmus had associated Plato's description of the spiritual realm with the purest elements of Christian faith, Voltaire linked it with the superstitions and corruptions promoted by Christianity.

The "reason" that Voltaire commended is not quite the same as that which Plato praised. Voltaire identified it at various times with such things as good sense and scientific thinking. He would have none of Plato's talk about discerning timeless, transcendent essences or about the divinity of the soul. To the extent that he saw the Platonic Socrates as the classical proto-type of the sensible moralist struggling against superstitious dolts and crooked manipulators, Voltaire was an heir to the Platonic tradition of cul-tural criticism. But in other ways he stood apart from that tradition and was one of its enemies. Plato and Voltaire represent two types of "reasonable" people, and their proffered solutions to the problem of phoney culture, while similarly conceived in the spirit of good will, are ultimately divergent. Even people who disapprove of those features of Plato's philosophy that offended Voltaire can still think of Plato as the paradigmatic philosopher; while even those who agree with Voltaire on the essential points are some-times given to wondering whether he was a philosopher at all.

Though not a very original or profound thinker, Voltaire serves well as a symbol for a series of modern intellectual movements that focused cultural criticism increasingly on forms of manipulation and manipulability associ-ated with "traditional" types of institutionalized Christianity. The "pious" followers of the Augustines and Erasmuses now found themselves more and more regarded as reactionary enemies of the growing spirit of freedom, rea-son, and progress. If they were uneducated, they were dismissed as supersti-tious fools, and if they were educated, they were perceived as manipulative deceivers.

But in the Renaissance, the Age of Reason, and the Enlightenment, the philosophical solution to inauthentic culture was not seen as essentially a matter of responding to subjectivism or relativism. Rather, empirical scien-tific inquiry, liberal social institutions, and the limitation of religion to the status of a form of culture and experience came more and more to be seen by intellectuals as the proper responses to the superstition of the masses and the authoritarianism of political and ecclesiastical puppeteers. Thus either the classical analysis of inauthentic culture was gradually replaced by an altogether new type of criticism of inauthentic culture, a "modern" form; or the classical analysis had at least been transformed into something substan-tially new. Throughout the eighteenth and nineteenth centuries, both intel-lectual and political struggles were significantly related to conflicting conceptions of inauthentic culture on the part of liberal defenders of one ideal of truth, reality, and value and conservative defenders of a rather dif-ferent ideal of truth, reality, and value.

NIETZSCHE

By the late nineteenth century, it was clear to many that a new "crisis of culture" had developed partly as the result of such intellectual movements as

positivism, radical socialism, Marxism, higher criticism, and Darwinism –
and the authoritarian, irrationalist, and traditionalist attempts to counter
them. The time seemed right for a dramatic new philosophical reworking of
the classical critique of inauthentic culture. Though several major thinkers,
such as Ernest Renan, Paul Rée, and Eduard von Hartmann,[46] contributed
to this new spirit of traditional philosophical cultural criticism, the name
that we now generally associate with it is that of Nietzsche. Nietzsche is, after
Plato, the most influential of all philosophers of culture, and his influence
on all major schools of recent philosophy of culture has been more direct
and more obvious than Plato's. Thus close familiarity with his work has
become in the last few years almost a prerequisite to academic cultural theory. There is even less agreement among scholars now than there was earlier
in the century about what precisely Nietzsche was saying about culture. It
would appear that Nietzsche himself, despite his characteristic assertiveness,
did not know exactly what he wanted to say about culture. Most of us who
are prepared to learn from him still find in his work a provocative "medley
of a hundred promiscuous paradoxes and heterodoxies," rather than the
"logical results of a perfectly definite philosophical *sensibility*" that he hoped
we would uncover there.[47]

Nietzsche's many provocative and somewhat inconsistent claims about
authentic and inauthentic culture are too numerous for us to consider here,
but we will look at those aspects of his philosophy of culture that are directly
relevant to his reworking of the classical analysis of inauthentic culture.
Though Nietzsche did make, despite his announced intentions, contributions to metaphysics, epistemology, and moral philosophy, he was above all
else what he so often conceived himself to be – a philosopher of culture. This
was readily apparent to the first major expositor of his work, George
Brandes, with whom he had a lively correspondence in the last years before
he went mad. Brandes, widely credited with having "discovered" Nietzsche,[48]
appreciated the broad range of his insights on the various subjects with
which he has come to be associated. These include the prejudices of philosophers, the Jewish (and Christian) inversion of natural morality, the corrupting influence of Christianity, the distinction between philosophy and mere
scholarship, aristocratic versus conventional virtues, master versus slave
morality, the will to power, the essence of nobility, the primacy of the Diony-
sian, *ressentiment*, the paramount importance of the great man, and so forth.

But Brandes believed that the key to understanding the entire corpus, and
the unity of his philosophical project, could be found in his attack, early in
his career, on the degraded state of European (and particularly German)
"culture," which he saw as represented by the scholar-critic David Strauss.[49]

In this essay, along with Nietzsche's first major work, *The Birth of Tragedy*,[50] we find the core of his vision, even though he had not yet developed such notions as eternal recurrence and the primacy of the will to power. Their basic theme is that the culture of the so-called civilized world has been increasingly weakened by passive acceptance of ideas and attitudes that are antagonistic to the development of the type of individual, creative genius who is necessary for the emergence of a true culture that represents a stage in the advancement and eventual transcendence of the human "type." Nietzsche heartily approved of the name that Brandes had given to his philosophy of culture – "aristocratic radicalism"[51] – and he saw in Brandes's well-known essay on his work a sound understanding of what the cultural state of affairs was that Nietzsche regarded as the basic philosophical problem of both his own age and the entire history of Western civilization.

According to Brandes's account, Nietzsche was from the start convinced that what his fellow Germans regard as culture is not culture at all.[52] Maintaining in the essay on Strauss that culture is essentially a unity of artistic style running through every expression of a nation's life, Nietzsche looked on the "cultural" products of his own society as empty and phoney.[53] He regarded what passed for culture in that society as a mockery of the true culture that elevates rather than keeps down the human "type."

Though Nietzsche saw the degradation of culture as having deep roots in ancient Jewish and Christian metaphysical, theological, and moral conceptions, he believed that he was writing at a key moment of history. Individual national cultures were about to give way to a European or European-American culture, and he saw himself as urgently working for the rearing of a caste of pre-eminent spirits who would be able to grasp the central power. He felt that to carry out his task, it was necessary for him to confront the "Culture-Philistines" and expose them for the promoters of phoney culture that they were. Culture-Philistines regard their own impersonal education as the real culture; but lacking creativity, intellectual depth, genuine ambition, discipline, willingness to suffer, and kindred qualities of the superior human being, they simply derive their basic ideas, attitudes, and values from the masses.[54]

We can see a parallel here with Plato's contempt for the sophists, who advertised themselves as exemplars and promoters of high culture but were ultimately motivated only by a slightly refined version of the shallow, conventional morality that they had passively derived from the herd. As a young man, Nietzsche had looked on Richard Wagner as a genius who was working to free Germany from its dependence on Christian conceptions; but with the appearance of Wagner's *Parsifal*, with its Christian piety and advancement of ascetic ideals, Nietzsche came to see Wagner as the paradigmatic creator and promoter of phoney cultural products.[55]

In time, Nietzsche came to perceive himself as something of a philosophical liberator who would lead the worthy out of the cave world of late-nineteenth-century European "culture." He would help to free those few who were capable of envisioning a higher type of humanity by helping them to remove the chains of Christianity and slave-morality that had kept them from creatively realizing imaginative personal projects. They could then go back to the cave to use the largely uneducable mass, with its truncated will to power, for whatever purposes they saw fit in their task of elevating the "type" Man.[56]

Nietzsche's scheme is very different from Plato's, as he well realizes. Nietzsche is not concerned with promoting a culture that will provide the various classes of society with whatever "happiness" they are capable of attaining. He is interested in the superior individual and his project; those who are not capable of advancing the human "type" are, in Nietzsche's view, proper subjects for whatever exploitation and manipulation the truly noble person deems appropriate in carrying out his grand designs. In advocating such exploitativeness on the part of the higher man, Nietzsche echoes the preaching of those sophists whom Plato most despised, such as Callicles and Thrasymachus, so that William Temple has characterized his philosophy as "Thrasymachus turned into poetry."[57]

Nietzsche's attitude towards the sophists is in fact highly respectful, whereas his feelings about Plato are markedly ambivalent. But Plato saw the more manipulative sophists not as "higher men" in Nietzsche's sense of the expression but as culture-Philistines who manipulate people in order to satisfy trivial, materialistic interests. And though in *The Birth of Tragedy* Nietzsche blames Socrates and Plato for spoiling Hellenic culture with their rationalism, idealism, and moralism,[58] and he does in places sound very much like Callicles and Thrasymachus, his own philosophical criticism of inauthentic culture is in the very spirit of Plato's attack on the sophists. But before we consider the amalgam of Platonic and anti-Platonic elements in that criticism, let us consider briefly how the mature Nietzsche contrasts Plato and the sophists.

Nietzsche was a professor of classical philology; he knew the works of the ancient Greek philosophers well. He thought it imperative for modern students of culture to know those works thoroughly, because of both their immediate and long-term influence and their emphasis on the central themes of cultural theory. Here and there in his works, Nietzsche acknowledges the brilliance and nobility of Plato, an aristocratic genius who contrasted the philosophical Guardian with those who have only base metals in their soul.[59] But just as Nietzsche began his career as a philosophical writer by attacking Socrates and Plato in *The Birth of Tragedy*, he was still able to write in a late work, *The Twilight of the Idols*:

Plato is boring. In reality my distrust of Plato is fundamental. I find him so very much astray from all the deepest instincts of the Hellenes, so steeped in moral prejudices, so pre-existently Christian – the concept 'good' is already the highest value with him, – that rather than use any other expression I would prefer to designate the whole phenomenon of Plato with the hard word 'superior bunkum,' or if you would like it better, 'idealism'. Humanity has had to pay dearly for this Athenian having gone to school among the Egyptians (– or among the Jews in Egypt? ...). In the great fatality of Christianity, Plato is that double-faced fascination called the 'ideal,' which made it possible for the more noble natures of antiquity to misunderstand themselves and to tread the *bridge* which led to the 'cross'. And what an amount of Plato is still to be found in the concept 'church', and in the construction, the system and the practice of the church![60]

In contrast, consider these words on the sophists written by Nietzsche near the end of his career: "The moment is a very remarkable one: the Sophists are within sight of the first *criticism of morality*, the first *knowledge* of morality ... They postulate the primary truth that there is no such thing as a 'moral *per se*', a 'good *per se*', and that it is madness to talk of 'truth' in this respect ... The Greek culture of the Sophists had grown out of all the Greek instincts; it belongs to the culture of the age of Pericles as necessarily as Plato does not ... And – it has ultimately shown itself to be right: every step in the science of epistemology and morality has *confirmed the attitude* of the Sophists."[61] Contrasting the sophists with a Plato whose very integrity he calls into question, Nietzsche even suggests that their realism was more authentic than Platonic idealism: "The *Sophists* are nothing more nor less than realists: they elevate all the values and practices which are common property to the rank of values – they have the courage, peculiar to all strong intellects, which consists in *knowing* their immorality."[62]

It almost goes without saying that Christian and other "traditional" critics of Nietzsche have exploited the distance that Nietzsche places between himself and Plato (and his corresponding respect for the customarily despised sophists) as a device for diminishing his stature as a serious philosophical thinker. Some have drawn attention to how far Nietzsche can stray from the classical approach to culture. Frederick Copleston, for example, grants that there is some truth in what Nietzsche has to say about the aristocratic basis of culture,[63] but he goes on to explain why the Platonic analysis of culture, which Nietzsche has in fact greatly misunderstood,[64] is vastly superior to Nietzsche's, which is the "way of madness."[65]

But Nietzsche is not merely a modern Thrasymachus, and he is not consistently the radical relativist, or even the hard believer in exploitation and manipulation, that he sometimes believes and at other times pretends. If he were, sophisticated contemporary philosophers of culture would not be able to take him as seriously as they do. Indeed, when Nietzsche attacks inauthentic culture, he sounds in certain ways very much like Plato. What I have in mind here is not the sophisticated and provocative argument of Heidegger and others that Nietzsche, despite his claim to be providing an "inversion" of Platonism, has unwittingly ended up as a Platonist in his approach to Being.[66] Rather, I am thinking simply of the tone and much of the detail of Nietzsche's attack on the decadent "culture" of his society, with its empty or phoney "cultural" products in all artistic domains, promoted by small-minded, narrowly self-interested, manipulative types who satisfy their trivial, materialistic interests at the cost of preventing development of a real culture that would help advance all humanity and the "human type."

G.A. Morgan provides a useful summary of Nietzsche's comprehensive critique of the inauthentic culture of modernity, and the twin Platonic obsessions of corruptive manipulativeness and manufactured "appearance" recur frequently in the survey. Thus, for example, in society Nietzsche sees the "disintegration of institutions," and in politics, "state idolatry, prostituting culture to barbarous ends." In economic life he observes "a contemptible money-economy infecting all society with commercialized values, debasing cultural interests for business purposes," and, in science, "the undermining of older moral and religious ideas without the power to create a substitute." He sees further "the emancipation of specialists from the control of philosophy" and a new form of pseudo-intellectual inquiry that is "lacking any sustaining ideal." In education, Nietzsche finds "preferment of mediocrity," the "degrading [of] the standards of the old education, disguising the ugliness of the modern philistine." Education has actually become "the worst obstacle to a purified and rejuvenated culture." In art, there are "bizarre combinations of charlatanism and virtuosity," the "demand for 'effect at any price'," and the "cult of passion," and artists "pandering to the tastes of the mob, the over-worked, the neurotic." He sees an enfeebled religion "losing hold of its dogmatic foundations but still professing them outwardly before the populace." In philosophy, or what is dishonestly promoted as such, he detects "a plethora of timid, second-rate minds, devoid of real vocation, perverted to the service of material ends, who ignore and are unfit for the royal task of true philosophy."

In general, Nietzsche conceives of his society as one in which "people live in such haste that they receive numerous, therefore superficial, impressions; nothing has a chance to sink deep, take root, mature; man is becoming a marionette of external stimuli. There has been a break with tradition; continuity of development has been destroyed, and men live disconnectedly 'by the day.'"[67] Was this not substantially how Plato saw the decadent culture of his own society?

Morgan follows Brandes in seeing at the heart of Nietzsche's philosophical project, from the beginning to the end of his short career, a contempt for, and a mission to counter, the sickness, degeneracy, and decadence of modern "culture." And despite his antipathy to the proto-Christian idealism and moralism of Platonism, with its invocation of transcendent reality and absolute morality, and its promise of salvation for the soul, Nietzsche's cultural criticism echoes Plato's. Though he sometimes indicts Plato for himself having been a destructive manipulator, his criticism generally is significantly tempered by his realization that Plato was a noble, honest thinker, who, along with a few fellow Greeks and with the Jews of antiquity, brought about the most monumental event in the history of culture – the inversion of natural morality – the most imposing manifestation yet of creative will to power. If Plato and the ancient Jews let loose on the world the sick Christian priests, they nevertheless were themselves anything but mediocrities. So while Nietzsche despises much of the content of the Platonic and Jewish world-views, he is not being inconsistent when he expresses his deep admiration of the "grand style of morality."[68] Nor on reflection is it all that strange that in his role as cultural critic he should sound so much like Plato and the Hebrew prophets.

Though we may well be troubled by the licence that Nietzsche gives to great men to exploit and manipulate the masses, we should put his advocacy of exploitation into proper perspective. Nietzsche gives encouragement only to noble, honest human beings to exploit only the mediocre "herd animals." He does not generally regard exploitativeness and manipulativeness as such as evidential marks of nobility and greatness. In fact, a central theme of his cultural criticism is that mediocrity and the corruption of cultural products have been largely the result of the corruptive manipulation of the masses by those who, unlike the higher man, have nothing in the way of a noble purpose or vision. Nietzsche recognizes that the sick priests and their ilk, with their phoney values and institutions, have been "successful" at their own ignoble project: they have satisfied their trivial interests at the expense of the masses and of all humanity. But such a "success," derived as it is from shallow conceptions that are only slightly refined versions of the herd's, is finally as worthless as the "success" that Plato saw the ancient sophist as having achieved. Just as the manipulative sophist derived his standards of success ultimately from the "Great Sophist" to which he saw himself as vastly superior, the high functionaries and agents of the decaying institutions of Christendom have accomplished nothing of real significance through their manipulation.

So while Nietzsche at times does seem to be advocating manipulative exploitation for its own sake, as the very essence of natural morality, his cultural criticism indicates that he generally regards such activity as instrumental, as a device for the promotion of real or phoney culture. He is advocating only manipulative exploitation that will counter the trivially "successful" but corruptive manipulative exploitation of the agents of mediocrity and cultural deterioration. Plato had encouraged the wise to learn how to communicate better with the masses; but even Plato, being well aware of the intellectual limitations of the masses, could see the necessity of the "noble lie."

Nietzsche's advocacy of egoism can be understood along similar lines. For Nietzsche, the great man is not concerned with narrow self-interest, as are the promoters of phoney culture; rather, he is someone with a mission – to elevate humanity and the human "type." He is highly disciplined and prepared to suffer and make sacrifices; he has his own special "virtues" – the "Stoic" virtues of the higher man.[69] In the *Republic*, Adeimantus had criticized the Platonic Socrates for insisting that the lives of the philosophical Guardians must be so hard and so demanding; and the answer that Plato had Socrates give is the prototype of Nietzsche's own position.[70] The superior person does not seek what the masses seek; he is engaged in a process of personal and communal advancement that demands that he distance himself as much as possible from the pleasures and other spiritually trivial things that preoccupy the masses. As Plato does, Nietzsche sees the great man's mission as complementary to his concern for self-as-individual. But Nietzsche is in his own way even more demanding than Plato, in that he associates nobility with concern for the advancement of not only communal culture but the developing human order that will some day transcend its own humanity.

If Nietzsche's analysis of inauthentic culture is as "traditional" as I have suggested, then why is his solution to the problem of inauthentic culture so different from that of an Aristophanes, Plato, Augustine, or Erasmus? How can one see something akin to the "classical" analysis in the philosophy of a writer who is profoundly antipathetic to so much for which Plato and his company stand, such as transcendent reality, absolute morality, sympathetic concern for all of one's fellows, and the need for a return to religious commitment? First, it should be possible to distinguish, if perhaps only with some difficulty, between the form and the content of the classical criticism. Those that one regards as being responsible for manipulative exploitation in one's own society may be quite different from the sophists and dramatists of Plato's day, and their products may be "unreal" or "illusory" in a less metaphysical sense than Plato had in mind. Yet it might still be appropriate to see criticism of a comparable inauthenticity as belonging to a classical tradition. Moreover, there is no good reason for believing it necessarily inappropriate to respect someone for some things and be critical of him for others, or to agree with someone's view of a problem and yet disagree with him on the proper solution, or to see someone as having done the very thing that he has been critical of others for doing.

Second, Nietzsche's philosophical style is distinctive. His work is filled with intentionally provocative paradoxes, curved sentences, ambiguities, and experimental proposals. Like Emerson (an avowed Platonist of sorts, an eloquent proponent of the classical analysis of inauthentic culture, and someone who had an enormous influence on Nietzsche's thought), he was inclined to regard a "foolish consistency" as the "hobgoblin of little minds."[71] Nietzsche neither wants nor expects readers to take whatever he says literally, though sometimes scholars who should know better see him as a systematic philosopher. I take Nietzsche's contempt for inauthentic culture to be rather more fundamental to his outlook than are most of the bizarre hypotheses that he entertains along the way. Nietzsche wrote: "Whatever is profound loves masks."[72]

Third, there are places in Nietzsche's writings where his views are not as contradictory to Platonic and religious views as he sometimes makes them appear. Despite his attacks on Platonic and Christian talk about transcendent reality, Nietzsche has no use for the garden variety of empiricism, positivism, materialism, or "common sense" realism. Much of his discussion of the will, eternal recurrence, and kindred subjects is – if not "news from nowhere"[73] of the kind served up by metaphysical system-builders, or evidence of an out-and-out mysticism – then at least heady stuff for people not given to speculation on high matters. For a relativist and perspectivist who condemns and ridicules those who promote belief in absolute morality, Nietzsche also does a remarkable amount of preaching, judging, and ranking. Though a self-proclaimed "immoralist,"[74] he seems to believe that he knows a great deal about what is "good" – at least "good" as opposed to "bad" rather than to "evil."[75] And he does not merely regard master-morality as different from slave-morality; he thinks of it as higher and nobler.[76] Again, his comments on something such as pity are not really inconsistent with the Platonic world-view; and, like Plato, he can see the great-souled man as capable of a kind of generosity of which ordinary people are not. Even with respect to religion, Nietzsche sometimes shows himself open to an appreciation of the positive value of many of its styles for people of all ranks.[77]

To many students of the history of ideas, Nietzsche represents the outstanding example of a thinker who, all but overwhelmed by cultural rubbish, is drawn into a flirtation with nihilism. But as Helmut Thielicke observes, Nietzsche eventually realized that for the serious thinker reflective nihilism can never be more than an interim state.[78] As for Nietzsche's contribution to the analysis of inauthentic culture, and to cultural theory in general, he was an heir to the classical tradition of perfectionist or self-realization ethics. Though a favourite author of many cynics, Nietzsche ultimately had little use for cynics; and though brimming with resentment, he provided perhaps the most powerful description ever given of its corruptive influence. As a young man, Nietzsche was drawn to Schopenhauer's pessimistic philosophy, but he soon outgrew it. He saw utilitarianism as shallow and superficial and deontologism as the outgrowth of neurosis. But with the Greek philosophers, particularly Socrates and Plato, it was different; though he initially identified them as the principal subverters of the highest Hellenic culture, they never ceased to influence his thought. There were two major foci to Nietzsche's historical interests – his own century and ancient Greece.[79] He consistently rejected Plato's rationalism and idealism, yet traces of both lingered in his thought; and though he never stopped railing against the influence of Platonic moralism, its charms were too powerful for a classically trained cultural critic to resist entirely.

Nietzsche's perfectionist ethic is at the core of his response to the social and philosophical problem of inauthentic culture. As Plato does, he teaches that real culture can develop only when the best and brightest people are allowed to cultivate in themselves and their society a unified "artistic style" that is in harmony with the highest potentialities and aspirations. Nietzsche's ethical, social, and cultural perfectionism is inferior to Plato's: it has little if any metaphysical foundation; it fails to account for the social nature of culture; and it is diluted with relativism. However, Nietzsche also transformed and extended the classical perfectionist ethic by emphasizing things that Plato had undervalued – novelty, individuality, and creativity. By doing so, Nietzsche helped to pave the way for the existential philosophers who have been the most influential reflective critics of inauthenticity in our own century. Even so, Nietzsche's list of virtues is not very different from Plato's. For in spite of his talk about the higher man's "creation" of values,[80] Nietzsche believes that anyone who warrants being regarded as "higher" possesses most of the following: strength of will, integrity, honesty, purity, sincerity, hatred of the charlatan, subtlety, delicacy, intellectuality, nobility, magnanimity, measure, and individuality.[81]

Nietzsche's application and transformation of central themes of the classical analysis of inauthentic culture tell us a great deal about the staying power and adaptability of that classical analysis. In the eyes of many philosophers and cultural theorists of our own time, particularly in continental Europe, Nietzsche is the key figure standing on the threshold of modern philosophy and cultural theory. To these people, he represents the spirit of modernity. Yet when he got down to the business of explaining what was wrong with the culture of his own society, he was still looking at things in much the way that Plato had. Here we have a professed enemy of rationalism, idealism, moralism, transcendentalism, metaphysical system-building, religious piety, and almost everything that Plato stands for – not to mention of Plato himself. He is regularly taken to have been a proponent of nihilism, perspectivism, relativism, irrationalism, atheism, and immoralism. But when this classically trained philosopher dealt with cultural corruption, he gave his readers a stylish rendition of the old Platonic song.

To talk about a "tradition," especially with reference to something such as the history of philosophical ideas, is inevitably to blur significant differences. The admirer of Nietzsche, mindful of the master's emphasis on novelty, individuality, and creativity – and the importance of geniuses or great men – may particularly object to locating Nietzsche's cultural criticism in a tradition, especially a very old one represented by so many thinkers with whom he would have felt uncomfortable being grouped. It would be inaccurate and misleading to say that Nietzsche's analysis of the corrupt culture of his day is plain and simply the "classical" analysis. Even Augustine and Erasmus do not just give their readers the "kind" of cultural criticism that an Aristophanes, Socrates, or Plato offered in his day.

The distinctions are ultimately as important to note as the similarities, and though I have indicated some of those distinctions, I have placed more emphasis here on similarities and continuities. One of my main objectives has been to show that inauthentic culture is not an entirely new social and philosophical problem that has arisen as a result of the unique circumstances of contemporary life. It is rather a very old problem that, despite the somewhat different forms it has taken over time, has arisen from the human situation itself and is thus clarified through reference to insights of some of the great philosophers of the past.

Of course, our contemporary problems can also usefully be contrasted with those of cultural critics and social reformers of other ages. But it is not enough, I think, to observe that philosophers of culture have responded to inauthenticity in numerous ways. It is worth our while to consider the general "philosophical" way in which they have come to terms with a problem that is both transcultural and traditional.

6

THE CLASSICAL ANALYSIS REWORKED:
TWO RECENT STUDIES AND AN OVERVIEW

Inauthentic culture is not simply a philosophical problem, and it is most certainly not one that Plato "invented." Plato's criticism of inauthentic culture was a response to certain conditions that he saw as pervasive in his declining society. Later philosophers, and later theologians, scientists, and literary scholars, have confronted comparable problems, and not just because Platonic thought influenced them, consciously or unconsciously. And the social problem of inauthentic culture can be approached theologically or scientifically as well as philosophically. But cultural criticism, while it can be essentially theological rather than philosophical, can never be purely empirical-scientific, for empirical science as such cannot generate the value judgments that criticism requires. At some point the empirical-scientific critic must start talking philosophically or theologically. She can do so in ignorance of what theologians and philosophers have said about inauthentic culture; or she can draw on their insights.

With these considerations in mind, let us turn to one of the most famous modern critics of inauthentic culture, Thorstein Veblen. Veblen's credentials in this area would appear impeccable, as it was he who introduced such expressions as "conspicuous consumption," "pecuniary emulation," and "invidious interest." A striking feature of his thought is the underlying tension between his scientific objectivity and his passionate contempt for the "pecuniary culture" of American capitalist society. Some scholars see the dry, objective tone of most of his work as primarily a device for augmenting the bite of his satirical attack on the character types and cultural products that he sought to expose and undermine. George Soulé, for example, writes: "His method was to describe some institution with the most distant objectivity, as if he were a visiting anthropologist from a higher civilization. The effect was more devastating than the angriest invective; no eloquence was required to drive his points home."[1]

This view is not quite correct. Veblen is primarily remembered today, especially by non-specialists, as a sardonic critic of a corrupt socio-cultural system based largely on predatory exploitation. But he does not seem to have been all too certain about whether he was primarily an objective social scientist or a leftist cultural critic and social reformer. He had a deep hatred for the wealthy and powerful who indulge their foolish tastes at the expense of the poor, downtrodden, and genuinely productive. It was important for him to expose the shallowness of the leisure class's values and tastes and to vindicate the virtues of the "common man."

But Veblen was also conscious of his hard-earned status as a scientific scholar, and he so often turned uncritically to the positivistic and deterministic assumptions of natural and social scientists that he frequently left his more reflective readers with the impression that he was doing little more than describing the "way of the world." Though his views have certain obvious affinities with those of Marx, to whom he paid considerable attention,[2] he "felt himself put off by Marx's dual role as scholar and propagandist; he cared too much for an objective science to be comfortable with Marx's mixture of strategy and prophecy."[3] Veblen rarely speaks to us unequivocally in the voice of the ardent critic-reformer. His work is in large measure a consequence of what he regarded as "idle curiosity"; and, though he could on occasion play the role of the social activist,[4] his "uncommitted griping"[5] never developed into a full-fledged, practical strategy for cultural reform.

Nevertheless, Veblen is an astute critic of phoney cultural products, and his analysis of them is partly philosophical as well as social-scientific. It was the philosophical aspect that allowed him to move from analysis to criticism. His early academic training was as a philosopher. He not only majored in philosophy at Carleton College, to which his father had sent him in the hopes of his entering the Lutheran ministry,[6] but went on to do extensive graduate work at Johns Hopkins and Yale and earned a doctorate in the field. Though he later moved into the professional area of academic economics, he carried with him various ideas, attitudes, and concerns that he had picked up in his philosophical studies. There was always something of the philosopher of culture in Veblen, though, despite his extensive study of classical Greek and traditional moral philosophy, he was more obviously influenced by the Social Darwinism of Herbert Spencer and his own teacher at Yale, W.G. Sumner. Early in his career he reacted against the Spencer-Sumner intellectual defence of capitalism, but many of Social Darwinism's methods and assumptions were to leave a lasting impression on him.

Veblen is best known for his first major work, *The Theory of the Leisure Class*. This is a remarkable work and, among other things, a subtle, semi-philosophical critique of a certain type of anatropic culture. Though thoroughly devoid of metaphysical content, the book offers an analysis of phoney culture and cultural products that has much in common with traditional philosophical analyses. Veblen conceives of the entire culture of American capitalist society as systematically pervaded by phoney, unnatural, corruptive values and the products that they generate. He sees the "common man" as the victim of exploitation, and the genuine intellectual as marginalized because educational and religious institutions are controlled by self-serving agents of the status quo. Cultural institutions in general are in the control of a manipulative, exploitative wealthy class that, though victimized by the false values that it promotes, has imposed those values on the middle and working classes. And he believes that intellectuals such as he can, through publication of the results of their intellectual inquiries into cultural institutions and values, greatly enhance people's understanding of the need to return to the purer, truer values of a much earlier, peaceable way of life, based on workmanship and sympathy.

In the cultural criticism of his great study, here concisely summarized by Soulé, Veblen focuses on the unnatural – one might perhaps say "unreal" – quality of the cultural products of his society:

The theme of *The Theory of the Leisure Class* (1899) is that the social standards which determine behaviour under Western capitalism are, beneath their modern trappings, much the same as those characteristic of barbarian societies. The money economy and the struggle for accumulation of wealth constitute new counters in the game, but the game exercises the same human traits.

The sign of high rank in both types of culture is "exemption from industrial toil." The barbarian rulers were warriors or priests; their status was won by predatory rather than productive exploits. Aristocratic virtues are the same today as then – "ferocity, self-seeking, clannishness, disingenuousness, and a free resort to force and fraud." Modern aristocrats, engaged in high finance and big business, exhibit these same "virtues," as do the retainers of financiers and big businessmen – bankers and lawyers.

The one distinction of the higher classes is that their activities are absolutely useless from the point of view of the humble citizen. The sign of success is lavish expenditure, which satisfies no real need but is a mark of prestige. Fine clothing in which one could not do any manual labor, a bejeweled wife, rich food, or useless learning constitute the "conspicuous waste" and "conspicuous consumption" which mark the man whom everyone wishes to emulate.[7]

Much of the book is curious, highly speculative evolutionary anthropology, but the force of his cultural criticism is largely independent of such theorizing, brought to life by the keen perception that he brings to his descriptions of the shallowness and emptiness of most cultural products in relation to real human needs. Veblen is as offended by the wastefulness institutionalized by his society's anatropic culture as he is by the power that the culture gives to an exploitative, unproductive class over productive, and potentially very much more productive, human beings. In the manner of Plato, he portrays the ship of state as being in the hands of worthless incompetents who have undermined respect for knowledge and true craftsmanship. The "vested interests" represent the new barbarians, and while Veblen sees the degradation of culture as a process that has gone on for millennia, he regards that process in his own society as particularly disgusting in light of its pretence to high civilization.

In the spirit of traditional philosophical criticism of inauthentic culture, Veblen excoriates the corruption of institutions of higher education. He initially regarded such institutions as important primarily because they can provide useful knowledge to the craftsmen who do constructive work.[8] In *The Theory of the Leisure Class*, he looks at higher learning as an expression of the pecuniary culture. His aim is to illustrate the "method and trend of the leisure-class influence in higher education,"[9] particularly the unproductive teaching, learning, and research. Later, in *The Higher Learning in America* (1918), he emphasizes the value of universities in relation to the instinct of "idle curiosity," which he takes to be, along with the instinct of workmanship and "parental bent,"[10] one of the three most fundamental human instincts. Having concluded that "idle curiosity" both is to be valued for its own sake and can have immense practical utility, he concentrates on the control of institutions of higher learning by business entrepreneurs who subvert them by putting them to their own narrow ends. Like Plato and Nietzsche, he was concerned with preserving the independence and integrity of the intellectual.

But despite its affinities with traditional philosophical analysis of inauthentic culture, Veblen's analysis of the anatropic culture of American capitalism is also much farther from the classical analysis than any of those considered in our survey. By the time he wrote *The Theory of the Leisure Class*, he had come to regard himself as a social scientist rather than a philosopher, and his analysis of inauthentic culture is rather more social-

scientific than philosophical. In spite of the moralistic strain in his personality, and his desire to subvert the pecuniary culture that he saw as a rever-
sion to barbarism and an inversion of civilization, Veblen was often
preoccupied with simply understanding things as they are; and his cast of
mind was for the most part materialistic and positivistic.

For one thing, like Marx, he was convinced that economic factors are at
the heart of all cultural development and deterioration.[11] All his work was
concerned with interpretation of the origin and development of social institutions under the dominant pressure of economic forces.[12] Cultural critics
such as Plato, Erasmus, and Nietzsche had surely undervalued economic
factors, and Veblen here provides a useful emendation. But his emphasis on
economic factors is reductionistic and plays down other cultural factors,
such as the religious, philosophical, political, and aesthetic, all of which he
subsumes under the economic.

He even associates these economic factors with biological ones. As the
years passed, he came to take more seriously the view of his friend Jacques
Loeb that "only a social science shaped in the image of post-Darwinian
biology could lay claim to being 'scientific,'"[13] and his "emphasis on the
rationality and wholeness of human behavior grew less and less."[14] As a
result, the determinism implicit in his early work became more explicit. As
his analysis of inauthentic culture became more empirical-scientific and less
philosophical, his effectiveness as a cultural critic declined. At one point he
had gained from William James and John Dewey a renewed sense of the
human person as an active being who selects her environment as well as
being shaped by it.[15] But in focusing in his later work on the role of instincts,
he "emphasized conscious human purposes less than biological drives, and
cultivated purposes less than 'natural' or inherited ones."[16]

Even in *The Theory of the Leisure Class*, Veblen had often suggested that
most individuals are passive puppets of economic processes that they cannot
control or comprehend, leaving individuals with little if any freedom to
"withdraw from the unceasing chase for pecuniary reputability."[17] In time,
Veblen could conceive only of "a society which did not give other meaning
to the universe than that blind play of cumulative forces studied by Darwin;
a society in which men admitted their insignificance, their kinship with other
animals, and their helplessness in the slow working out of the evolutionary
drift."[18]

To the end, Veblen was as anti-relativistic as Plato. He was never prepared
to be permissive with respect to the exploitative class's promotion of false,
unproductive values and institutions. Veblen's three fundamental instincts
– workmanship, idle curiosity, and care for the young (parental bent) –

remained for him "not only a substratum of human nature but a source of moral absolutes."[19] These "moral absolutes," though vastly different from Plato's timeless, transcendent Forms, could at least be known through rational inquiry.

Even so, Veblen's very short list of the primary instincts from which moral absolutes are derived is not at all satisfactory. From a purely empirical-scientific point of view, it is quite arbitrary. It is easy to see Veblen's list as based on a concealed moral choice[20] and as reflecting certain puritanical and ascetic feelings.[21] Also, Veblen is unable to explain how, if these instincts are so basic, they are so easily "contaminated." "It is of a piece with this bio-logistic thinking that Veblen never seems to have asked himself how species-serving workmanship could be so readily contaminated by the desire for approval, nor does he ask in what way emulation can result in workmanlike behavior, ... nor does he try to explain how the very nature of group life may lead a culture to prefer other values to the workmanship which this descendant of peasant Lutherans took too much for granted."[22] The empirical-scientific student of culture can hardly be expected to embrace a metaphysical or theological grounding of basic values. Still, he may well be able to appreciate the reasonableness of Plato's thesis that immoral, destructive behaviour ordinarily involves a lack of moral understanding, not just a supposedly "basic" instinct's mysterious failure to operate.

David Riesman's reference above to Veblen's Lutheran background reminds us both that social-scientific inquiry is rarely if ever "value-neutral" and that it cannot by itself generate the value judgments involved in cultural criticism. It also indirectly reminds us of traditional philosophical and theological discussions of the relations between religion and culture. Veblen's attitude towards religion in general, and Christianity in particular, is interesting. In *The Theory of the Leisure Class*, especially in the chapter on "devout observances," Veblen makes it plain that he believes the typical religious cultural product of his society to be as inauthentic as the typical secular product.[23] Recognizing the historical and anthropological importance of religion as a fundamental form of culture and experience, he sees the corruption of secular institutions as to a great extent having historically followed on the corruption of religious ones, especially in earlier stages of cultural development.

However, Veblen does not make the corruption of religion the focus of his cultural criticism, largely because of the primacy of the economic factor but also because of his positive view of what he takes to be the ideals of primitive Christianity. His view of Christianity is ambivalent; he sees it, "on the one hand, as a patriarchal religion of futile subservience to extravagant earthly representatives of a leisure-laden heavenly hierarchy; on the other hand, as a religion of brotherhood and abnegation at odds with pecuniary culture."[24]

Veblen's admiration for early Christianity's rejection of the values and other products of an anatropic culture is most apparent in his 1910 essay, "Christian Morals and the Competitive System."[25] J.P. Diggins, who regards this as Veblen's "most desperate and inconsistent" essay,[26] holds that while Veblen may have hoped for a revitalization of the "instincts" of a primitive, "natural" Christianity that could prevail over the institutions of capitalism, his own "faith" rested solidly on the evolution of empirical progress.[27] Though Veblen found it useful to distinguish the early principles and communal ethos of a pure Christianity from the modern practices and competitive ethic of a corrupted version,[28] he could not in theory regard a revitalized, purified Christianity as anything more than an instrument for the decontamination of the instincts that are directly conducive to the material well-being and biological success of a race.[29]

Yet D.W. Noble has shown that much of Veblen's socio-economic theory can be translated into the theological language of a puritan jeremiad,[30] and Veblen's 1910 essay appeared at just the time that "social gospel" theology was receiving its most powerful expression in the major works of Walter Rauschenbusch and Shailer Mathews.[31] That a positivist and materialist should have entered into even the practical spirit of this movement may perhaps tell us more than Veblen himself understood about a principal source of the values that animated his cultural criticism.

The need for a return to a revitalized, purified religious spirituality has traditionally been emphasized by philosophical critics of inauthentic culture – even Nietzsche acknowledges something akin to it. The value system that animates Veblen's cultural criticism may reflect the influence of traditional philosophical critics of inauthentic culture in an even more basic way. Theodor Adorno, the Frankfurt critical theorist (and himself a semi-philosophical critic of inauthentic culture), while admiring aspects of Veblen's cultural criticism, has concluded that he is ultimately an empiricist without an ethic,[32] and his deterministic language lends credence to that interpretation.

Yet Veblen's talk about workmanship, care for the young, and idle curiosity, though served up in the context of a biological (or pseudobiological) framework, has something of a classical-philosophical ring to it. Veblen had studied moral philosophy as a young man and decided early on that he had little use for hedonism.[33] The three basic "instincts" on which he settled are actually Platonic values. Riesman has pointed out that the instinct of workmanship is the thing that comes closest to being a basic entity in Veblen's theory.[34] It corresponds closely to something stressed by Plato, especially in so far as Veblen sees the "mutual furtherance" of the instincts of workmanship and parental bent as so broad and intimate "as often to leave it a matter of extreme difficulty to draw a line between them."[35]

You may recall that, in the *Republic*, Plato has Socrates correct Thrasymachus's "inverted" conception of craftsmanship even before he argues for a sound division of labour as the foundation of the just society. Plato's main thesis in this regard is that the true craftsman competently and conscientiously creates cultural products that serve not only his own interests but those of the "weaker party" and indeed the society at large. In relation to the state as a whole, the just person is someone who not only is personally just but performs his proper vocational role and does not attempt any roles for which he is not naturally suited and properly trained.

As for parental bent, Veblen understands it broadly. He sees it as having "a large part in the sentimental concern entertained by nearly all persons for the life and comfort of the community at large, and particularly for the community's future welfare."[36] This too sounds rather Platonic, as does his stress on "idle curiosity," for though his phrase does not immediately suggest anything like the "reason" or "understanding" promoted by Plato, his association of "idle curiosity" with the activity of academic scholars calls to mind the Platonic Socrates' well-known observation that philosophy is derived from the sense of wonder.[37] Veblen well knew that his own "idle curiosity" was of a different order from that of the "common man"; whatever his contempt for most "aristocratic virtues," he took his academic vocation seriously, and there was clearly a great deal of old-fashioned perfectionism in the world-view by which he himself lived.

One admirable feature of Veblen's analysis of inauthentic culture distinguishes it from other well-known analyses that stress the economic factor. That is his keen insight into the role played by invidious interest in the production and promotion of inauthentic cultural products. Veblen attaches much more importance than most social scientists and cultural theorists do to matters of "status" – perhaps too much. But he has at least left his readers with a fine sense of how phoney things can be when they are contrived simply to establish, perpetuate, or serve invidious distinctions that are unrelated to, or in conflict with, any meliorative function.

If much of what Veblen says about status, ostentation, social climbing, and the like now seems obvious to so many of his readers, it is in part because of the impression left on several generations, particularly in North America, by Veblen's astute observations about conspicuous leisure, conspicuous consumption, and conspicuous waste.[38] Here too, however, Veblen is heir to the "tradition": Plato had warned in the *Republic* of the limitations of "honour" as a motive to morality and had made it clear that people who attach much value to social status have a way of becoming concerned more with appearing worthy of honour than with being worthy of it.[39]

Veblen's criticism of inauthentic culture is of interest here for several reasons. It is an outstanding example of the mixture of philosophical and non-philosophical elements in such an analysis. It illustrates how specifically philosophical (or theological) judgments rather than empirical-scientific ones generate the critical aspect of such analyses. It reminds us of the durability and adaptability of certain themes of the classical philosophical analysis of inauthentic culture. And it provides us with some insight into the contemporary analyses that emphasize the economic factor. I am not saying that the weaknesses (or strengths) in Veblen's cultural criticism are all to be found in the similar studies of the contemporary schools of Marxism, critical theory, and radical theory, but the similarities may be as important as the differences.

ALLAN BLOOM

We have examined the cultural criticism of six philosophical or semi-philosophical writers from diverse backgrounds. They lived in different times and places and faced very different circumstances. Plato, an ancient Greek, endeavoured to promote "reason" in a world in which he was one of the few who knew what it was. Augustine of Hippo, scourge of the heretics, was a North African father and doctor of the church who bridged the ancient and medieval worlds. Erasmus, Dutch humanist of Renaissance and Reformation times, was himself a bridge between the medieval and modern worlds. We took a brief look at the world-view of Voltaire, a famous voice of the Enlightenment, and we then turned to Nietzsche, a late-nineteenth-century German who flirted with nihilism. Veblen, an eccentric American social theorist, indulged his "idle curiosity" by looking through the "idle rich."

These six also lived in the *same* world – one of schemers, operators, and self-promoters; of deceivers, hypocrites, and con artists; of bullies, manipulators, and exploiters. It is a world also of suckers, victims, and innocents. It has as well pious believers, honest doubters, and materialists; sages, clever guys, and dullards; aristocrats, plutocrats, and democrats; prisoners, puppeteers, and liberators.

In chapter 1, we considered inauthentic culture as a social and philosophical problem of today. We reflected on the culture of modern Western democracies, and we took note of a certain kind of criticism often directed at it by high-minded individuals. In chapters 2 and 3, in an examination of culture itself, we examined a few more instances of such criticism. Some of the critics whose words we looked at were philosophers by vocation, but others were amateurs who were probably not even aware that they were philosophizing. The issue that all these critics have addressed is contemporary. But we have now seen that it has much in common with, and in a sense is, a "traditional" problem; and so what earlier thinkers said with respect to it may help us understand our own situation.

The late Allan Bloom's 1987 best-seller, *The Closing of the American Mind*, is perhaps the most notable example of a recent North American contribution to this tradition of criticism.[40] W.A. Galston has observed that while Bloom "took on his subject in a manner utterly contemptuous of current fashion, and virtually guaranteed to enrage," the book was "reviewed in tones ranging from respectful to rapturous in the nation's most respected newspapers and journals."[41] Though the work's prominence is undoubtedly largely the result of shrewd marketing by a major commercial publishing house, many readers were receptive to the kind of cultural analysis that Bloom was offering.

As Galston has remarked, the book's reception was itself "an indication of the deep foreboding just beneath the complacent surface of contemporary culture."[42] Galston sees the study as having three distinguishable but closely related strands: "[a] detailed description of modern American society, viewed through the prism of university students; an historical-analytical explanation of the ills revealed by that description; and finally, a proposed cure for those ills."[43] Here we can recognize the usual elements: Bloom sees cultural corruption as pervasive, attaches special importance to corruptive influences on future leaders, identifies the principal corruptive forces, proposes means to neutralize their influence, and argues for a return to absolutes mediated by way of religious and philosophical traditions.

Bloom's intellectual interests, attitudes, and methods were very close to those of his teacher, Leo Strauss, with whom he shared a deep interest in and respect for the works of Plato. Prior to the publication of *The Closing of the American Mind*, Bloom was probably best known in the academy for his translation and edition of Plato's *Republic*. Following in the spirit of Plato's attack on the sophists, Bloom identifies the promotion of an alien relativism as the key to the cultural sickness of his society. Bloom realizes that the "common man" is not yet much attracted to relativistic notions, but he is convinced that the old pattern is at work: "Influential changes of opinion begin at the top and gradually filter downward. First comes dangerous philosophy, then the corruption of the intellectuals, then the students, political leaders, and finally the general public."[44]

"Why has the elite American mind deserted its founding convictions – the rights of man, the Bible – in favor of an openness that cannot make moral distinctions and eventually undermines all convictions? Bloom's official answer, which provides the plot line for much of his book, is that relativistic German philosophy gradually imposed the yoke of alien thought on what had been a sturdy Enlightenment tradition."[45] While Galston and most other critics have seen Bloom as overestimating the influence of German ideology, they are impressed by his catalogue of the marks of relativism in the emerging anatropic culture of American society. "Liberal tolerance fosters relativism when it seeks to widen its scope by placing more and more claims to superiority outside the realm of knowledge (pp. 30–31). Liberal freedom fosters relativism when it seeks to become absolute by denying all rational limits (p. 28). Democratic egalitarianism fosters relativism by denigrating heroism and delegitimating rank-ordering among human beings (pp. 66, 90). Egoistic individualism fosters relativism by denying natural relatedness among, and duties toward, other human beings, a trend exacerbated by the liberal-contractarian view of the family (pp. 86, 112). In short, Bloom's own account suggests that modern liberal democracy is not stably well-ordered unless it is somehow mitigated by external forces (religion, traditional moral restraints, aristocracy) with which it is at war and which it tends to corrode (see especially pp. 251–252)."[46] Bloom's analysis is thus close in content as well as spirit to the classical philosophical analysis of inauthentic culture.

Though Bloom, like Plato, can summon up sincere respect for the sophisticated relativistic theories of reflective, high-minded thinkers, he is astounded by the dogmatism with which relativism is accepted by shallow thinkers, by the generally uncritical response of the many who are unconcerned about what relativism means for our lives.[47] Bloom's fellow Straussian H.V. Jaffa, while recognizing that Bloom is very different from "Bible thumpers" and other shallow, dogmatic critics of the "new morality," astutely observes that his critique of relativism is most eloquently conveyed in these poignant personal comments:

My grandparents were ignorant people by our standards, and my grandfather held only lowly jobs. But their home was spiritually rich because all the things in it, not only what was specifically ritual, found their origins in the Bible's commandments, and their explanation in the Bible's stories and the commentaries on them, and had their imaginative counterparts in the deeds of the myriad of exemplary heroes. My grandparents found reasons for the existence of their family and the fulfillment of their duties in serious writings, and they interpreted their special sufferings with respect to a great and ennobling past. Their simple faith and practices linked them to great scholars and thinkers who dealt with the same material, not from outside or from an alien perspective, but believing as they did, while simply going deeper and providing guidance. There was real respect for real learning, because it had a felt connection with their lives. This is what a community and a history mean, a common experience inviting high and low into a single body of belief.[48]

The tradition to which Bloom refers here is not the Christian but the Jewish. But even though Bloom is not a quasi-pragmatic Christian apologist in the manner of the Christian philosophers of culture Dawson and Eliot, there is an unmistakable affinity between his cultural criticism and theirs.

The historian Fred Matthews has pointed out that underlying all these recent attacks on inauthentic culture are common themes: "the revulsion from intellectual modernism, and from corrosive social modernity (the loss of traditional hierarchy and status, the acceptance of universal mobility and equality), the need for hierarchy, for tight communities of belief and reverence led by a clerisy as the basis of civic order and personal self-development."[49] Bloom focuses on the need for "close study of classic texts to deduce authoritative understanding,"[50] and his cultural conservatism was anticipated a half-century earlier by the neo-Aristotelian, neo-Thomistic educational critics Robert Hutchins and Mortimer J. Adler, who had emphasized the corruptive influence not of alien German ideology but of then intellectually fashionable forms of empiricism, positivism, and pragmatism.[51] Though narrower and more dogmatic than Bloom, Hutchins and Adler had also stressed the timeless value of the "great books" and the need for scholars to keep in close touch with established intellectual and religious traditions.

Though *The Closing of the American Mind* was warmly received in many circles, both within and beyond the academy, and it provoked a salutary debate in scholarly and popular journals about the proper direction of American higher education and American culture in general, it is not clear that its cultural criticism will be any more successful in the long term than that of Hutchins and Adler in reversing the prevailing trends in academic teaching and scholarship. An academic "establishment," like any other, will invariably resist reform, and it will be even more tenacious in holding on to its familiar and comfortable ways when it feels that it has been unfairly blamed for pervasive cultural corruption.

As it happens, it is not hard to find flaws in Bloom's specific historical, philosophical, and cultural analyses; and the arrogant, contemptuous tone of his work is in itself almost enough to turn an open-minded reader away from it. The sympathy with which Bloom's argument has been received by many outside the academy can be interpreted in very different ways. It can be seen as a sign that scholars may not be serving their society as well as they like to believe; or it can be seen as just one more piece of evidence of traditional hostility to intellectuals, who from Socrates on have been convenient targets for the condemnation and ridicule of resentful, indolent types who have no desire to be liberated. Besides, against the dangers of relativism, egalitarianism, positivism, and the like must be weighed the very great threat represented by certain forms of conservatism and authoritarianism, and by intolerance, ethnocentrism, and uncritical traditionalism. The "cure" for cultural sickness, if carelessly administered, can turn out to be worse than the disease. In any case, we have good reason to suspect that many of the strengths and weaknesses of Bloom's analysis are strengths and weaknesses not of his analysis alone but of the traditional form of philosophical cultural analysis that it exemplifies.

A CRITICAL OVERVIEW

Several factors complicate general evaluation of this traditional form of philosophical cultural criticism. Every contribution is highly distinctive, and when one tries to separate out the traditional themes from the distinctive ones in a particular critique, one sees that the traditional themes have themselves been substantially transformed through being combined with the other themes. Also, since each critique incorporates most but not all of the themes of the classical analysis, questions arise as to how much it fits into the tradition, and one's judgment in this regard depends on what one takes to be the central and characteristic features of the classical analysis and the tradition that has grown out of it.

This or that reader will be puzzled and perhaps irritated by my inclusion of, for example, Nietzsche or Veblen, as exemplars. That response may reflect in part the reader's judgment about the essential features of the tradition. The specific combination of themes that marks the classical analysis of Aristophanes, Socrates, and Plato is *sui generis*, at least in fact if not in theory. And each particular theme of that analysis had a precise significance for Plato that it could not have had for the cultural critic of another time, place, and situation. Moreover, even when we have been able to pick out common (or similar) themes in the various analyses, we cannot be sure that a particular theme was as appropriate in one philosopher's society as in another's.

Nevertheless, having worked hard to detect similarities and continuities (while not ignoring significant differences), I would like to venture some general evaluation. We may observe first that the critics considered above were all hypercritical by temperament and also felt personally threatened or marginalized in some way. Their general assessment of the cultural products of their society was extremely severe; and in attributing motives to those whom they perceived as their rivals they were less generous than they might have been, and certainly less than a more open-minded observer would have been. They were cranky and somewhat self-righteous, largely blind to both the positive aspects of what they attacked and the dangers posed by their own prescriptions for cultural reform. Though they were generally more reasonable than most people of their age, they could not consistently rise above resentment, self-justification, meanness, and dishonesty; and they often fell short of the high-mindedness that they found lacking in others. In key places, their cultural analyses are marked by ambiguity, inconsistency, and inadequate evidential support. They were all splendid writers – and have almost universally been recognized as such – but their writing is marred in places by excessive cleverness and a rhetorical manipulativeness as bad in its own way as that which they attributed to their rivals. At times they were extremists, even fanatics.

The immediate incentive to their cultural criticism was their belief that their own society was pervaded by cultural corruption and undergoing rapid cultural deterioration. Though each of them made a powerful case to support this contention, they generally overstated their point, and they were themselves at times prepared to acknowledge the soundness of many of their society's cultural institutions. That their societies survived, and in certain ways thrived, after their death can be to some extent explained by their own positive influence; but none of them, not even Plato, can be reasonably credited with having single-handedly, or with the aid of his disciples, saved his society. Most of these critics looked back to a better time, some to a "golden age," but to the limited extent to which their rear vision was clear, it was mostly unrealistic. None of them had experienced anything much better than what they were condemning; and none of them had sufficient warrant for believing that such a culture had ever existed.

What really makes their cultural criticism work is their awareness of how far the culture of their society falls short of an ideal. While right to esteem respect for certain declining traditions, they have generally been more valuable for their account of what might be than their account of what once was. We saw in chapter 4 that if Plato was a traditionalist, he was certainly a critical one; and we think of him today less as a great defender of tradition than as the first major utopian theorist. Even that other great ancient Greek critic of inauthentic culture, Aristophanes, could laugh at defenders of the "old ways," as is perhaps especially apparent in *The Birds*.

Central to traditional philosophical criticism of inauthentic culture is the image of the many being manipulated by the crooked, self-serving few.

Though here again the various critics made a powerful case in support of their view, they themselves expressed grave doubts about the ability of the "common man" to motivate himself to participate actively in the dual program of personal and communal advancement. Plato despised democracy partly because he saw the mob as easily swayed by demagogues; but he also believed that few people would amount to much if they were left on their own to care for their souls and their community. In Plato's view, the masses need to be led by philosophical Guardians so that they can live in peace and be liberated to the extent of their natural potential. Plato advocates reasoning with the general public where possible, but he never forgets the limits of the general public's reasonableness, and he explicitly acknowledges that there are circumstances under which the people have to be manipulated for their own good and that of the state.

All our critics knew that the unphilosophical masses require guidance yet do not consistently respond well to attempts to reason with them. Moreover, they recognized that manipulative elites derive their most basic values from the general public. They did not simply regard those who are manipulated as essentially "better" than those who manipulate them; and though they thought of the manipulated as victims, they also saw manipulability as evidence of weakness of will, of intellect, of ambition, and of imagination. In criticizing the manipulators, they portrayed them as people whose values do not rise significantly above the mob's.

Even those among them who praised democratic institutions were aristocratic at heart, not the least because they could not abide the mob's perpetration of injustices against noble figures, vulnerable minorities, and itself. Our critics also sometimes noted that ordinary people are manipulated not only by elites but by each other. The inauthenticity of the sophist's product or the poet's mirrors that of the products of ordinary craftsmen with which the sophist and poet have grown up. To put the primary blame for cultural corruption on manipulative elites may be far too lenient on "simple folk." Our critics were all aware of this, but it did not suit their strategy for reform to emphasize it. Nietzsche is the exception – he believed that it was "natural" for the "common man" to be manipulated. But Nietzsche was troubled by two related facts: that the "common man" is routinely manipulated by other inferior men rather than by higher men for higher purposes; and that the potential higher man is himself routinely manipulated by inferior men. The question arises, of course, of why a potential higher man would need a Nietzsche to tell him what to do.

Our critics must have realized that they owed much of their own influence, and much of their education, to the patronage of the "manipulative few." Throughout most of history, it has largely been the political, business,

and ecclesiastical elites that have provided most of the wherewithal for institutions of higher learning and the other institutions of high culture. Intellectual cultural critics who empathize with the victims of manipulation
generally grant that the masses tend to be less appreciative of humanistic
learning than are the operators who exploit them. The masses would perhaps
eventually come to appreciate true intellectuals if they were not kept down
by the operators. But as Plato had observed, in their unenlightened condition
the masses ordinarily cannot recognize the true intellectual who has come to
liberate them, though they can sense to some extent that the phoney intellectual is himself nothing more than a clever operator.

The critics considered above were almost always at their best in uncover-
ing and describing the methods of leading cultural manipulators. They
deserve a great deal of credit in this regard, for this form of empirical inquiry
requires psychological, sociological, and anthropological imagination. However, in their analysis of the motivation of manipulators, they generally relied
too heavily on the assumption that the typical manipulator is essentially a
greedy, acquisitive materialist, ever concerned with adding to his wealth,
pleasure, and social power. Nietzsche and Veblen did venture into the
domain of depth psychology, and with useful results, but generally our critics
made the manipulator seem as shallow as possible so as not to elicit any
respect, envy, or compassion for him. The utility of such a strategy is obvious; but our critics could have enlightened us more had they been willing to
take a closer, deeper look at the operator's mind. What light, for example,
would Adlerian psychology shed on the manipulator's neurotic technique of
life?[52]

It is probably with respect to the "unreality" of phoney cultural products
that we see the greatest transformation of a classical theme. In positing the
existence of a realm of timeless, transcendent, unchanging Forms, Plato
explained what the philosopher knows that makes him an appropriate leader
for the community; and at the same time he was able to contrast true Justice
and the like with the mere "appearances" or "shadows" on which operators
and victims base their judgment and behaviour. It is tempting for the practical-
minded thinker to regard Plato's invocation of the Forms as simply a sym-
bolic device for indicating the possibility of an objective value-knowledge to
be attained by means of rational, dialectical processes. After all, Plato gives
numerous examples in his dialogues of how the employment of reason can
enhance our understanding of things that are for most people matters of
mere "opinion." But it is clear from Plato's middle dialogues that he actually
believes in these Forms of which visible objects are simply "likenesses." His
confidence in the reflective person's ability to attain moral and political

knowledge is tied to his metaphysical commitment to a realm of transcendent essences.

Plato's insight into the world of the Forms was as much mystical as rational, and in the sun analogy of the *Republic*, the supreme Form of the Good is assigned a role comparable in important ways to that played by God in Western monotheistic world-views. In his later dialogues, Plato was much occupied with correcting weaknesses in his metaphysic, but he seems to have remained committed to the view that it is lack of knowledge of the relevant Forms that leads the manipulator and the incompetent to produce and promote cultural products that are divorced from reality in a way and to a degree that the products of those who know the Forms are not.

Some philosophical critics of inauthentic culture have accepted an attenuated version of Plato's metaphysic, which they have seen as corresponding in large measure to the account of the spiritual world offered by Western monotheism. But even for a Platonist of sorts such as Augustine, what basically renders the unbeliever's world illusory is its distance from the reality that is to be known by way of revelation.

Erasmus was directly influenced by Platonic and medieval metaphysical conceptions, and though he emphasizes a different dimension of "folly" than Plato and Augustine do, he at least follows them in regarding the highly placed operator as someone who does not know or even wish to know certain things that a cultural leader needs to know. Such an operator lives in a world of illusion and self-deception because he refuses to see things for what they are.

In Voltaire's account, inauthenticity is largely a consequence of superstition rather than of scientific understanding of reality. Voltaire ridicules the metaphysicians because he regards their account of reality as riddled with superstition. He contrasts their "falsehoods" with the objective truths attained through empirical inquiry.

Nietzsche attacks classical metaphysicians and Enlightenment rationalists alike and sees their talk about "objective" truth and reality as lacking subtlety and showing no insight into relevant existential considerations. But despite his dissatisfaction with the limits to personal development posed by Platonic essentialism, he ends up with a dogmatic account of reality. He sees both the sick priests and the herd as lacking insight into what really matters, and nobility, creativity, honesty, and the like thus take on for him a status akin to that which Plato attributed to the Forms.

In Veblen's model, what makes the cultural products of American capitalist culture phoney is their distance from the real needs of human beings. These products are not what they appear to be to most of the people who create, promote, and appropriate them, and so they merely appear to have a value and importance that in reality they do not. Veblen believes, however, that moral and political understanding can be attained through scientific inquiry.

These accounts are notably different, and each has its charms; perhaps each gives us an insight into an aspect of inauthenticity. There is also, however, a pattern to be noted. All these accounts portray the producer of phoney products as not only being manipulatively deceptive but as failing to know what one needs to know in order to be able to produce "the real thing." The product is phoney not only because the promoter has made it appear to be what it is not but because the promoter, not understanding reality, does not even know what the product is supposed to be. He may have some narrow understanding of its proper function, but he does not have an adequate moral, metaphysical, theological, or scientific understanding of its significance as a cultural product.

This may be the point at which traditional philosophical cultural criticism has been most profound. A cultural product has no meaning apart from the intellectual framework in which it is understood. That framework may be very narrow, in which case the meaning of the product will be very limited. When one seeks to attain a deeper understanding of the product, one considers it in the context of a wider framework – moral, metaphysical, theological, or scientific. One may thereby arrive at a deeper appreciation of the product; but the product may now seem much less important – perhaps even "meaningless," "insignificant," "empty," "unreal."

When one considers a cultural product in a wider framework, one almost invariably attains a better understanding of its significance as a *cultural* product, and one considers it in relation to an ideal of *culture* (though one may not associate the ideal with this term). One realizes that the domain of culture is not something simply given by nature, but the ever-changing domain of products fashioned and promoted by people very much like ourselves, all of whom have understood the products in the context of a particular framework, narrow or wide. It is almost inevitable then that one will be moved to consider certain products in relation to what one takes to be the understanding of their producers and promoters.

All the critics examined want us to understand cultural products in the context of some framework, one that is wider than that to which we are accustomed in everyday life. They disagree about its precise nature, but they all believe that once we have it we shall find it easier to make useful, reasonable judgments of the form, "What appears to be x is in reality y." For example, "What appears to be an economic policy beneficial to society as a whole is in reality a device for increasing the wealth of an elite." Or, "What appears to be a religious ritual that will increase our chances of salvation is in reality an instrument for enhancing the prestige of the priests." Or, "What appears to be a beautiful dress is in reality a dress that is no more or no less beautiful than most other dresses, but has been promoted as 'beautiful' by advertisers who want rich people to buy it and poor people to regret that they cannot afford it." In such cases, that sort of context helps us to see through the deception of the creators.

But our critics have also suggested another level of interpretation. Why has the producer put forward an "appearance" rather than something real? In most cases, it is partly because he does not know how to produce the real thing. At the heart of his manipulation, which may or may not also involve some degree of self-deception, is a pretence to know. The sophist does not know how to make people better; the corrupt politician cannot solve social problems; the crooked television evangelist does not know how his flock can be saved; the pop artist and her promoters do not have the ability to create beautiful things; and so forth.

Even if the producer did know how to "deliver the goods," his decision not to do so would appear to indicate lack of understanding of another sort. If he is willing to put forward a product that he knows to be significantly inferior to what he could have produced, then he apparently lacks the deeper understanding of the cultural importance of the product that becomes clear within a wider moral, metaphysical, theological, or scientific framework. Of course, he may think to himself that he simply thinks of the product (and his promotion of it) in a different framework from others' and one – for example, a "materialistic" one – not necessarily narrower than any alternative. Still, those who can envision a framework that involves an ideal of culture can attain a richer understanding of what that product is and what it is not. Moreover, they can work to promote an appropriately wider view of cultural products.

It is characteristic of philosophers to encourage people to take a wider view of things so that they can be wiser, happier, and better human beings. They also typically seek to elevate our moral and metaphysical conceptions simultaneously. If they have rarely been able to get people to view all things "under the aspect of eternity," the great philosophers have at least urged many people away from the shallow "ethical" and "metaphysical" views appropriately labelled "materialism." (Even a semi-philosophical positivist such as Veblen wants us to reject a shallow materialistic ethic in favour of an ethic that focuses on workmanship, concern for others, and intellectual curiosity.)

When a philosopher takes on the role of cultural critic, he realizes that sooner or later he has to put some of his ethical and metaphysical positions on the table. He tries to show us why his wider framework merits our appropriation. He reasons with us, and he places before us moral and metaphysical arguments and, where appropriate, theological and scientific ones. If he is a real philosopher, his offerings are authentic; he aims at meliorating our condition and our fellows'. But in any case, the value of his cultural criticism obviously depends in large measure on the soundness of the theories of morality and reality that he associates with it. Now, we cannot do justice in this type of inquiry to the complex ethical and metaphysical theories of Plato or most of the other philosophers considered. It will have to suffice for us to note, first, that they all believe in the importance of at least occasionally taking a wider view of cultural products than that which we usually take in everyday life, and second, that ultimately we must decide for ourselves, in an act of commitment, what the widest view is that we are capable of taking.

Most of our critics saw certain kinds of religious faith as providing a helpfully wide view of cultural products and processes. With the exception of Augustine, none was a full-fledged religious apologist; and all of them, including Augustine, were keenly aware of how institutionalized religion can be drowned in inauthenticity. But none underestimated the power of genuine religious commitment to influence one's attitude towards cultural products and processes; and all of them, including Voltaire and Nietzsche, were prepared to grant that there are ennobling forms of religious spirituality. They all also recognized that, for better or for worse, religion functions on a certain plane as the philosophy of the masses, and, being practical-minded men as well as lovers of truth, they gave considerable weight to that fact in their prescriptions for cultural reform. Nietzsche is particularly interesting in this regard; while generally regarding religion as a cultural field in which the higher man can carry out his projects, Nietzsche was also sometimes very troubled by what the "death of God" may ultimately mean for European civilization. He saw the rapid decline of traditional forms of religious commitment as capable of precipitating destructive forms of nihilism wholly incompatible with advances in humanity; and the horrors of the twentieth century have shown him to be prescient in this regard.

Nevertheless, we should resist any temptation to dismiss the attitude towards religion of an Erasmus, Nietzsche, or Veblen as merely pragmatic, utilitarian, or fictionalist. In chapter 3, we took note of the complexity of certain religious conceptions of culture; and in chapter 4, we considered the folly of dismissing Plato's attitude towards religion as purely pragmatic. Deep thinkers are ordinarily given to reflecting on religion and religious subjects, and rarely just in the spirit of the debunker. Even the most rationalistic are at least occasionally inclined to mystical reflection, and it is not hard for them to summon up a profound respect for one or another form of saintliness. None of our critics, except Augustine, was a "religious believer" in the sense conventionally accepted in his day; but in the highly personal way that they came to terms with traditional religious symbolism they were generally more meditative than sceptical. Despite their heightened sensitivity to the inauthenticity of most conventional religious products, they could conceive of a purified form of faith compatible with promotion of the highest and most authentic cultural products. Thus when they mused about the salutary cultural value of a communal return to an extensively refined form of traditional religious faith, they were not merely thinking about social control and social stability but also reflecting on the profundity of a way of looking at things that dramatically enhances human dignity and frees the agent from manipulativeness and manipulability.

In this respect, we may contrast them with an unphilosophical cultural theorist such as Freud, who could never see religion as much more than "an illusion inspired by infantile belief in the omnipotence of thought, a universal neurosis, a kind of narcotic that hampers the free exercise of intelligence, and something man will have to give up."[53] By the end of *Civilization and Its Discontents*, Freud is left wondering whether culture itself may be a source of neurosis: "If the development of civilization [*Kultur*] has such a far-reaching similarity to the development of the individual and if it employs the same methods, may we not be justified in reaching the diagnosis that, under the influence of cultural urges, some civilizations, or some epochs of civilization – possibly the whole of mankind – have become 'neurotic'?"[54]

With the exception of Augustine, our critics were not inclined to regard religion as such as a panacea for all forms of cultural corruption. They were, however, firmly convinced that if people are to be persuaded to get beyond their manipulativeness and manipulability, they must be shown, or at least reminded of, the possibility of a richer, nobler life than that to which they have become accustomed. At the end of his discussion of the significance of the cave parable, Plato offers what may be his most eloquent defence of his thesis that political and cultural leadership should be put in the hands of the philosopher rather than the sophisticated but corrupt man of the world. He has Socrates observe: "You must contrive for your future rulers another and a better life than that of a ruler, and then you may have a well-ordered State; for only in the State which offers this, will they rule who are truly rich, not in silver and gold, but in virtue and wisdom, which are the true blessings of life. Whereas if they go to the administration of public affairs, poor and hungering after their own private advantage, thinking that hence they are to snatch the chief good, order there can never be."[55] The life of true philosophy, we are told, is the only life that "looks down" on the life of political ambition;[56] and it is only those who know this "better life" that can function effectively as the vanguard of political, social, and cultural reform.

7

CONTEMPORARY APPLICATIONS

THE CASE OF TELEVISION

The basic aim of this inquiry has been to shed light on a social and philosophical issue that for want of an available label has been called here the problem of inauthentic culture. We began by considering it in a contemporary context. Chapter 1 demarcated the matter by considering the ordinary language that people use to express concern about the "phoney" quality of many cultural products of their society. With a working conception of the problem, we considered, in chapters 2 and 3, relevant issues in the philosophy of culture. Chapters 4–6 were given over largely to studies in the history of philosophical cultural criticism that indicate that the problem is not entirely new but rather the most recent manifestation of a traditional problem that from ancient times has troubled certain reform-minded intellectuals.

While of humanistic interest in its own right, the historical pattern that we have detected is of practical relevance to our concern about inauthentic culture today. Though our critics lived in different times and (with the exception of the last) in a world very different from ours, the cultural corruption that they confronted has much in common with the pervasive inauthenticity of our own society. Thus what they have said provides a richer understanding of a problem that is both contemporary and traditional. Every so often in the course of our historical studies, we noted the contemporary relevance of a certain idea, but more needs to be said in this regard. I conclude this inquiry by considering some applications of the classical analysis to our own times.

Of course, we must allow for the distinctiveness of our situation. It is distinctive mainly with respect to three orders of development. First, the culture of our advanced societies is generally more complex than that of earlier societies in so far as it has deeper historical roots. Not only have more historical factors entered into determining the character and condition of our culture, but people have more historical phenomena on which to reflect when philosophizing about culture or simply participating in a cultural process. Many events have taken place since the time of Plato, Erasmus, or Veblen, and they have influenced culture and shed light on culture in ways that it would be unwise to ignore.

Second, and more specifically, those who have an interest in cultural products and processes can know much more about culture than could students of culture in earlier societies. There are more relevant data available to them, and more theories for them to take into account. That is the main reason why analyses such as Plato's or even Veblen's seem so out of date in certain ways. Today's typical North American or western European university student of the humanities or social sciences knows much more about culture than Plato or Nietzsche did – or, for that matter, Tylor, Simmel, Renan, or Freud. Students of culture now have access to the insights of all these thinkers, and to the results of recent research and reflection in such new fields as sociobiology and hermeneutics, as well as in older, more established fields of cultural study. Not only are we now in a better position to understand the traditional problem of inauthentic culture, but cultural corruption in our society is generally promoted by people who know considerably more about what they are doing than their predecessors did.

Third, and still more specifically, we must make allowance for advances in technology. Cultural processes, including educational liberation and manipulative deception, have been transformed by the new media in which they are carried on.[1]

It is not surprising then that today's cultural critics have concentrated on recent developments that have contributed to the growth of inauthenticity. We live in interesting times, and there have been remarkable new developments in the realm of cultural processes that call for disciplined investigation and creative response. Still, our problem is not as new as most cultural critics believe; many of the features that they describe were already present in earlier societies in a way and to a degree that they have not recognized. In describing the contemporary situation, these critics often make use of language and imagery that would have been as appropriate in ancient times as it is now. Were one to reconsider the comments of the cultural critics cited in the first three chapters – Lasch, Schiller, Berdyaev, Dawson, and the rest – one would see that much that they have taken to be new and strange is old and all too familiar. And so, having dutifully acknowledged the distinctive aspects of the contemporary problem, and having recalled that critics of inauthentic culture generally focus on what they rightly or wrongly take to be distinctively contemporary matters, we can now return to the main theme.

In that context, we should consider two phenomena that regularly receive attention from critics of inauthentic culture – television and professional public relations. Television has obviously had an immense influence on Western societies. This remarkable cultural product gives countless millions access in their own homes to images of the past and future, to events actually taking place all over the world, to ideas and information, to truth, falsehood, and fantasy, to other cultural products, and to natural phenomena. It has proven extremely effective in both education and manipulative deception; it makes some people much wiser, and some much duller, and most people wiser in some ways and duller in others. It pacifies and enrages, amuses and depresses, stimulates and narcotizes, inspires and embitters. What kind of general judgment can we reasonably pass on such a phenomenon, especially when many of our brightest cultural theorists hold that it is still too early to know what the thing "means"?

Yet there is a widespread feeling among both cultural theorists and less reflective observers that for all the good it has done and can do, television has also done a great deal of harm to the culture of their society. Much criticism has focused on how its popularity has led to increasing neglect of other cultural products that may be of higher and perhaps irreplaceable value. According to this view, television has pushed into the background meliorative cultural products that cannot successfully compete with it for the less reflective person's attention. The accessibility of television can hardly be overemphasized, and it is constantly increasing. More than a decade ago, A.A. Berger could observe: "It is estimated that 96 percent of American homes have television receivers (33 percent have more than one receiver), and the average set is on more than six hours per day. Many children in America watch four to six hours of television each day. It is estimated that by the time an American child reaches high school, he or she will have been exposed to something like 15,000 hours of television, including 650,000 commercials."[2] How can school teachers, religious teachers, writers, or parents compete with such an instrument of education and miseducation?

Marshall McLuhan, who believed that criticisms of television that focus on content are generally naive,[3] was nevertheless troubled by how the mode of perception that it demands represents a powerful challenge to the culture of literacy. "Perhaps the most familiar and pathetic effect of the TV image is the posture of children in the early grades. Since TV, children – regardless of eye condition – average about six and a half inches from the printed page. Our children are striving to carry over to the printed page the all-involving sensory mandate of the TV image."[4] Convinced that "not even the most lucid understanding of the peculiar force of a medium can head off the ordinary 'closure' of the senses that causes us to conform to the pattern of experience presented," McLuhan concluded in *Understanding Media*: "To resist TV, therefore, one must acquire the antidote of related media like print."[5] As the years passed, McLuhan came to be so awed by the power of media technology to alter our basic mode of perception that he lost much of his ability to function as a media and cultural critic.

While McLuhan rightly observed that it is not on the level of content alone that television has had its enormous influence, his fascination with the impact of technology on perception was not accompanied by an adequate appreciation of the fact that some perception gives insight into truth and reality while some prevents it. The content of television programming – what viewers are induced to see and hear – is largely what renders the perception significant. Plato himself attached much significance to the various modes of apprehension by which people arrive at their world-view; and he was mindful of the sophists' claim that they could alter people's perceptions and teach their students how to do the same. Yet Plato rightly insisted that some modes of apprehension yield knowledge while others can yield only "opinion." He realized that a primary task of the educator is to enable his fellows to see better than they do by developing modes of apprehension that give them access to a higher order of objects. Television allows the viewer to see on different levels. What one sees when one watches a serious discussion of social problems is vastly different from what one sees when one watches a hockey game or a soap opera, and what one apprehends when one is being told the truth by an honest politician or religious teacher is of a different order from what one apprehends when being conned by a crooked politician or preacher.

What then does television provide in the way of content? Having closely studied American television programming, Berger came to the conclusion that there are only a dozen basic genres or program types: news and documentaries, commercials, sports, game shows, culture, crime shows, humour (including situation comedies), soap operas, love and sex, food preparation, variety shows, and movies.[6] It is noteworthy that Berger here regards "culture" as provided by only one type, especially since he professes to appreciate the culture of the "common man" and the extent to which "high" culture is permeated by "low" culture.[7]

In fact, specific cultural products in the other eleven categories can be highly meliorative and authentic. When we peruse Berger's list, however, we realize that most cultural products put forward for our appropriation by television programming executives tend to be rather less meliorative than others that might have been offered. As well, they have been put forward often by people who are generally concerned less with improving the condition of viewers than with looking after their own material interests. It is only a small step from that insight to realization that while television is a distinctively contemporary phenomenon – a remarkable piece of technology, with its own distinctive forms of influence – it conceives and offers inauthentic cultural products in much the same spirit as such products have always been. Its products may be more or less meliorative, more or less authentic, and more or less conceived in the spirit of responsible craftsmanship. Sometimes, however, power over television programming has been concentrated in the hands of professional, business, and political elites that, while regularly professing to be concerned with the educational value of the medium, indicate by their behaviour that they are more concerned with self-promotion. For the television executives themselves that often means increasing "market share" and maximizing profits.

When we considered Plato's attack on the dramatists in Book X of the *Republic*, we noted how easy it would be to adapt his analysis for most cultural products put forward on television. As for violence, sexual titillation, escapism, stereotyping, sensationalism, materialism, and anatropic values routinely served up by television – for all of which it has been condemned by thoughtful critics – long before television was invented, all these things were already being served up by dramatists, novelists, journalists, and similar producers of cultural products who were themselves severely criticized by high-minded thinkers.

But in fact television programming lends itself much better than most other fields of cultural production to the imagery that Plato offers in the cave parable. Consider in this regard these chapter and section titles from Jerry Mander's *Four Arguments for the Elimination of Television*: "The Walling of Awareness," "Mediated Environments," "Expropriation of Knowledge," "Popular Philosophy and Arbitrary Reality," "The Creation of 'Value,'" "Commodity People," "Domination of the Influencing Machine," "How Television Dims the Mind," "How We Turn into Our Images," and "The Irresistibility of Images."[8] Mander makes no reference to Plato, and there is no evidence that he was influenced by Plato's description of life in the cave. But he approached a distinctively contemporary phenomenon such as television along lines familiar to those who have been exposed to traditional philosophical criticism of inauthentic culture.

Let us consider Mander's four arguments. First, "As humans have moved into totally artificial environments, ... we cannot know up from down or truth from fiction. Conditions are appropriate for the implantation of arbitrary realities. Television is one recent example of this, a serious one, since it greatly accelerates the problem."[9] Second: "It is no accident that television has been dominated by a handful of corporate powers. Neither is it accidental that television has been used to re-create human beings into a new form that matches the artificial, commercial environment. A conspiracy of technological and economic factors made this inevitable and continue to."[10] Third: "Television technology produces neuro-physiological responses in the people who watch it. It may create illness, it certainly produces confusion and submission to external imagery. Taken together, the effects amount to conditioning for autocratic control."[11] Fourth: "Along with the venality of its controllers, the technology of television predetermines the boundaries of its content. Some information can be conveyed completely, some partially, some not at all."[12]

Though Mander emphasizes the technology itself, he has otherwise described life in the cave world. The prisoners and puppeteers live in the artificial environment of the cave, incapable of attaining genuine knowledge. Disconnected from reality, with their eyes fixed on the cave wall before them, they are exposed to an order of arbitrary realities, of mere "appearances" or "shadows." The puppeteers constitute a small manipulative elite, and, in fashioning the world-view and way of life of the prisoners in the way that they do, they make it all the more difficult to liberate the captives. The prisoners are confused and submissive to the imagery created by the puppeteers, who control their minds and lives. The prime motive of the puppeteers appears to be venality, but even they are limited by the artificial environment and empty technology from which they need to be liberated.

To Mander's analysis we may add that the would-be liberator has for the most part been marginalized. Most of those who could be liberators have looked on the denizens of the cave with contempt and declined to play their proper role in advancing the quality of thought and life of those now confined to the anatropic cultural processes of producing and appropriating mere images.

To keep the prisoners occupied, the puppeteers promote a system of invidious distinctions. They will not share the limited knowledge and power they have with the prisoners, and they lead the prisoners to orient their whole lives around the artificial status to be derived from being an expert on the shadows on the cave wall. It is through such expertise that the prisoners derive their sense of competence and social standing. The media of mass communications, perhaps television above all, routinely create such hierarchies. The puppeteers derive some sense of self-importance from their power over the world-view and way of life of the ignorant. Yet in their concern for artificial status, they are themselves committed to the foolish values of those for whom they perform their shadow-play.

The world of television, like that of the cave, is in large part one of invidious distinctions and artificial criteria of worth and importance. Television programming is substantially a field for the creation and promotion of celebrities, and the people who perform those tasks derive their self-importance both from their ability to do so and from their association with the phoney celebrities whom they have invented. Most programmers thus mirror the mediocrity of those whom they manipulate, including those whom they elevate to positions of "importance" by enabling them to become experts on shadows.

"It is obvious," C. Wright Mills observes, "that prestige depends, often quite decisively, upon access to the publicity machines that are now a central and normal feature of all the big institutions of modern America"[13] – specifically the mass media.[14] These present-day heirs to the sophists use a powerful medium to create and promote artificial celebrities and artificial criteria of success and competence. Simultaneously, many worthy and knowledgeable individuals who are truly capable of elevating the condition of the prisoners, puppeteers, and community are marginalized by being dismissed in the medium as bores or cranks who cannot possibly have anything useful to say to people in the "real world" of the cave. "Nowadays what we are up against is precisely the absence of mind of any sort as a public force; what we are up against is a disinterest in and a fear of knowledge that might have liberating public relevance."[15] Television programmers were not imaginative enough to have invented all this anatropic culture on their own; they have merely reinforced it, having derived their basic "ideal" of culture from the Great Sophist itself.[16]

There is a good deal for observers of television and its programming to be troubled about, and it is appropriate that criticism should come from many directions, but few critics have taken a wide, philosophical view. While being grateful for the work of people such as Mander who are prepared to consider the medium in relation to cultural ideals, we may still be disappointed that so few critics of contemporary culture have used the insights of great cultural critics of the past, especially when they have to start from scratch or, worse yet, start out with unsound assumptions or too narrow a perspective.

That much of what cultural critics of the distant past had to say is still relevant today is itself disquieting. Can humanity have made so little progress? There has, of course, been much advance in many domains, not the least because we have to some extent been willing to learn from the past.

Mander informs us: "Imagining a world free of television, I can envision only beneficial effects."[17] We can appreciate the conditions that have driven him to such an overstatement, but we should not forget that television has much good to offer and that it has already put forward many cultural products of high authenticity and overall quality.

THE CASE OF PROFESSIONAL PUBLIC RELATIONS

We turn now to another phenomenon not nearly as well known as television programming – professional public relations (PR). Many people do complain from time to time about the pervasiveness of hype and PR, and one occasionally hears it said that the characteristic attitudes and methods of professionals in that field have infected even the highest and most spiritual cultural domains, such as institutionalized religion, higher education and research, and the performing arts. Yet professional public relations has rarely received close enough attention from cultural critics; and that is just as the specialists would have it, for their success is attributable in large part to their ability to avoid drawing attention to themselves. Joyce Nelson has observed: "The PR industry is so unexamined and hidden, and at the same time, paradoxically, so pervasive, that it is usually not even considered in any political analysis of current events, or in any serious discussion of the role of the media."[18] Indeed, "The power of the PR industry is demonstrated not only by its hegemonic manœuverings within and for every area of government and business, but also by its remarkable ability to function as a virtually invisible 'grey eminence' behind the scenes, gliding in and out of troubled situations with the ease of a Cardinal Richelieu and the conscience of a mercenary."[19]

In chapter 1, we took note of the opinion of Packard and McLuhan that the new scientific public-relations experts pose a great danger to society. In their concern about new tendencies, these observers share the view held by most public-relations specialists that PR is essentially something that has emerged in this century. In 1923, the most influential of all recent teachers of public relations, E.L. Bernays, remarked that his profession was so new that it had not yet come to be designated by a generally accepted name.[20] The rapid rise of professional public relations in Bernays's day, particularly in the United States, can be attributed to several factors, including advances in the behavioural and social sciences, development of business education, and erosion of the character ethic that followed on the declining influence of traditional forms of religious commitment.[21]

But actually how new is professional public relations? In their popular public-relations text, H.F. Moore and B.R. Canfield state that public relations is "a relatively new, emerging concept"[22] and a "20th century American phenomenon,"[23] but they qualify these statements by adding: "The origins of public relations ... can actually be traced back to the dawn of civilization." Further, "Its fundamental elements – informing people, persuading people, and integrating people – were basic to earliest society just as they are today."[24] For example, "In ancient Egypt, priests were experts in public opinion and persuasion,"[25] and, with the growth of Hellenic civilization, influencing public opinion became a "key factor in public life."[26] That is no news to us; but even some students of public relations have recognized the continuity.

Defining "public relations" is no easy task, and it may not be prudent for the specialist to attempt to do so. Irwin Ross points in this regard to "Bernays' famous shorthand definition of PR as 'the engineering of consent' – a phrase whose manipulative ring (which Bernays did not intend) in itself constituted a grievous PR blunder."[27] We can see then why L.L. Knott prefers to conclude: "No dictionary definition can do the job. Only through reports of Public Relations in action can Public Relations be adequately demonstrated or defined."[28] Moore and Canfield characterize it as "a social philosophy of management expressed in policies and practices, which, through sensitive interpretation of events based upon two-way communication with its publics, strives to secure mutual understanding and goodwill."[29] They see the practitioner as making use of four basic tools: advertising ("paid, nonpersonal communication through various media of communication by an identified individual or organization"); lobbying ("the attempt to influence the voting of legislators"); press-agentry ("the promotion of an individual or organization through obtaining favorable publicity in the mass media"); and publicity ("the technique of securing public notice, or ... the public notice itself").[30] This list is not comprehensive, but it gives us an idea of some of the main fields in which public-relations specialists now ply their craft.

Professional public relations can be viewed from numerous perspectives, and, as we would expect, specialists are generally adept at putting their vocation in a more favourable light. Knott writes: "All the Public Relations activities, all the things that are done to create good Public Relations, are simply the outward expression of the good, honest principles which every government, business, institution or individual must believe in and practise in order to have good relations with the public."[31] Laurence Evans insists: "A chasm exists between propaganda and public relations practice": "Propaganda seeks to make the masses believe in a ready-made dogma irrespective of truth or reality. Public relations seeks to inform the public and, by giving accurate helpful information, to create a better understanding of things as they really are."[32]

Bernays, who already in the 1920s had to acknowledge the extent to which people "condemn the entire profession generally and all its members individually,"[33] took a different approach from Evans: "Mr. [Walter] Lippmann says propaganda is dependent upon censorship. From my point of view the precise reverse is more nearly true. Propaganda is a purposeful, directed effort to overcome censorship – the censorship of the group mind and the herd reaction. The average citizen is the world's most efficient censor. His own mind is the greatest barrier between him and the facts."[34] But like Evans a half-century later, Bernays found it convenient to portray the public-relations specialist as not essentially different from the educator: "The only difference between 'propaganda' and 'education', really, is in the point of view. The advocacy of what we believe in is education. The advocacy of what we don't believe in is propaganda. Each of these nouns carries with it social and moral implications. Education is valuable, commendable, enlightening, instructive. Propaganda is insidious, dishonest, underhand, misleading."[35]

Why do critics of professional public relations such as Packard and Nelson not appreciate the educational or quasi-educational role of these providers of "helpful information"? Why are many people troubled by what they perceive as the manipulativeness of these promoters of cultural products? Here is a situation in which our historical consciousness can serve us well, for, thinking back to Plato's attack on the sophists, we can consider whether there is anything in the public-relations specialist's "social philosophy" that corresponds to that of the sophist. Knowing what to look for, we shall not be disappointed.

The public-relations specialist, like the sophist, wants his potential client and potential disciple to appreciate what he has to offer them. Thus, for example, the forthright H. Gordon Lewis writes: "Since benefits seldom come to those who fail to seek them out, seek them out; since no one else will start the promotional machinery working for you, you start it; since so many worthwhile image-builders and attention-getters depend on nothing other than intelligent application of time and effort, apply time and effort intelligently; and since the only missing component may well be technique, not intent, borrow the techniques. Whatever happens, you'll be way ahead of the person who has done nothing at all."[36] Can this be the old song of the sophists?

Listen further: "Always act as though you know what you're doing. In public relations, confidence (or the appearance of it) often is a valid replacement for knowledge, especially when dealing with media people."[37] A "valid replacement for knowledge"? Valid in what sense? "The challenge of public relations is not merely the dissemination of information of interest to the disseminator; it is, rather, the creation of materials that are apparently of interest to the recipient, but that benefit the originator."[38]

This certainly sounds a lot like sophistry, but perhaps this fellow's enthusiasm has gotten the best of him. We need to consider the relevant attitudes of a "serious" student of public relations, and none has been more influential than Bernays. "[The public-relations counsel's] ability to create those symbols to which the public is ready to respond; his ability to know and to analyze those reactions which the public is ready to give; his ability to find those stereotypes, individual and community, which will bring favorable responses; his ability to speak in the language of his audience and to receive from it a favorable reception are his contributions. The appeal to the instincts and the universal desires is the basic method through which he produces his results."[39]

Is the public-relations specialist not obliged to recognize the primacy of certain basic moral and political truths? "Political, economic and moral judgments, as we have seen, are more often expressions of crowd psychology and herd reaction than the result of the calm exercise of judgment. It is difficult to believe that this is not inevitable … Society cannot wait to find absolute truth. It cannot weigh every issue carefully before making a judgment … In the struggle among ideas, the only test is the one which Justice Holmes of the Supreme Court pointed out – the power of thought to get itself accepted in the open competition of the market."[40]

Bernays goes on to suggest that it is in "creation of a public conscience" that the public-relations practitioner is destined to be most useful to his society.[41] But in the absence of knowledge of absolute truth, where are the appropriate elements of "conscience" to be found? "What they ['the people'] want and what they get are fused by some mysterious alchemy. The press, the lecturer, the screen and the public lead and are led by each other."[42] And so here we are, back in the old, familiar world of the cave.

Public-relations techniques are on one level "value-neutral." They can be put to socially constructive as well as manipulative use. Oliver Thomson has suggested that before we condemn all forms of propaganda, we should make an effort to appreciate the "myriad small rites" that "help societies to function,"[43] and what is true of propaganda in this regard is true of public relations in general. Moreover, reformers as well as exploiters must be realistic enough to face the fact that the manipulative and the manipulated will always be with us; in Evans's words, "Fear, intimidation, strong and weak personalities are part of living."[44] Did not even the greatest critic of the sophists grant that the uneducated, irrational masses need to be "led" and even at times deceived for their own good?

It is precisely at this point that we may benefit most from drawing on the classical philosophical analysis of inauthentic culture. For standing at a certain distance from the contemporary scene, we can better see the public-relations specialist for what he is and what he is not. He is not an educator; he is not a liberator. He provides information (and misinformation); he keeps people occupied; and in certain ways he may even make people happier and better. But he does not free people from their chains; he leaves them in chains. He has much in common with the puppeteer in the cave. And when he promotes the products (and the social status) of corrupt and incompetent politicians, artists, and craftsmen, he stands to them in approximately the same relation that the sophist of Plato's day stood in relation to various "authorities" and "celebrities" of that distant world.

By the very nature of her occupation, the public-relations specialist is obliged to regard as of secondary importance at best the meliorative value of the products that she promotes. In fact, her basic offering is not the political platform or consumer product that she is being paid to promote but rather the ability to influence the judgment of those who can be induced to appropriate a product. Such an ability or influence is not a "cultural" product in any familiar sense of the word. A person will ordinarily be able to see some of the meliorative value of what an educator offers him, but it is hard to see a corresponding value in being induced to appropriate products for the good of the producers themselves. The educator rightly or wrongly believes that he is improving the lot of his student; but the public-relations expert is concerned only with helping another producer or promoter. The "weaker party" that he serves is not the public with which he "relates" but the individual or group that stands to benefit materially by his ability to make things "appear" a certain way to the public. So while he is a craftsman of sorts in relation to those who pay for his services, he himself offers no cultural product to those whom he is working to influence.

To say that the public-relations person offers "helpful information" to people concerning "things as they really are" is to misunderstand the nature of his peculiar craft. An advertiser, lobbyist, press agent, or publicity woman may enlighten or deceive, tell the truth or tell lies, make those who appropriate cultural products happier and better or unhappier and worse. But the only "weaker party" that she is obliged to serve is the individual or group that has contracted with her to promote a product that may or may not be beneficial to those who are being induced to appropriate it. Once the specialist departs from her "value-neutral" stance, she is no longer simply involved in the craft of "public relations"; she has adopted an attitude of concern for the "public" and is now genuinely interested in what cultural products are being put forward for appropriation by the public.

But the professional public-relations expert, like the professional rhetorician or lawyer or any other creator of "appearances," puts her techniques at the service of those who are prepared to pay to have their product promoted. Like the educator-liberator, she aims at influencing the judgment and behaviour of people; but unlike the educator, she is required by the nature of her calling to set aside questions about whether she is serving those people, for they are not the party that she has contracted to serve. Indeed, while she may more than occasionally offer the public helpful information, the nature of her enterprise regularly brings her into conflict with the educator, who is committed not only to the betterment of those he seeks to influence but to the promotion of truth and understanding of reality. And while the educator who miseducates is essentially doing her job badly, the public-relations specialist can be doing her job well even when promoting the most inauthentic and corruptive cultural product.

Though people do grumble about the pervasiveness of hype and PR in our society, they are generally more permissive with respect to advertisers, lobbyists, and the like than with the producers of inauthentic products that these people serve. They regard them as technicians and are sometimes not even surprised when they hear about a case like that of the noted American public-relations specialist Ivy Lee, who took money to advise the Nazi government.[45] But the public-relations practitioner is a modern heir to the classical sophist. He symbolizes the inverted form of culture; much of the most powerful influence over the public mind is put into the hands of an individual who, having no commitment to the promotion of objective truth or knowledge, practises his strange "craft" by altering "appearances" in a way that will materially benefit whoever can compensate him well for his efforts. This is not education; in a sense, it is the inversion of education.

There is another dimension to the anatropic quality of professional public relations. In their basic advertising text, the advertising professors Rotzoll, Haefner, and Sandage defend advertising as a "classical liberal institution" – a response to the consumer's freedom to choose from among alternative products put forward for her appropriation.[46] Yet they realize that they need to explain the widespread mistrust that people have of those in the advertising profession, as indicated, for example, in a Gallup poll that "ranked people in the advertising business 24th out of 25 occupational groups in terms of honesty and ethical standards."[47] These professors believe that, to some extent, "Advertising's areas of inherent ethical encounter are part of its institutional milieu."[48] Yet they also recognize that despite her "value-neutral" stance on one level, the advertising specialist is generally inclined to adopt a materialistic conception of human motivation that makes little allowance for individual and communal self-realization. They invite us to contrast the "seven deadly sins" (greed, lust, sloth, pride, envy, gluttony, and anger) with the "seven cardinal virtues" (wisdom, justice, temperance, courage, faith, hope, and love), and they observe: "Critics would contend that advertisers are far more likely to use appeals to the first than to the second, and consumer goods advertisers are far more likely to be charged."[49]

What bothers critics in this regard is that the "value-neutrality" of the advertising specialist and other public-relations professionals is not simply a function of their perception of themselves as technicians but also partly a result of the conceptions of human nature and human potential that have enabled them to take on the social role that they have. There is a certain amount of cynicism at work here in the attitude that there is little point in appealing to higher motives when "natural morality" is so decisive for the vast majority of consumers. Thus for semi-philosophical or scientific reasons, public-relations specialists have felt it appropriate to set aside the classical ideal of culture. To the extent that they are willing to allow that cultural advancement of individuals and societies is possible, the defenders of advertising and the like "may contend, in sound pluralistic argumentation, that there are other institutions (e.g., churches, schools, etc.) attending to many of the cardinal virtues, and if advertising does indeed espouse their counterparts, it is only one voice among many to which the individual may or may not attend."[50]

But the fact is that the public-relations person is not merely "one voice." He can carry out his aims only by subverting in the process the ideal of culture promoted by those who believe in the possibility of human perfectibility. Indeed, he regards his success as evidence of the superiority of his own conception of "natural morality" to the moral absolutism of high-minded but naive dreamers who long for the widespread realization of ideals. So though he is on one level a value-neutral technician, what enables him to pursue with confidence his curious vocation is an underlying commitment to a materialistic world-view according to which the domain of "culture" is ultimately reducible to "appearances," emotions, and appetites.

Classical and traditional insights into inauthentic culture could offer today's critics valuable insights into new varieties of sophistry. The public relations expert is not just one more voice in contemporary culture; his program calls for him to subvert the influence of traditional promoters of culture, and he has promoted his own cynical attitude among agents of the very institutions – churches, schools, and the like – that have traditionally "attended to many of the cardinal virtues." He sees his views on "natural morality" as vindicated by the high degree to which established institutions have been taken over by "operators," and by how even ordinary agents of these institutions have accepted that domination as the "natural order" and the "way of the world." Of course, every cultural critic is at least vaguely aware of this new sophistry and prepared to contend with it in some way, but few have had the philosophical and theological wherewithal to see it for precisely what it is and to deal with it accordingly.

Moreover, even when the critic is able to overcome guilt about his own hypocrisy, he is often so much in awe of the advanced technology of contemporary sophistry, and of the entrenchment of the spirit of sophistry in the highest cultural institutions, that he either retreats to the "ivory tower" or seeks solutions only to concrete "practical" problems through direct political involvement. Plato believed that escapism is irresponsible and that political adventuring is ordinarily imprudent and ultimately ineffective. He was inclined by temperament, conviction, and strategy to look mainly to education and religion, which he sought to restore to the dignity of which they had been deprived by shallow, self-serving schemers and functionaries. The classical analysis of inauthentic culture would be considerably less useful to us if Plato and his "disciples" had not given us insights into what we can do about all this cultural rubbish.

THE ROLE OF THE ACADEMY

Socrates had recognized the primary role of education but had been limited by his essentially critical approach and had left himself vulnerable to the hostility that follows on being provocative in the agora. Plato, less modest and more prudent, had a better strategy. He would work towards the development, through higher education, of enlightened, progressive communal leaders. His attempts to do so in Syracuse failed,[51] but the institution that he established in Athens proved successful. His school of higher studies, the prototype of all universities and most other institutions of higher learning, was precisely the forum that reform-minded intellectuals needed for going about their work of cultural reform.

Plato's Academy was not conceived as an "ivory tower"; it was a place not only where people would be free to pursue the highest and purest intellectual inquiry possible but where knowledge would be acquired that would enable intellectuals to serve their fellows in the corrupt world outside. Future leaders, armed with moral and political insights and with general knowledge, would be trained up there, and the masses would gradually come to appreciate the value to society of these wise, unselfish scholars. Books would be written to pass on the results of intellectual investigations carried on within its precincts. Its denizens would be protected from the corruptions of the cave world, but they would be able to return to the cave when appropriate in order to carry out their task of educational liberation and could do so without losing their minds or souls in the chaos of conventional politics and art.

This was a remarkable piece of strategy on Plato's part, and his plan has worked fairly well ever since. It is no wonder that such philosophical cultural critics as Erasmus, Nietzsche, Veblen, and Bloom turned to the academy as the best available forum in which to carry out their own work of cultural reform. But these later critics were also aware of how the academy itself can be corrupted. Without the commanding presence of a Plato to lead it, the academy can fall under the control of sophists, politicians, entrepreneurs, and others given to treating it as one more field, and a very rich one, for carrying out their own schemes.

The corruptibility of the academy is not the only relevant concern. Relations between the academy and the "outside" world – the cave world, or as detractors of the academy often describe it, the "real" world – are necessarily complex. They must have already been so in Plato's time. Having emphasized the intellectual's obligation to return to the cave to perform his duties as liberator, Plato could not have allowed the academy to become a refuge for those who wish to cut themselves off from the rest of society. He obviously desired that the academy should be kept free from corruptive values and attitudes of the cave world, but he must have realized that the academy is essentially a social institution if not a "public" one in the conventional sense. He knew that the students at his own Academy had not received the kind of primary education outlined in the *Republic* and had brought with them character traits, ideas, and attitudes derived from their cultural experience in a society that was far from ideal. He also probably realized that there will always be people outside the academy who will be concerned for one reason or other about what is going on in the semi-cloistral precincts of an institution of higher learning and research.

Plato's Academy, and its students and teachers, belonged to the real world, and Plato must have given considerable thought to the actual and possible interactions between his scholars and the puppeteers and prisoners whom they were being trained to liberate. For reform-minded intellectuals of later periods, the vulnerability of the academy and the academic scholar was all the more obvious, for by their time the academy already had a long institutional history, which included problems arising from its past interactions with various political, ecclesiastical, and commercial institutions.

Cultural critics today, while still sustained in large measure by much of the traditional philosophy and cultural apparatus of the academy, have had good reason to worry. There is cause for concern about the ways in which the academy has been corrupted, about ways in which it can be further corrupted, and about its declining prospects as a ground for personal and communal cultural development. But no serious cultural critic would dismiss outright the role of the academy in a strategy for combatting inauthentic culture. Whatever its failings and limitations, the academy still represents one of the domains in which the cultural reformer can best do constructive work. Still, for the scholar today, the idea of "returning to the cave" carries with it many more concrete associations than it did in Plato's day.

We have yet to see any society accept the necessity of philosophical leadership, though occasionally an academic or even an intellectual with a philosophical bent attains a position of high political influence (and without necessarily having to throw away all her moral principles). Moreover, even in advanced societies, it is rarely clear when the time is right for the academic intellectual to return to the cave and enter directly into political processes. Academic cultural critics are now rarely willing to wait for the "right" moment; more and more feel obliged to become involved immediately in some way in cave life. Even when premature, such involvement has often been beneficial, especially for victims of inauthentic culture who have benefited directly from the work done for them by activist scholars.

But the academic intellectual who is not careful enough in carrying out his liberating tasks is a threat to communal development on several levels. He may harm those whom he wishes to help, he may make all intellectuals look worse, and in moving back and forth between the academy and the cave he may infect the academy with the corruptive values and attitudes of "worldly" types. Still, the academy is a force for cultural reform in ways that Plato could not have imagined. In providing liberal education to large numbers of people who go on to positions of influence in many different fields, in obtaining and disseminating useful information derived from a wide range of empirical sciences, in promoting a broad range of cognitive skills and methods, and in serving as a forum for constructive debate and creative reflection, the academy has carried on the war against inauthentic culture on fronts that Plato could not have envisioned.

In considering the relevance of Plato's proposals for dealing with inauthentic culture, we find that almost all involve education on some level. In the first book of the *Republic*, Plato shows how philosophical analysis can increase a person's awareness of what cultural products he has already appropriated, particularly in the way of ideas, attitudes, and values. Philosophical analysis can also provide the individual with tools for assessing the cultural products that he has previously "accepted" largely unconsciously, and even with some idea of alternative products available to him. In his treatment of Thrasymachus's theory of justice, Plato shows further how philosophical analysis can help one to understand the motives of promoters of cultural products. Such "consciousness raising" is as valuable now as it was in Plato's time.

In chapter 1, we took note of Vance Packard's remark: "We cannot be too seriously manipulated if we know what is going on."[52] The kind of manipulability that concerns us in this study is based largely on ignorance. Knowing "what is going on" will not in itself make one free, for one may still be subject to determining factors, including brute force and psychological compulsion. But such knowledge is always contributive to freedom. We should take responsibility for that aspect of our manipulability over which we have control, especially because of the dangers involved in leaving it to experts or authorities to determine when we are being manipulated. Oliver Thomson suggests: "The answer to worries about manipulation by any group, commercial or otherwise, is not to censor them, but to make audiences more aware that various groups are trying to manipulate them, how they do it, why and when."[53] This is generally true, though censorship may sometimes be a necessary evil, and, in any case, people do not ordinarily have a right to expect others to inform them when they are being manipulated. But the critic of inauthentic culture should still begin, as Plato did, by "consciousness raising."

THE RESTORATION OF CRAFTSMANSHIP

Plato's observations on craftsmanship are also as valuable today as they were in his time. In assessing cultural products, we should consider the extent to which they have been created and promoted by people who properly consider themselves "craftsmen" – that is, individuals who have a cultivated ability to serve their fellows with the products that they put before them. Many people tend to be permissive in response to the venality, indifference, callousness, and indolence of some who profess to be craftsmen, professionals, and skilled labourers. This permissiveness has contributed to the decline of standards in such diverse fields as teaching, medicine, fine art, and religious ministry, just to mention fields with which Plato himself was familiar.

The very term *craftsmanship* now seems rather dated, not only because many cultural products are mass produced but because people rarely deal directly with a carpenter, potter, or weaver but instead deal through merchants, sales personnel, and advertisers. We tend to speak more now of "tradesmen" than "craftsmen," with the emphasis shifted away from the creative to the commercial dimension. Even such terms as *profession* and *vocation* have increasingly become associated more with "making a living" than "performing a service."

It is generally not much easier now than in Plato's day to see through the phoney "teacher," "healer," or "statesman." Sometimes it is obvious to most people that a certain individual is a sophist, quack, crook, charlatan, or imposter, but most cases call for closer scrutiny. Craftsmanship in fact is something of an ideal and virtue to be realized as much as possible through dedication and discipline. Questions may appropriately arise as to what constitutes craftsmanship in a particular situation, just as they do about courage or temperance in certain circumstances. We are not being fair or reasonable when we expect too much of people, but it is also a mistake to expect too little. When we suspect that a cultural product is highly inauthentic, that is often a reliable sign that the creator or promoter has not done her job in accordance with a suitably high standard of craftsmanship.

People sometimes remember with pride and a sense of accomplishment how they "told off" their lazy dentist, blackened the reputation of the repairman who cheated them, or worked hard in a political campaign to establish the unworthiness of a crooked incumbent. Fair and reasonable criticism is instructive both to the chastised craftsman and to observers, and it can strengthen people's resolve to stand up not only for their own rights but for those of their fellows. However, if the actual standard of craftsmanship in most fields is indeed declining, as is widely suspected, that itself suggests that most of us are still too timid.

It is one thing to stand up to a dentist and another to stand up to the dental profession; and it is one thing to speak out against a crooked politician and a rather different thing to fight against a corrupt political system. Though effective measures are possible even when responding to large-scale, institutionalized contempt for the ideal of craftsmanship, we cannot take on the whole world, and we must avoid expecting too much of ourselves or our fellow critics. But most of us can do much more than we have done to counter our society's declining standard of craftsmanship and professionalism.

Most important, it is very much within the typical individual's power to work in accordance with a higher standard of craftsmanship than that which she has followed in the past. This is a crucial point. The critics considered above are at least indirectly appealing to the reader herself not to participate in the creation and promotion of inauthentic products. They never criticize the reader directly – they do not know the typical reader personally, they have nothing to gain from offending the reader, and they have some reason to believe that anyone who would read a book or article advocating cultural reform must already be somewhat high-minded. Even so, they are still encouraging the reader to work as hard as she can to avoid joining the ranks of the operators, schemers, and irresponsible, undisciplined craftsmen. They want to help the reader to avoid being manipulated, but they are also reminding her that she should always be mindful of her own integrity and responsibility.

This may be especially true of Plato, who ends Book IX of the *Republic* by observing that it is the establishment of an ideal constitution in one's own soul that must be one's foremost concern. The republic that interests Plato most is the republic of the soul, and he had introduced political theory into the *Republic* as a way of clarifying personal morality. Plato understands that neither he nor his reader can single-handedly reverse corruptive cultural tendencies. But he believes that most people can make some contribution towards dealing with the problem. And further, the starting-point is establishing for oneself a high standard of craftsmanship conducive to the creation and promotion of superior cultural products in one's field of work. One thereby not only increases the amount of authentic culture in one's society but provides a sound example or role model for other people, some of whom may be deeply impressed by the manifestation of excellence and social interest. Again, it behoves one to praise a high standard of craftsmanship whenever possible, particularly when one finds it manifested in cultural products put forward by people with whom one has direct personal contact. Criticism of inauthentic culture ordinarily becomes offensively self-righteous when it is not accompanied by a sincere willingness to appreciate and praise highly authentic culture and to honour the craftsmanship of those who have shared it with their fellows.

Though Plato associates craftsmanship with professionalism, it is consistent with the spirit of his analysis to regard it as proper for people to bring something akin to craftsmanship to the non-vocational, non-professional ways in which they share cultural products. When, for example, a parent, friend, or well-meaning neighbour proffers an ostensibly meliorative cultural product for our appropriation, it hardly seems fair to hold such a person to the same standard of responsibility as we hold a professional. If a lower standard is deemed suitable, it is mainly because we believe that a strong personal relationship, one that involves sympathetic concern far deeper than that to be expected from a stranger, more than compensates for the would-be benefactor's limitations in competence. Nevertheless, we must not assume that love or good will by itself equips a person with all she needs in order to provide meliorative cultural products to those in whose welfare she has a special interest.

Given the complexity of human judgment and human relationships, we should not even assume that the cultural products put forward for our appropriation by those closest to us are entirely authentic. Plato understood this well; indeed he thought it best to have children of the Guardian class taken away from their parents at birth and brought up by professionals. While few people today would go along with the scheme recommended in the *Republic*, in modern Western democracies, children are usually sent off at an early age to be educated by competent professional teachers. While advanced societies still allow parents considerable authority over their children, they indicate in various ways that parents who wish to maintain such authority must give evidence of a certain degree of concern, competence, and responsibility. In general, even when producers and promoters of cultural products are not acting in some professional capacity, they are still expected to work towards the realization of an ideal akin to craftsmanship.

It is useful for us to pause every so often to consider how much craftsmanship or professionalism we ourselves are currently bringing to our work and to assess our actual personal standard of craftsmanship in relation to both our ideal of craftsmanship in our field and what we perceive to be the conventional standard. Whatever our evaluations, we shall probably be moved to take certain obligations somewhat more seriously than we have been accustomed to taking them. Empathetic projection is especially useful in this regard; we usually attain valuable insights when we ask ourselves whether our actual standard of craftsmanship is comparable to that which we would like to see observed by the craftsmen and professionals in other fields with whom we have to deal. People who regularly complain about the callousness and indifference of teachers, physicians, lawyers, and producers of consumer goods rarely reach anything close to the high standard of craftsmanship that Plato held up and personally observed.

The critic of inauthentic culture is being hypocritical when she fails to acknowledge the profound limitations of her own actual personal standard of craftsmanship; and the disposition of people to such hypocrisy greatly limits the effectiveness of criticism of inauthentic culture. Consider how easy it was for their detractors to dismiss the cultural criticism of such imperfect human beings as Erasmus, Voltaire, Nietzsche, Veblen, and Bloom. Humility and the capacity for sound self-criticism are great assets to the cultural reformer. He should not allow undue humility to take away his critical voice, but he should avoid self-righteousness as much as possible, should work harder than he expects others to work at maintaining a high personal standard of craftsmanship, and should clearly distinguish his own actual standard of craftsmanship from his ideal of perfect craftsmanship.

MAKING DEMOCRACY WORK

The contemporary relevance of most of Plato's more specific proposals for cultural reform should be fairly obvious; and to some great extent his advice has been heeded, which is one reason why so many societies are advanced as they are. The value of sound primary education was recognized long before Plato's time, but Plato has provided a paradigmatically clear and impressive statement of the relevant themes, particularly with respect to moral education. However, in an age of sophisticated educational theory, supported extensively by knowledge obtained through behavioural and social-scientific research, most educators understand much more than Plato did about the conditions and methods of a sound system of basic education. Educational options are now so much more numerous than they were in Plato's time – or Plato's imagination – that his concrete proposals are as dated in detail as they are commendable in spirit.

Plato's defence of a simple life unencumbered by phoney, corruptive luxuries has found a modern counterpart in the combined appeals of environmentalists, promoters of health and fitness, and critics of conspicuous consumption and other forms of rampant consumer materialism. Perhaps especially notable is the relevance of Plato's warning about unnecessary dependence on medical and legal professionals. Cultural critics should not undervalue his observation that people need to be constantly reminded of their obligation to look after the condition of their bodies and their souls so that they will not need to rely as much as they do on the costly services put forward for their appropriation by physicians, jurists, and others.

Plato's attacks on egalitarianism and democracy pose a more serious challenge. Even those of us who have not personally experienced the evils of totalitarianism have sufficient familiarity with the history of political oppression to be disinclined to adopt elitist attitudes of the kind promoted by Plato. We have seen how absolute power can corrupt even the most high-minded political leaders, and we have seen how difficult it can be for benevolent types to understand the needs and interests of those whom they sincerely aspire to look after. While most of us can appreciate some of Plato's specific

complaints about egalitarianism and democracy, we have persuaded ourselves that democracy generally is, despite its faults, the least of various
constitutional evils realistically available to a community. Plato himself recognized that democracy is greatly superior to tyranny, and we may thus
assume that he would have been sympathetic to our inclination to tolerate
the former in order to avoid the latter. The best that we can do now is to
work towards minimizing the destructive consequences of those aspects of
democracy and egalitarianism that have consistently troubled idealistic political theorists since Plato's time – specifically, those related to the arbitrary and
irrational rule of a "mob" vulnerable to manipulation by self-serving elites
gifted in the arts of public relations.

The cultural reformer must tread lightly here. She cannot afford to ignore
the civil liberties of which Plato could not conceive, much less understand
or appreciate. She is wiser in this regard to follow the example of Spinoza,
who could lament, in the manner of his great ancient predecessor: "The
fickle disposition of the masses drives anyone who experiences it to despair,
for they are governed not by reason but only by their passions."[54] Yet he was
still able to conclude that democracy is the best and most natural form of
government,[55] and he affirmed the paramountcy of freedom of thought and
speech.[56]

But when one has concluded that democracy is the best and most natural
form of government, one is even more obliged than Plato was to consider
carefully the methods by which the general public can be politically educated. Plato assumed that if philosophers were the leaders of the state, they
would be in a position to provide such instruction. But how is political
education of the general public possible when so much power is already
concentrated in its hands and few people appreciate the wisdom that a
learned person has to offer them?

The general public is not much more inclined in modern Western democracies to accept the leadership of intellectuals than it was in Plato's day.
Perhaps that is a good thing, for the academic-political machinations of
many leading intellectuals in their own small community leads one to
wonder whether they would be any better leaders than the sort of people
typically entrusted with high office by the Great Sophist. Still, the Great
Sophist is wiser now than it was in Plato's day, and in recent years it has
generally expected its leaders to be "well educated." Sometimes the masses
still take a fancy to a charismatic crackpot, but usually there is a preference
for bright, fairly reasonable, university-educated types.

Politicians are still often manipulative, and some are extremely corrupt,
but they have not received their education solely from sophists. The influence

of the academy on them should not be taken lightly; most of them have read great books, engaged in serious discussions of moral and political problems, reflected on the deeper meaning of the religious faith of their ancestors, and even been exposed to the ideas, attitudes, and intellectual methods of Plato and other philosophers. Plato would be impressed, though he would have seen the survival of manipulative exploitation and other forms of corruption as evidence both of the inadequacy of much of the academic training offered to future leaders and of the price to be paid for admitting into the academy people who do not belong there and cannot properly benefit from what it has to offer.

However, Plato also mistakenly believed that if bright, promising people were properly educated, they would eventually, in coming to see the "Forms," agree on all fundamental moral and political issues. Had he been able to gaze into the future, he would have had to acknowledge that even the best, brightest, and wisest cannot agree on all those fundamental issues. He would obviously look with favour on those who now regard themselves as heirs to the classical humanistic tradition, but he would see that even among his "disciples" there are profound disagreements. The academy does not turn out clones of Plato, and, as the case of Aristotle shows, it did not do so even in Plato's time. A sound philosophical and liberal education encourages and helps people to be appropriately independent-minded. Thus those "returning to the cave" do not share precisely the same idea of what liberation involves, and such would-be liberators are engaged in a competition of their own. The prisoners in the cave world of modern life are offered a bewildering variety of "paths to liberation," and it is thus even harder for them to distinguish the true liberators from the imposters. These are matters that people such as Voltaire, Veblen, and Bloom have understood better than Plato.

Nevertheless, those who would play the role of liberator can still benefit from Plato's advice. They should seek the wisdom necessary for leadership, allow their eyes to become accustomed to the darkness of the cave, and find the right words for communicating with those whom they wish to help. They should offer enlightenment in stages appropriate to the student's level of advancement, be prepared to make personal sacrifices, counter the influence of operators and deceivers, and proceed in accordance with a high personal standard of craftsmanship and public service. In their endeavour to bring about a just state, they would also do well to remember Plato's observation that when a fragile democracy is undermined, the result is ordinarily worse – tyranny or despotism. Indeed they should consider the emphasis that Plato places on the improvement of individuals.

Again, they should realize that direct political involvement, though not to be ruled out in principle, is risky on several planes and is only one option available to an intellectual cultural reformer. In any case, when one fulfils one's responsibility to "descend again among the prisoners in the den, and partake of their labours and honours, whether they are worth having or not,"[57] one must not forget what one has learned about "what the several images are, and what they represent, because you have seen the beautiful and just and good in their truth."[58] The cultural reformer must always bear in mind that she is committed to the values of a higher life and to making those values known to others.

RELIGIO-CULTURAL REVIVAL?

How much importance should a cultural critic and reformer attach to the religious dimension of the classical philosophical response to inauthentic culture? Much will inevitably depend on one's personal world-view. Given their background, temperament, and cast of mind, it was natural for Augustine, Erasmus, Temple, and Dawson to be impressed by the religious aspect of Plato's attack on the subverters of culture. In the eyes of a Voltaire or Nietzsche, in contrast, Plato's conservative religious piety, and the metaphysical theory that it in part inspired, constitute the core weakness in his cultural critique.

Plato's interest in "political religion" is most evident in the *Laws*, with its religious authoritarianism, theological arguments, and invocation of "God the measure." But the *Laws* has generally not interested philosophers of culture as much as the *Republic*, and Plato's approach to religion and culture is subtler in the earlier and more famous dialogue. Plato's critical-traditionalist approach in the *Republic* to the relation of religion to culture manifests itself in several ways. When Plato has Adeimantus request in Book II that Socrates explain how justice benefits a person without referring to the justice supposedly dispensed by the gods, Plato is drawing our attention to, among other things, the dangers inherent in relying unreflectively on traditional theological explanations and appeals in formulating one's world-view. It is Plato the rational moralist who has Adeimantus speak these remarkable words: "But what if there are no gods? or, suppose them to have no care of human things – why in either case should we mind about concealment? And even if there are gods, and they do care about us, yet we know of them only from tradition and the genealogies of the poets; and these are the very persons who say that they may be influenced and turned by 'sacrifices and soothing entreaties and by offerings.'"[59] Yet while Plato has Socrates comply with Adeimantus's request on one level, his general outlook can hardly be regarded as agnostic.

In his outline of the primary education suitable for future Guardians, Plato appears thoroughly sincere in acknowledging the continuing value and profundity of what he takes to be the fundamental conceptions underlying the traditional religious world-view of the people among whom he lives. He respects many aspects of traditional religious faith and practice and, like Aristophanes, is deeply troubled by the radicalism of certain sophistic critics. But as a rationalist and a *critical* traditionalist, he feels it necessary to attack certain features of the theologian-poets' portrait of the gods. That portrait, he believes, needs to be corrected not only because it gives people flawed role models to follow but because reason reveals to us that it is false and unsound. We are intellectually as well as practically obliged to associate the higher order exclusively with goodness.

In chapter 4, we took note of the complex amalgam of traditionalist, radical, practical, and intellectualist elements in Plato's religious vision; and we saw that even though Plato appreciated the role of religion in promoting and protecting personal and social morality and the authenticity of cultural products, his own religion was not merely "pragmatic." He realized that the cultural reformer must work with the pre- and quasi-philosophical theological and ethical material provided by his society. But mindful of certain of its weaknesses, Plato took it on himself to refine, extend, and elevate traditional religious conceptions and to combine them with both rational philosophical considerations and insights derived from Orphic teaching. We may recall here Despland's remark: "Plato is a great philosopher because he ventures, openly, into the management of the inauthentic. He tries to find a *modus vivendi* between philosophy and public religion."[60]

Plato's concerns are partly political, but they are more generally cultural, and, as a philosopher of culture, he cannot entirely avoid considering religious phenomena with respect to their own distinctive nature. Impressed by religious conceptions as such, and particularly those of Orphism, Plato does some of his managing by synthesizing. Just as he brings together Athenian and Spartan ideals in his political philosophy, he joins Olympic and Orphic conceptions in his religious philosophy. But he goes beyond synthesizing, and, in the sun analogy and elsewhere, he gives evidence of his capacity for mystical religious insight of a highly personal kind. At these places in Plato's writings, philosophy itself goes beyond reasoning and argumentation, and readers find themselves confronted with a higher form of philosophy that complements the higher form of religion to which the author has been drawn.

Reflective religious commitment is both a highly personal, existential matter and something substantially influenced by cultural factors. Even if one wanted to see things in precisely the way that Plato did, an act of the will would probably not be enough to bring one's thoughts in line with his. Reviewing the cultural analyses considered in chapters 5 and 6, we see that it is the personal modes of orienting themselves towards traditional religious ideas, attitudes, and practices that more than anything else distinguish these versions of the traditional criticism. Moreover, while Plato was aware of the danger involved in relying unreflectively on traditional theology, the philosophical cultural critic today has more and deeper reasons to worry about excessive reliance on religion. She probably knows vastly more about religion than Plato did. She knows about various religions, about their history, and about evils perpetrated by their professed adherents. She has probably considered religion from depth-psychological, behavioural-scientific, and social-scientific perspectives, and she is regularly reminded of the many different varieties of religious experience, belief, and communal participation.

Yet again Plato's situation was not so different from that of today's critic, who also must work with the religious inheritance of one or more communities, which is more complex and has deeper roots than that with which Plato had to deal. With all the lessons he has learned from the Enlightenment and modern behavioural and social-scientific investigations of religion, the philosopher of culture will obviously have a more sophisticated understanding of religion than even the wisest of the ancients. But he may be no less impressed than Plato, Augustine, or Erasmus was by the power of religion as a force in personal and communal life. He can see that even those who regard themselves as working against traditional forms of religion cannot entirely avoid living off the conceptual, ethical, and emotional capital of communal religious inheritance. Such writers as Dawson and Eliot overstate this point, but the cases of Voltaire and Nietzsche are instructive. And the positivistic materialist who dismisses religion as corruptive primitive superstition almost invariably has a hard time convincing most of his fellows that he himself has purely scientific reasons for holding on to the lofty spiritual precepts and attitudes of his ancestors.

In electing to work whole-heartedly with the religious inheritance of his fellows, Plato was not merely being cowardly or uncritical. He well knew that his own personal religion and that of Socrates were vastly different from the popular religion of less reflective men and women. But he also understood that authentic Athenian culture was grounded in traditional religious conceptions, and he realized that little was to be gained by dismissing traditional religion outright as an obstacle to philosophy and cultural reform. Though he could not accept popular religion whole, he treated it as something worthy of respect, and he worked towards purifying it and bringing it together harmoniously with philosophical and Orphic conceptions.

Today's critic too should at least make an honest effort to "take religion seriously." He should not pretend to believe what he does not, and he should not teach others to believe what he does not. But the critic of inauthentic culture may well have an obligation to work towards appreciating the importance of religion. Not only is it a rich, complex form of human experience and culture, but it is also a traditional conceptual ground for culture and an especially powerful incentive to the production and promotion of authentic cultural products. It is wholly appropriate for the philosopher of culture to draw the attention of his fellows to the historical development and continuing importance of religion as a "given" in culture and to the need for people to consider their attitudes towards religion in relation to those that they bring to their appropriation and promotion of cultural products. If she concludes after serious reflection that she cannot, as Plato, Augustine, or Erasmus did, work whole-heartedly with communal religious inheritance as it manifests itself in popular religion, then she should at least recognize, with Nietzsche, that her repudiation of the ideal of a religiously grounded culture may carry with it the obligation to provide an alternative incentive to the promotion of authentic culture.

Though his views on the relation of religion to culture were not purely pragmatic, Plato was highly appreciative of the social utility of religion. He recognized its value as a source of communal unity, an incentive to virtue, and a restraint on emotions and appetites that might otherwise lead individuals to deal unjustly with their fellows. Plato understood how religion itself can become inauthentic, and he indicated clearly that religious piety is not entirely an adequate substitute for rational, reflective morality. But he also realized that the philosophical liberation of the prisoners in the cave would inevitably be a very slow process and that some people in the cave could never be philosophically liberated.

Thus he was in a good position to appreciate the useful role of high-minded, socially constructive religious teaching, which is ordinarily accessible to the general public in a way that recondite philosophical speculation and disciplined, sustained ratiocination are not. Plato could well have agreed with a modern philosopher of culture such as Berdyaev that religion is the only possible "meeting-place of the masses with the aristocratic cultural class."[61] Plato seems to have been sincere in his contention that philosophy and religion are not rivals but complementary forces in personal and cultural development. But again, his attitude towards religion and its relation to culture was never purely pragmatic. He clearly believed that sound religious teaching brings people much closer than they would otherwise be to the highest moral and metaphysical truths. When faced with what he took to be the limitations of argumentation and dialectic, he gracefully moved to a mode of discourse that is as much religious as philosophical.

The religious dimension of Plato's philosophy of culture is perhaps most pronounced in some of his discussions of the soul. As a philosophical writer, Plato aims at getting his readers to see certain important matters in a somewhat new and instructive light. He is not presenting empirical data but rather suggesting what he considers to be a better way of understanding certain important matters. His talk about the soul provides us with a certain way of understanding human existence and personality; his model enables some readers to consider human effort in relation to a higher order and by doing so imparts to human effort a certain meaningfulness or significance for them that it might otherwise not have.

Plato's ideas about the soul are vulnerable to rational criticism; but once we consider them as instructions for understanding matters that cannot be resolved by ordinary empirical inquiry, it gradually becomes apparent that we are moving into the domain of faith and existential commitment.[62] One can interpret Plato's talk about the soul in a variety of ways; and one can pick and choose what in his model one finds believable, insightful, or useful. But in any case, if one thinks about human effort and the creation, promotion, and appropriation of cultural products in the context of even a vaguely Platonic conception of the relation of human existence to higher realities and eternal truths, then one is apt to regard the materialistic beliefs and values of promoters of inauthentic culture as shallow, empty, or unsound. So it is with religious world-views in general. If, for example, one can believe in some way that human beings have been created in the image of God, then even though one's theological and anthropological ideas may be rather vague and undefined, one will probably be much less inclined to take lightly the matter of sharing cultural products with others than one would be if one conceived oneself as essentially a material object determined to "action" by forces wholly beyond one's control.

When Plato says at *Republic* 427b–c that the ordering of the "greatest and noblest and chiefest things of all" – religious institutions and rites – should be left to the established religious authorities, not to philosophical Guardians, he may be exhibiting prudence; he could hardly forget the fate of Socrates, who had been convicted of impiety. But if we are prepared to be generous in our interpretation, then we may believe him when he says: "These are matters of which we are ignorant ourselves." In insisting that traditional religious institutions and practices, unlike ordinary secular ones, are not to be left in the hands of either the philosophical rationalist or the purely practical-minded social reformer, Plato almost seems to have a modern insight into the need for "separating" religious and secular authority.[63]

But as his comments here and in the *Laws* show, he did not have sufficient experience, understanding, or imagination to appreciate the dangers of religious repression and the positive value of religious liberty and religious pluralism. Reactionary religionists are following Plato when they insist that the need for communal unity takes precedence over the need for religious liberty, individuality, and creativity. Still, Plato did not believe that the communal return to traditional religion was in itself the key to doing away with inauthentic culture. As a defender of Socrates, a critic of inauthentic religion, a refiner of traditional religious conceptions, and an independent-minded religious visionary, Plato was also a forerunner of modern advocates of religious liberty and religious liberalism. Even Voltaire, who despised Plato's metaphysics, could see that.

Though the contemporary critic may believe that there would be a substantial decline in inauthentic culture if her fellows embraced her particular religious creed, values, and ways, she should also be able to see that repressive religious authority inevitably promotes inauthentic culture on a large scale. Authentic religious culture, and all that grows out of it, is possible only when there is communal respect for the need for sincerity in religious and ideological commitment. There cannot be authentic culture without the kind of personal authenticity involved in existential commitment.[64] Thus, in promoting religion as an incentive for authentic culture, the cultural reformer must focus more on promoting serious commitment as such than on narrower, more conventional forms of religious proselytizing. She must be able to see beyond whatever wisdom is inherent in her own personal faith so as to be able to recognize the value of faith itself.

That faith may in some cases be religious in only an attenuated sense, and perhaps some secular forms of faith are capable of sustaining respect for cultural authenticity. But for historical, psychological, and anthropological reasons that we have yet to grasp entirely, ideological commitments that approach the status of secular faiths, such as the more earnest forms of positivism, Marxism, and psychoanalysis, do not seem to satisfy the spiritual needs of very many people, despite their trenchant criticism of the inauthenticity of traditional religion. Most of the major existential philosophers have been religious thinkers and vigorous promoters of religious commitment, though this fact has been obscured somewhat by the tendency of most journalists and even many scholars to associate "existentialism" primarily with Nietzsche, Sartre, and Heidegger.

The monotheistic faith that has been so dominant in advanced Western societies is an incentive to cultural authenticity in more than one way. When the products associated with it have themselves been largely kept free of inauthenticity, it can elevate and inspire people. Of course, if one believes that God as Judge is closely observing cultural processes, that in itself will have a tremendous influence on one's mode of participation in cultural processes – one will be concerned with the kinds of participation that can contribute to one's chances of attaining some form of "salvation." But the philosophical or social-scientific student of religion is only scratching the surface when he thinks of religious commitment primarily in relation to rewards and punishments.

More important in the long run is the true believer's respect for the role model represented by God as a dedicated, able, compassionate Creator and Sustainer, who takes unremitting sympathetic interest in creatures endowed with capacities for aspiration, reflection, creativity, and compassion. The rewards and punishments that such a Being could dispense matter less than the meaningfulness that such a Being imparts to cultural products and processes by situating them within a cosmic context that, though not entirely comprehensible to mortals, enables them to see beyond the "success" to be derived from the ability to exploit one's fellows with cultural rubbish.

All the traditional philosophical critics of inauthentic culture whom we considered in chapters 5 and 6 sensed the value of religion in this regard. None, except possibly Augustine, was religious in a conventional sense, and most remained troubled about certain implications of religious commitment. Yet all were able to see religion, when it approaches some purer or more authentic form, as carrying human beings beyond the emotions and appetites that make them susceptible to inauthentic culture. Though few if any were able to rise to the religious-metaphysical vision of a Plato, they all at least suggested important connections between the growth of inauthentic culture and the growth of shallow secularist, materialist attitudes. The vagueness or ambiguity that marks their approaches to religion is a result of their contempt for inauthentic religion, of an existential commitment that was inevitably mixed with doubt and reservation,[65] and of the continuing development of their personal world-views.

It is, in any case, important to appreciate the distance between the philosophical moralist's understanding of the practical cultural value of religion and that of the narrower, less reflective, self-justifying religious apologist.

Even such humanist-pragmatist philosophers as William James and F.C.S. Schiller have seen religious commitment as more than merely a psychotherapeutic and socially efficacious orientation to experience.[66] These pragmatist philosophers were much influenced by Kant, whose approach to the moral and cultural role of religion is not nearly as apologetical or pragmatic as it might initially appear:

We can easily see now that all worthiness is a matter of moral conduct, because this constitutes the condition of everything else (which belongs to one's state) in the concept of the highest good, i.e., participation in happiness. From this there follows that one must never consider morals itself as a doctrine of happiness, i.e., as an instruction in how to acquire happiness. For morals has to do only with the rational condition (*conditio sine qua non*) of happiness and not with means of achieving it. But when morals (which imposes only duties instead of providing rules for selfish wishes) is completely expounded, and a moral wish has been awakened to promote the highest good (to bring the kingdom of God to us), which is a wish based on law and one to which no selfish mind could have aspired, and when for the sake of this wish the step to religion has been taken – then only can ethics be called a doctrine of happiness, because the *hope* for it first arises with religion.[67]

The philosophical cultural critic cannot reasonably be expected to take lightly the inauthenticity of so many products associated with religion. On the contrary, she is obliged to take it very seriously and to work wholeheartedly to counter it. The cultural reformer's defence of religion may well begin with her ability to uncover the corruptions of traditional religion. Charles Hartshorne goes too far when he argues: "The divine attributes are abstract types of social relationship,"[68] but the critic of inauthentic culture would do well to reflect on these suggestions of Hartshorne's:

Man cannot live without ideal aims which relate his endeavor and his suffering and his joy to something more lasting and more unitary than the sum of individual human achievements taken merely at face value. Without such an aim, he falls into cynicism or despair, by which the will to live is indefinitely nullified. The conduct of affairs cannot long remain in the hands of persons thus weakened. History seems so far entirely on the side of the doctrine that when the gods go the half-gods arrive. There is never a vacuum of religious power … If human reason seems to discredit known religious forms, what ensues is not a sober rational appraisal of merely human factors accepted as such. What ensues is Lenin worship, party worship, state worship, self-worship, despair, sensuality, or some other vagary. The proper reaction to this apparent fact is not necessarily the advocacy of a "return to religion," meaning by that to a religion whose deficiencies were the very reason why men of the highest integrity and wisdom felt dissatisfied with it, and which is deeply entangled in vested interests. What we need is to make a renewed attempt to worship the objective God, not our forefathers' doctrines about him.[69]

Still, there are some who may qualify as people "of the highest integrity and wisdom" who cannot see their way to regarding religion as such as itself more than an immense vagary, and perhaps even the foremost vagary, the most destructive, and the principal source of most others. Such people, armed with social science and secular philosophy and ideology, can still participate in substantial measure in the "traditional" program of cultural reform by exposing manipulative exploitation, promoting the ideal of craftsmanship, and so forth. Whether or not such philosophical cultural critics as Marx, Sartre, and Marcuse can reasonably be regarded as people of the highest integrity and wisdom, they have made significant contributions to philosophical criticism of inauthentic culture. Many of their theories deserve a more respectful hearing than even some of the most reflective and open-minded religious thinkers have been prepared to give them. In some ways, the task that these earnest thinkers have set for themselves is harder than that at which "traditional" philosophical critics have worked.

Even so, promoting respect for a refined form of religious commitment is not an easy task, especially in a society so much influenced by commercial television programming, scientific public relations, widespread academic indifference or hostility towards religion, and the like, in addition to the ever-present evidences of inauthentic religion and the Great Sophist's persistent resentment of anything approximating a prophetic voice. And precisely what kind of respect for religion is to be promoted? And for what kind of religion? Today's critics are not more likely to agree on these perplexing matters than were the representatives of the tradition considered in chapters 5 and 6. When we consider even the significantly different attitudes of the early, middle, and later Plato, we may be struck by the apparent futility of attempting to get these high matters "right" once and for all.

CONSERVING A CULTURAL INHERITANCE

Philosophical and other humanistic critics of inauthentic culture are constantly vulnerable to forms of discouragement and despair that threaten to develop into paralysing cynicism. There are times when they must worry about whether they are little more than arrogant, petulant cranks. Though they may take some pride in their alienation, they probably cannot help occasionally looking with envy on those who are not troubled by the things that bother them, people who have made peace with their fellows and come to terms with the "way of the world." Criticizing one's fellows can be satisfying in its own way, but it can offend people whom it is very imprudent to offend, and it can hurt people whom one never meant to hurt.

People are often quite tolerant and sometimes appreciative of our criticism of others, but when we criticize *them*, they are just as often resentful and angry. Sometimes they are genuinely puzzled as to why we are "coming down" on them, especially when the world is populated by so many people demonstrably more callous, malevolent, and destructive than they are. Even when we do not criticize them directly, they may feel that we are excessively negative in our appraisals and that we are inclined to be self-righteous, severe, or at least unrealistic in our expectations. One who attacks his community and its culture, or a substantial part of it, is apt to strike many observers as especially arrogant, particularly in so far as he is at least implicitly critical of most people for taking corruptive forces and injustices too lightly.

But the philosophical cultural critics whose views concern us in this inquiry were not merely cranks, and, however strong sometimes their sense of alienation and their resentment and despair, they were not for long reduced to paralysing cynicism. They carried on with their broad intellectual and practical mission in the deeply felt belief that the lessons that they taught were meliorative cultural products that could improve the lives of their students and readers and could even help to elevate the quality of the culture of one or more communities. Though hypercritical, they were able to appreciate many authentic cultural products and the dignity and integrity of those who produce them. They were not, for the most part, given to concentrating on such specific social problems as poverty and racism, or one or two specific types of inauthentic culture, but they rightly believed that what they had to say about inauthentic culture is relevant to all other social problems and to all types of inauthentic cultural products.

Led by temperament, vocation, and conviction to take a wide view of things, they approached the human condition and the state of civilization from a wide perspective, a philosophical one. If they were disinclined to move closer to the level of the concrete and to get their hands dirty by involving themselves more directly and more frequently in the politics, social work, and agitation immediately relevant to the plight of concrete flesh-and-blood human beings, they nevertheless provided encouragement and support to those actively involved in social reform on that level. Some of them could reflect with satisfaction on the fruits of their labours; all were aware that to some extent they had been successful in getting their message out. They all believed, rightly, that the influence of their teaching and writing would continue after they had departed from this world, and whatever success they have had in this regard should be an encouragement to today's humanistic cultural critics and reformers.

While their cultural criticism is generally clearer and more impressive than their actual suggestions for cultural reform, it would be unfair to dismiss them as "mere critics." Their proposals, though vague and in places dangerous or unsound, carry along with them lofty spiritual conceptions of human and social potentiality that are admirable in their own right. Their cultural criticism can itself be seen to have been animated by their confidence that improvement of individuals, societies, and humanity as a whole is not only possible and worthy of vigorous, disciplined promotion but already well represented by great achievements to which they have whole-heartedly and helpfully drawn our attention. However flawed, their own cultural products merit being considered alongside of such achievements.

Though most of them considered it important for intellectuals eventually to learn how to speak to the Great Sophist, they themselves generally addressed a more specific audience. Their academic lectures and philosophical tomes and tracts were designed for the consumption of at least moderately educated, moderately reflective individuals, people who have already undergone some degree of philosophical liberation. Taking a wider view than the political revolutionary, the social worker, and the charitable doer of good deeds – all of whom most of them could genuinely respect and sincerely praise – they focused on education, the most crucial of all cultural processes, and they sought mainly to provide insight and encouragement to fellow and potential educators. They realized that philosophical liberation is ordinarily slower and less dramatic than other processes of cultural reform, and they knew that it could take years, perhaps generations, before their wisdom would begin to filter down to those still staring at the cave wall.

Though they could probably appreciate the impatience of those reformers more concerned with the here and now, and with the immediate needs of those oppressed in the here and now, they chose, as Socrates did, to go where they thought they could do the most good for their fellows. They too could be impatient at times, particularly with their fellow intellectuals; and sometimes their philosophical judgment was distorted as a result of their impatience. No human being is simply a philosopher; even the calm, deliberate Spinoza at least once in his life was so enraged by the senseless murder of good people that he went out in the streets to confront the irrational mob, but he managed to pull himself together in time. The philosophical liberator is rarely worldly enough to be a man or woman of "action"; when he tries, he usually bungles the job. But in appraising the work of our critics, we can afford to be fairly generous and to emphasize the good that they accomplished rather than the good that their personality and outlook prevented them from doing.

With that in mind, contemporary humanists and cultural theorists should also take care not to anticipate too much of themselves. It is unreasonable for them to expect themselves or their fellow humanists to carry the entire burden of solving the urgent social problems of the here and now. Similarly, it is unreasonable for them to believe that they and their fellows can solve once and for all the kind of philosophical problem that has taxed the understanding, imagination, and optimism of thinkers from Plato's time to our own. Even simply as educators, academics, and their counterparts in religious, political, artistic, and other institutions, they can do only so much and no more in the struggle against something such as cultural corruption. If they do not do as much as they could, they may still be more admirable in this regard than those who do much less. Indeed, it is not to the credit of Plato, Erasmus, and company that they could not properly appreciate the efforts and accomplishments of so many of their less brilliant, less dynamic co-workers in the cause of cultural reform; and in promiscuous attacks on so many of their fellow educators, such modern cultural critics as Nietzsche and Bloom extend an ignoble tradition or, rather, the ignoble dimension of what is generally a noble tradition.

Little is to be gained by excoriating, ridiculing, or browbeating the well-meaning, honest, hard-working academics, teachers, clerics, artists, and others who quietly and unobtrusively labour to elevate the quality of communal culture and to enrich the lives of those for whom they practise their craft. Such people are surely in need of further enlightenment – for who is not? – but they should be encouraged rather than discouraged, and whatever contributions they have made should be gratefully acknowledged. They are the front-line troops in the war against inauthenticity and kindred cultural corruptions, and whoever dismisses them as ignorant, worthless functionaries is no true liberator. The philosopher of culture practises his craft when he serves these people, when he helps them to see better or to recollect what they once knew. That is his most important role in the world of the cave, and if he does not perform it, he has not fulfilled his obligation to such people, or to those who liberated him, or to society.

Responsibility is at the heart of authenticity, both with respect to human beings and to the cultural products that they share. The philosopher of culture is no less obliged than others to put forward for the appropriation of his fellows authentic, meliorative cultural products that help them to be better and better off. Whether or not he is willing to engage in vigorous cultural criticism, the philosopher of culture can help those whom he seeks to serve by showing or reminding them that the realm of culture, as a realm of human products, has a great deal to do with responsibility. Culture is now so regularly associated by social scientists and even many humanists with determinism and relativism that it is easy to ignore or forget the fact that culture is not simply a "given" but something that human beings of more or less intelligence, creativity, imagination, compassion, and responsibility produce, promote, and appropriate in countless ways. It is proper to bestow praise on some of it, to bestow blame on some of it, and to bestow neither praise nor blame on some of it.[70]

Those who are troubled by the phoney quality of much of the culture put forward for their appropriation can, if they have reached a level of intellectual development at which traditional philosophical inquiry is accessible to them, benefit in various ways from a close consideration of traditional philosophical criticism of inauthentic culture. The relevant insights of such thinkers as Plato, Erasmus, Nietzsche, and Veblen can help them to understand better what it is that bothers them about a certain kind of cultural corruption, which in fact is not as new as they might suspect, and can suggest to them ways in which the destructive influences of such corruption can be countered and minimized. Moreover, since those who participate in the struggle against such cultural corruption are vulnerable to forms of discouragement and despair that can grow into a paralysing cynicism, it is important for them to know that, when they feel impelled to speak out against inauthentic culture, they are not merely deluded cranks but heirs to a long and honourable tradition, which has contributed much to the survival and advancement of civilization and the dignity and meaningfulness of human existence. They can then more fully appreciate the importance of their endeavour and their responsibility to take advantage of their personal influence on students, readers, friends, and associates to promote, by word and example, respect for the authentic culture that reflects the authenticity involved in personal commitment to truth, reality, and goodness, and to one's fellows, parents, teachers, ancestors, and divinities.

The cultural analysis that they share with others itself becomes part of a developing culture and civilization that will continue to enrich the lives of those who come after them. As Cassirer observes, "What the individual feels, wills, and thinks does not remain enclosed within himself; it is objectified in his work. These works of language, poetry, plastic art, and religion, become the 'monuments', the symbols, of recognition and remembrance of human kind. They are 'more lasting than bronze'; for within them there remains not only something material; in addition, they are the manifestation of a spirit – manifestation which can be freed from its material covering and awakened to new power whenever a sympathetic and sensitive soul encounters it."[71]

NOTES

ONE: A SOCIAL AND PHILOSOPHICAL PROBLEM

1 Cf. Alan Trachtenberg, "Foreword," to Miles Orvell, *The Real Thing: Imitation and Authenticity in American Culture, 1880–1940* (Chapel Hill: University of North Carolina Press, 1989), ix.

2 John Wild, *Plato's Theory of Man: An Introduction to the Realistic Philosophy of Culture* (Cambridge, Mass.: Harvard University Press, 1948), 6.

3 Robert Wuthnow, James Davison Hunter, Albert Bergesen, and Edith Kurzweil, *Cultural Analysis: The Work of Peter L. Berger, Mary Douglas, Michel Foucault, and Jürgen Habermas* (Boston, Mass.: Routledge and Kegan Paul, 1984), 7.

4 Cf., for example, F.R. Cowell, *Culture in Private and Public Life* (London: Thames and Hudson, 1959), 3; David Kaplan and Robert A. Manners, *Culture Theory* (Englewood Cliffs, NJ: Prentice-Hall, 1972), 3; *A Working Definition of Culture for the Canadian Commission for UNESCO* (Ottawa: Canadian Commission for UNESCO, 1976), 4.

5 A.L. Kroeber and Clyde Kluckhohn (with Wayne Untereiner and appendices by Alfred G. Meyer), *Culture: A Critical Review of Concepts and Definitions*, first pub. 1952 (New York: Vintage Books, 1963), 291.

6 Bronislaw Malinowski, *A Scientific Theory of Culture, and Other Essays* (Chapel Hill: University of North Carolina Press, 1944), 43.

7 Matthew Arnold, *Culture and Anarchy* (London: Thomas Nelson, 1869), 74.

8 Christopher Lasch, *The Culture of Narcissism: American Life in an Age of Diminishing Expectations* (New York: W.W. Norton, 1978), 58–9.

9 Ibid., 13.

10 Henri Peyre, *Literature and Sincerity* (New Haven, Conn.: Yale University Press, 1963), 339–40.

11 F.G. Bailey, *Humbuggery and Manipulation: The Art of Leadership* (Ithaca, NY: Cornell University Press, 1988), 3.

12 Marshall McLuhan, *The Mechanical Bride: Folklore of Industrial Man*, first pub. 1951 (Boston, Mass.: Beacon Press, 1967), v.

13 Ibid., vi.

14 Vance Packard, *The Hidden Persuaders* (New York: David McKay, 1957), 3.

15 Ibid.

16 Ibid., 4.

17 Herbert I. Schiller, *The Mind Managers* (Boston, Mass.: Beacon Press, 1973), 4.

18 Ibid.

19 Ibid., 29.

20 Arnold Itwaru, *Mass Communication and Mass Deception* (Toronto: Terebi, 1989), 60.

21 Packard, *Hidden Persuaders*, 265.

22 C. Wright Mills, *The Power Elite* (New York: Oxford University Press, 1956), 350.

23 Arthur Asa Berger, *Television as an Instrument of Terror: Essays on Media, Popular Culture, and Everyday Life* (New Brunswick, NJ: Transaction Books, 1981), 91.

24 Paul Blumberg, *The Predatory Society: Deception in the American Marketplace* (New York: Oxford University Press, 1989), 199.

25 Ibid., 205.

26 Ibid.

27 Ibid., 212.

28 Ibid.

29 Cf. Hyman E. Goldin, ed. in chief, *Dictionary of American Underworld Lingo* (London: Constable, 1950).

30 Nicolas Berdyaev, *The Fate of Man in the Modern World*, trans. Donald A. Lowrie, first pub. 1935 (Ann Arbor: University of Michigan Press, 1963), 25.

31 Ibid., 26.

32 Albert Camus, "The Myth of Sisyphus" (1942), in *The Myth of Sisyphus and Other Essays*, trans. Justin O'Brien (New York: Vintage Books, 1955), 11.

33 Thorstein Veblen, *The Theory of the Leisure Class* (1899), chap. 6.

34 Cf., for example, R.G. Collingwood, *The Idea of History* (Oxford: Clarendon Press, 1946), 213–14.

35 Cf., for example, R.G. Collingwood, *The Principles of Art* (Oxford: Clarendon Press, 1938), 139–44.

36 Cf. Patricia F. Sanborn, *Existentialism* (New York: Pegasus, 1968), 124–8.

37 Søren Kierkegaard, *The Present Age* (1846), trans. Alexander Dru (New York: Harper and Row, 1962), 35. This volume also includes a translation of Kierkegaard's *Of the Difference between a Genius and an Apostle*.

38 Herbert Marcuse, *An Essay on Liberation* (Boston, Mass.: Beacon Press, 1969), 6.

TWO: SOME RELEVANT ASPECTS OF CULTURE

1 David L. Hall, *The Civilization of Experience: A Whiteheadian Theory of Culture* (New York: Fordham University Press, 1973), 72.
2 Ernest Klein, *A Comprehensive Etymological Dictionary of the English Language* (Amsterdam: Elsevier, 1971).
3 Giles Gunn, *The Culture of Criticism and the Criticism of Culture* (New York: Oxford University Press, 1987), 6.
4 Ibid., 8.
5 A.L. Kroeber and Clyde Kluckhohn with Wayne Untereiner and appendices by Alfred G. Meyer, *Culture: A Critical Review of Concepts and Definitions*, first pub. 1952 (New York: Vintage Books, 1963), 3–4.
6 Ibid., 66–7.
7 Ibid., 54.
8 Ibid., 67.
9 Ibid., 283.
10 Ibid.
11 Ibid., 67.
12 Ibid., 60.
13 Werner Jaeger, *Paideia: The Ideals of Greek Culture*, trans. 1939 from the 2nd German ed. by Gilbert Highet, 2nd English ed., with notes (New York: Oxford University Press, 1947), I, xviii.
14 Ibid., xvii.
15 Ibid., p. 416–17, n.5.
16 Ibid., xvii.
17 Ibid.
18 Cf. Gunn, *Culture of Criticism*, 8–12.
19 John Walker, *A Critical Pronouncing Dictionary* (1791).
20 F.R. Cowell, *Culture in Private and Public Life* (London: Thames and Hudson, 1959), 105.
21 B.S. Sanyal, *Culture: An Introduction* (New York: Asia Publishing House, 1962), 44.
22 T.S. Eliot, *Notes towards the Definition of Culture* (London: Faber and Faber, 1948), 120.
23 Ibid., 27.
24 C.A. Van Peursen, *The Strategy of Culture* (Amsterdam: North-Holland Publishing Company, 1974), 8.
25 Ibid., 10.
26 David Kaplan and Robert A. Manners, *Culture Theory* (Englewood Cliffs, NJ: Prentice-Hall, 1972), 3.
27 Conrad M. Arensberg and Arthur H. Niehoff, *Introducing Social Change* (Chicago: Aldine, 1964), 15.

28 Ibid., 25.

29 Kroeber and Kluckhohn, *Culture*, 284.

30 Edward B. Tylor, *Primitive Culture: Researches into the Development of Mythology, Philosophy, Religion, Art, and Custom* (London: John Murray, 1871), I, 1.

31 Ina Corinne Brown, *Understanding Other Cultures* (Englewood Cliffs, NJ: Prentice-Hall, 1963), 3.

32 Ibid., 4.

33 Bronislaw Malinowski, *A Scientific Theory of Culture, and Other Essays* (Chapel Hill: University of North Carolina Press, 1944), 3.

34 Ibid., 48.

35 *A Working Definition of Culture for the Canadian Commission for UNESCO* (Ottawa: Canadian Commission for UNESCO, 1976), 3.

36 Ibid., 4.

37 Ibid., 6.

38 Kroeber and Kluckhohn, *Culture*, 60.

39 Eliot, *Notes*, 31.

40 Herbert J. Gans, *Popular Culture and High Culture* (New York: Basic Books, 1974), 3.

41 Ibid., 10.

42 Ibid., 19.

43 John Brenkman, *Culture and Domination* (Ithaca, NY: Cornell University Press, 1987), viii.

44 Nicolas Berdyaev, *The Fate of Man in the Modern World*, first pub. 1935, trans. Donald A. Lowrie (Ann Arbor: University of Michigan Press, 1963), 71–4.

45 José Ortega y Gasset, *The Revolt of the Masses (La Rebelión de las Masas)*, first pub. 1930 (Notre Dame, Ind.: University of Notre Dame Press, 1985).

46 Johan Huizinga, *Homo Ludens*, first pub. 1938, trans. from the German ed. (Boston, Mass.: Beacon Press, 1955), 205.

47 Karl Mannheim, *Man and Society in an Age of Reconstruction*, first pub. 1935, trans. Edward Shils (London: Routledge and Kegan Paul, 1960), 84–5.

48 Ibid., 95–6.

49 See note 29 above.

50 Ernst Cassirer, *The Logic of the Humanities*, trans. Clarence Smith Howe (New Haven: Yale University Press, 1961), chap. 3.

51 Ernst Mayr, *The Growth of Biological Thought: Diversity, Evolution, and Inheritance* (Cambridge, Mass.: Belknap Press of Harvard University Press, 1982), 622.

52 Ibid., 622–3.

53 Aristotle, *Metaphysics*, 1013a–1015a.

54 Cf. Aristotle, *De Anima*, Book I.

55 Cf. G.B. Kerferd, *The Sophistic Movement* (Cambridge: Cambridge University Press, 1981), chap. 10.

56 Cassirer, *Logic*, 157–8.

57 Leslie A. White, *The Science of Culture: A Study of Men and Civilization* (New York: Farrar, Straus and Cudahy, 1949), 15–16.

58 B.F. Skinner, *Beyond Freedom and Dignity* (New York: Alfred A. Knopf, 1971), chap. 3.

59 Hans Vaihinger, *The Philosophy of "As if"*, first pub. 1911, trans. from the 6th German ed. by C.K. Ogden, (2nd English ed. London: Routledge and Kegan Paul, 1924), 43.

60 Cf. Jay Newman, "The Fictionalist Analysis of Some Moral Concepts," *Metaphilosophy*, 12 (1981), 47–56.

61 Cf. R.G. Collingwood, *The New Leviathan* (Oxford: Clarendon Press, 1942), 176.

62 Ruth Benedict, *Patterns of Culture*, 2nd ed. (Boston, Mass.: Houghton Mifflin, 1934), 2–3.

63 Malinowski, *Scientific Theory*, 46.

64 Eliot, *Notes*, 43.

65 Benedict, *Patterns*, 252–3.

66 Ibid., 253.

67 Ibid.

68 Paul Radin, *Primitive Man as Philosopher*, first pub. 1927, 2nd revised ed. (New York: Dover, 1957).

THREE: THE RELEVANCE OF WHAT IS RELATIVE

1 Edward Westermarck, *Ethical Relativity* (New York: Harcourt, Brace, 1932).

2 William Graham Sumner, *Folkways* (Boston, Mass.: Ginn, 1906).

3 See, for example, Clyde Kluckhohn, "Cultural Relativity: *Sic et Non*," *Journal of Philosophy*, 52 (1955), 663–77.

4 See, for example, Paul W. Taylor, "Social Science and Ethical Relativism," *Journal of Philosophy*, 55 (1958), 32–44.

5 Melville J. Herskovits, *Man and His Works* (New York: Alfred A. Knopf, 1964), 61–78.

6 Ibid., 61.

7 Ibid., 63.

8 Ibid., 65.

9 Ibid., 66.

10 Ibid., 39.

11 Ibid., 17.

12 Ibid., 68.

13 Ibid., 78.

14 Ibid., 75.

15 Ibid., 77.

16 Ibid., 76.

17 David Riesman with Reuel Denney and Nathan Glazer, *The Lonely Crowd: A Study of the Changing American Character* (New Haven, Conn.: Yale University Press, 1950), 3.

18 Karl Mannheim, *Man and Society in an Age of Reconstruction*, first pub. 1935, trans. Edward Shils (London: Routledge and Kegan Paul, 1960), 81.

19 Herskovits, *Man and His Works*, 64.

20 Cf. Jay Newman, *Foundations of Religious Tolerance* (Toronto: University of Toronto Press, 1982), chap. 3.

21 A.L. Kroeber and Clyde Kluckhohn (with Wayne Untereiner and appendices by Alfred G. Meyer), *Culture: A Critical Review of Concepts and Definitions*, first pub. 1952 (New York: Vintage Books, 1963), 319–24.

22 Lionel Trilling, *Sincerity and Authenticity* (Cambridge, Mass.: Harvard University Press, 1972), 1–2.

23 Stephen Fuchs, *The Origin of Man and His Culture* (Bombay: Asia Publishing House, 1963), 277–8.

24 Bronislaw Malinowski, *A Scientific Theory of Culture, and Other Essays* (Chapel Hill: University of North Carolina Press, 1944), 91, 119–31.

25 T.S. Eliot, *Notes towards the Definition of Culture* (London: Faber and Faber, 1948), 19.

26 Westermarck, *Ethical Relativity*, 197.

27 Ibid.

28 Cf. R.G. Collingwood, *The New Leviathan* (Oxford: Clarendon Press, 1942), chap. 35.

29 Herskovits, *Man and His Works*, 17.

30 John Henry Newman, "Barbarism and Civilization" (1853) in "Lectures on the History of the Turks, in Their Relation to Europe," in *Historical Sketches* (London: Longmans, Green, 1908), I, 163.

31 Ibid., 164–5.

32 Ibid., 168.

33 Collingwood, *The New Leviathan*, 281.

34 Ibid., 289.

35 Ibid., 283–4.

36 Ibid., 291.

37 Ibid.

38 Ibid., 294–5.

39 Ibid., 342. Cf. Jay Newman, "Two Theories of Civilization," *Philosophy*, 54 (1979), 473–83.

40 Ibid., 281.

41 Cf. Jay Newman, *Fanatics and Hypocrites* (Buffalo, NY: Prometheus Books, 1986), chap. 3.

42 Ibid., 14.

43 Christopher Dawson, *Enquiries into Religion and Culture* (New York: Sheed and Ward, 1933), 95.

44 Ibid., 97.

45 Christopher Dawson, *Religion and Culture* (New York: Sheed and Ward, 1948), 49.

46 Ibid., 50.

47 Dawson, *Enquiries*, 303.

48 Dawson, *Religion and Culture*, 217.

49 Ibid.

50 Dawson, *Enquiries*, 306–7.

51 Dawson, *Religion and Culture*, 57.

52 Dawson, *Enquiries*, 115.

53 Eliot, *Notes*, 27.

54 Ibid., 28.

55 Ibid., 31.

56 Ibid., 122.

57 Emil Brunner, *Christianity and Civilisation* (London: Nisbet, 1948), I, 10.

58 Ibid., I, 10–11.

59 Ibid., II, 128, 131.

60 Ibid., II, 131.

61 Ibid., I, 2.

62 Paul Tillich, *Theology of Culture*, ed. Robert C. Kimball (New York: Oxford University Press, 1959), 6.

63 Ibid., 8.

64 Ibid., 42.

65 Ibid., 51.

66 Henry R. Van Til, *The Calvinistic Concept of Culture* (Grand Rapids, Mich.: Baker Book House, 1959), 7.

67 Ibid., 34.

68 Ibid., 43–4.

69 J.C. Shairp, *Culture and Religion in Some of Their Relations*, 3rd ed. (Boston, Mass.: Houghton Mifflin, 1872), 28.

70 Ibid., 30.

71 Ibid., 34.

72 Ibid., 169.

73 H. Richard Niebuhr, *Christ and Culture* (New York: Harper and Row, 1951), 40.

74 Nicolas Berdyaev, *The Fate of Man in the Modern World*, first pub. 1935, trans. Donald A. Lowrie (Ann Arbor: University of Michigan Press, 1963), 144.

75 Cf. Jay Newman, *On Religious Freedom* (Ottawa: University of Ottawa Press, 1991), chap. 4.

76 Cf. Newman, *Fanatics and Hypocrites*, chap. 4.

77 Cf. Jay Newman, *Competition in Religious Life* (Waterloo, Ont.: Wilfrid Laurier University Press, for the Canadian Corporation for Studies in Religion, 1989).

78 Cf. Friedrich Nietzsche, *Beyond Good and Evil* (1886), sec. 6.

79 François de La Rochefoucauld, *Maxims* (1665), no. 54.

80 Ibid., no. 20.

81 Ibid., no. 62.

82 Cf. Nietzsche, *Beyond Good and Evil*, sec. 260.

83 Ibid., sec. 222.

84 Ibid., sec. 226.

85 Ibid., sec. 257.

86 Oswald Spengler, *The Decline of the West*, 2 vols., first pub. 1918 and 1922, trans. Charles Francis Atkinson (New York: Alfred A. Knopf, 1966), I, 106.

87 Ibid., 104.

FOUR: PLATO AND THE CLASSICAL ANALYSIS

1 K.R. Popper, *The Open Society and Its Enemies*, vol. I: *The Spell of Plato*, first publ. 1944, 4th ed. rev. (Princeton, NJ: Princeton University Press, 1963), 142, 200. Cf. R.H.S. Crossman, *Plato To-day*, first pub. 1937, rev. ed. (London: George Allen and Unwin, 1959), 190.

2 Popper, *The Open Society*, vol. I, 171.

3 Ibid.

4 Ibid., 198.

5 Plato, *Republic*, 491d. All translations of passages in the *Republic*, unless otherwise indicated, are from *The Dialogues of Plato*, trans. B. Jowett, first pub. 1871, 3rd ed. (London: Oxford University Press, 1892).

6 Ibid., 492b–c.

7 Jay Newman, *The Journalist in Plato's Cave* (Rutherford, NJ: Fairleigh Dickinson University Press, 1989), especially chap. 3.

8 Plato, *Republic*, 516c–d.

9 Cf., for example, James L. Jarrett, "Introduction," to James L. Jarrett, ed., *The Educational Theories of the Sophists* (New York: Teachers College Press, 1969), 33.

10 Cf., for example, *Republic*, 499e–500a.

11 Jacob Burckhardt, *History of Greek Culture* (1898–1902), trans. Palmer Hilty from the 1958 abridged version published by Safari Verlag, Berlin (New York: Frederick Ungar, 1963), 156.

12 Eric A. Havelock, *Preface to Plato* (Cambridge, Mass.: Belknap Press of Harvard University Press, 1963).

13 Havelock, *Preface to Plato*, 4.

14 John Wild, *Plato's Theory of Man: An Introduction to the Realistic Philosophy of Culture* (Cambridge, Mass.: Harvard University Press, 1948), 2.

15 Ibid., 4.

16 Ibid., 35–6. Cf. Plato, *Sophist*.

17 Ibid., p. 36–8. Cf. Plato, *Gorgias* 464c–466a.

18 Ibid., 39.

19 Ibid., 38.

20 Ibid., 57

21 Ibid., 61.

22 Ibid., 273.

23 Ibid., 61–2.

24 Ibid., 276, 284.

25 Ibid., 308. Cf. Plato, *Sophist*.

26 Ibid., 311.

27 Ibid., 43.

28 Cf., for example, Mario Untersteiner, *The Sophists*, trans. Kathleen Freeman (Oxford: Basil Blackwell, 1962); Eugene Dupréel, *Les Sophistes* (Neuchatel: Éditions du Griffon, 1948); G.B. Kerferd, *The Sophistic Movement* (Cambridge: Cambridge University Press, 1981).

29 Alvin W. Gouldner, *Enter Plato: Classical Greece and the Origins of Social Theory* (New York: Basic Books, 1965), 193.

30 Cf., for example, H.D. Rankin, *Sophists, Socratics and Cynics* (London: Croom Helm, 1983), 13.

31 Werner Jaeger, *Paideia: the Ideals of Greek Culture,* first pub. 1939, trans. from the 2nd German ed. by Gilbert Highet, 2nd English ed., with notes (New York: Oxford University Press, 1947), I, 289, 303.

32 Cf., for example, Michel Despland, *The Education of Desire: Plato and the Philosophy of Religion* (Toronto: University of Toronto Press, 1985), 162.

33 Cf. Plato, *Apology*, 18c–d, 19c.

34 Gouldner, *Enter Plato*, 185.

35 Ibid., 184. Cf. Crossman, *Plato To-day*, 42–3.

36 Gouldner, *Enter Plato*, 193.

37 Jaeger, *Paideia*, I, 297. Cf. Plato, *Protagoras*, 313c.

38 Cf., for example, Michael Nill, *Morality and Self-Interest in Protagoras, Antiphon and Democritus* (Leiden: E.J. Brill, 1985), 13–51. Cf. Crossman, *Plato To-day*, 52.

39 Cf. Plato, *Phaedrus*. On Plato's distinction between true and sophistic rhetoric, see, for example, Richard M. Weaver, *The Ethics of Rhetoric* (Chicago: Henry Regnery, 1953), chap. 1; Keith V. Erickson, ed., *Plato: True and Sophistic Rhetoric* (Amsterdam: Rodopi, 1979); and Ronald B. Levinson, *In Defense of Plato* (Cambridge, Mass.: Harvard University Press, 1953), 432–3.

40 William Temple, *Plato and Christianity: Three Lectures* (London: Macmillan, 1916), 4.

41 Eric Voegelin, *Plato* (Baton Rouge: Louisiana State University Press, 1966), 69.

42 Plato, *Apology*, 18c–d, 19c. Cf. Leo Strauss, *Socrates and Aristophanes* (New York: Basic Books, 1966), 5, 311; Gilbert Murray, *Aristophanes: A Study*, first pub. 1933 (New York: Russell and Russell, 1964), 99–100.

43 Plato, *Apology*, 31b–c.

44 Ibid., 19d–e.

45 Ibid., 19d–e, 22e–23b, 33b.

46 Ibid., 32a–33a.

47 Ibid., 31c–32a.

48 Ibid., 31b.

49 Ibid., 37e–38a.

50 Ibid., 23c–24a, 38c–39b.

51 Maurice B. McNamee, *Honor and the Epic Hero: A Study of the Shifting Concept of Magnanimity in Philosophy and Epic Poetry* (New York: Holt, Rinehart and Winston, 1960), 5; Gouldner, *Enter Plato*, 194.

52 Leon Guilhamet, *The Sincere Ideal* (Montreal: McGill-Queen's University Press, 1974), 10–11.

53 Despland, *The Education of Desire*, 116; Popper, *The Open Society*, vol. I, 198.

54 Gouldner, *Enter Plato*, 194; Despland, *The Education of Desire*, 205; Strauss, *Socrates and Aristophanes*, 5.

55 Plato, *Republic*, 434d–445b.

56 Ibid., 520a–d.

57 Cf. Gouldner, *Enter Plato*, 198.

58 Plato, *Theaetetus*, 151d–152c, 161b–179c. Cf. Kerferd, *The Sophistic Movement*, chap. 9.

59 Plato, *Theaetetus*, 172b–177c.

60 Ibid., 161b–162a.

61 Ibid., 165e–168c.

62 Gouldner, *Enter Plato*, 194.

63 Kerferd, *The Sophistic Movement*, 165–8; W.K.C. Guthrie, *The Sophists* (Cambridge: Cambridge University Press, 1971), 234–5. The latter volume was first published as Part I of *A History of Greek Philosophy*, vol. III (Cambridge: Cambridge University Press, 1969).

64 Guthrie, *The Sophists*, 235–47.

65 Plato, *Apology*, 18c, 23b, 23d.

66 Ibid., 41c–d.

67 Popper, *The Open Society*, vol. I, 142.

68 Ibid., 143.

69 Cf., for example, Rankin, *Sophists*, 144–5.

70 Plato, *Laws*, X. Cf. Rankin, *Sophists*, 142–3.

71 Rankin, *Sophists*, 144.

72 Ibid., 145.

73 Ibid., 138.

74 Ibid., 90.

75 Ibid., 80.

76 Ibid., 142.

77 Jaeger, *Paideia*, I, 303.

78 Paul Elmer More, *The Religion of Plato* (Princeton, NJ: Princeton University Press, 1921), vii; Temple, *Plato and Christianity*.

79 Temple, *Plato and Christianity*, 28–9.

80 Ibid., 85.

81 Wild, *Plato's Theory of Man*, 74–5; Despland, *The Education of Desire*, 85, 98, 205–6; Gouldner, *Enter Plato*, 194.

82 James K. Feibleman, *Religious Platonism* (London: George Allen and Unwin, 1959), 17–18, 92.

83 Despland, *The Education of Desire*, 85.

84 Ibid., 98, 99.

85 Ibid., 191.

86 Ibid., 221.

87 Gouldner, *Enter Plato*, 198.

88 Ibid., 194.

89 Plato, *Laws*, 716c.

90 Popper, *The Open Society*, vol. I, 143.

91 Leo Strauss, *The Argument and the Action of Plato's Laws* (Chicago: University of Chicago Press, 1975), 2.

92 Gouldner, *Enter Plato*, 234–76.

93 Havelock, *Preface to Plato*, 263.

FIVE: FOUR STUDIES IN THE TRADITION

1 Cf. Brian Vickers, "Territorial Disputes: Philosophy *versus* Rhetoric," in Brian Vickers, ed., *Rhetoric Revalued* (Binghamton, NY: Center for Medieval and Early Renaissance Studies), 247.

2 Étienne Gilson, *The Christian Philosophy of Saint Augustine*, trans. L.E.M. Lynch (New York: Random House, 1960), 172.

3 Ibid., 174.

4 Ibid.

5 Étienne Gilson, *Reason and Revelation in the Middle Ages* (New York: Charles Scribner's Sons, 1938), 17.

6 Desiderius Erasmus, "The Godly Feast" (*Convivium religiosum*) (1522), in *The Collo-quies of Erasmus*, trans. Craig R. Thompson (Chicago: University of Chicago Press, 1965), 48.

7 Johan Huizinga, *Erasmus and the Age of Reformation* (*Erasmus of Rotterdam*), first pub. 1924, trans. F. Hopman (New York: Harper and Row, 1957), 106.

8 Desiderius Erasmus, *The Praise of Folly* (1509), trans. John Wilson (1668) (Ann Arbor: University of Michigan Press, 1958), 37–8.

9 Geraldine Thompson, *Under Pretext of Praise: Satiric Mode in Erasmus' Fiction* (Toronto: University of Toronto Press, 1973), 162.

10 Arthur E. DuBois, "Humanism and Folly," *Sewanee Review*, 40 (1932), 448–50.

11 James McConica, *Erasmus* (Oxford: Oxford University Press, 1991), 55.

12 Ibid., 83.

13 Walter M. Gordon, *Humanist Play and Belief: The Seriocomic Art of Desiderius Eras-mus* (Toronto: University of Toronto Press, 1990), 76.

14 Preserved Smith, *Erasmus: A Study of His Life, Ideals, and Place in History*, first pub. 1923 (New York: Frederick Ungar, 1962), 336.

15 McConica, *Erasmus*, 55.

16 Paul Oskar Kristeller, *Renaissance Thought and Its Sources*, ed. Michael Mooney (New York: Columbia University Press, 1979), 60.

17 Gordon, *Humanist Play*, 73.

18 Huizinga, *Erasmus*, 109.

19 McConica, *Erasmus*, 55.

20 Smith, *Erasmus*, 117.

21 Erasmus, *The Praise of Folly*, 53.

22 Ibid., 53–4.

23 Ibid., 67–8.

24 Ibid., 68.

25 Ibid., 70.

26 Ibid., 87–98.

27 Ibid., 98.

28 Ibid., 102.

29 Ibid., 112.

30 Ibid., 114.

31 Ibid., 116.

32 Ibid., 117.

33 Ibid., 118–19.

34 Cf. Smith, *Erasmus*, 421–3.

35 Huizinga, *Erasmus*, 190.

36 Erasmus, *The Praise of Folly*, 149.

37 Ibid., 144.

38 Ibid., 145–6.

39 Ibid., 150–1.

40 Cf., for example, Richard S. Dunn, *The Age of Religious Wars: 1559–1689* (New York: W.W. Norton, 1970), chaps. 1–2.

41 Cf. Jay Newman, *On Religious Freedom* (Ottawa: University of Ottawa Press, 1991), 107–10.

42 A. Owen Aldridge, *Voltaire and the Century of Light* (Princeton, NJ: Princeton University Press, 1975), 384.

43 Norman L. Torrey, *The Spirit of Voltaire* (Oxford: Marston Press, 1963), 258.

44 Ibid., 276–7.

45 Peter Gay, *Voltaire's Politics: The Poet as Realist*, first pub. 1959 (New Haven, Conn.: Yale University Press, 1988), 29.

46 Cf. George Brandes, "An Essay on Aristocratic Radicalism" (1889), in *Friedrich Nietzsche*, trans. A.G. Chater (London: William Heinemann, 1914), 33–7, 52–4.

47 Letter of Friedrich Nietzsche to George Brandes, 8 Jan. 1888, trans. A.G. Chater, in Brandes, *Friedrich Nietzsche*, 69.

48 Cf., for example, Walter Kaufmann, *Nietzsche: Philosopher, Psychologist, Antichrist*, first pub. 1950, 3rd ed. (New York: Vintage Books, 1968), 4, 490–1.

49 Friedrich Nietzsche, "David Strauss, the Confessor and Writer," in *Untimely Meditations* (1873).

50 Friedrich Nietzsche, *The Birth of Tragedy* (1871).

51 Letter of Friedrich Nietzsche to George Brandes, 2 Dec. 1887, trans. A.G. Chater, in Brandes, *Friedrich Nietzsche*, 64.

52 Brandes, "An Essay on Aristocratic Radicalism," 6.

53 Ibid., 6–7.

54 Ibid., 7–9.

55 Ibid., 3–4.

56 Cf., for example, Friedrich Nietzsche, *Beyond Good and Evil*, secs. 257–60.

57 William Temple, *Plato and Christianity: Three Lectures* (London: Macmillan, 1916), 59.

58 Friedrich Nietzsche, *The Birth of Tragedy*, secs. 12–20.

59 Cf., for example, Nietzsche, *Beyond Good and Evil*, secs. 14, 190, 191.

60 Friedrich Nietzsche, *The Twilight of the Idols* (1889), trans. Anthony M. Ludovici, vol. XVI of *The Complete Works of Friedrich Nietzsche*, ed. Oscar Levy, 18 vols., first pub. 1909–11 (New York: Russell and Russell, 1964), 114.

61 Friedrich Nietzsche, *The Will to Power* (1901, 1906), sec. 428, trans. Anthony M. Ludovici, vol. XIV of *The Complete Works of Friedrich Nietzsche*, ed. Oscar Levy, 18 vols., first pub. 1909–11 (New York: Russell and Russell, 1964), 348. *The Will to Power* was a posthumous collection of previously unpublished writings. Cf. Kaufmann, *Nietzsche*, 6–8.

62 Nietzsche, *The Will to Power*, sec. 429, p. 348.

63 Frederick Copleston, *Friedrich Nietzsche: Philosopher of Culture* (London: Burns, Oates and Washbourne, 1942), 41.

64 Ibid., 53–8.

65 Ibid., 209.

66 On Heidegger's thesis, see Richard Lowell Howey, *Heidegger and Jaspers on Nietzsche* (The Hague: Martinus Nijhoff, 1973), 55–7; Stanley Rosen, "Remarks on Nietzsche's Platonism," in Tom Darby, Béla Egyed, and Ben Jones, eds., *Nietzsche and the Rhetoric of Nihilism* (Ottawa: Carleton University Press, 1989), 145–63.

67 George Allen Morgan, *What Nietzsche Means*, first pub. 1941 (New York: Harper and Row, 1965), 324–7.

68 Nietzsche, *Beyond Good and Evil*, sec. 250.

69 Ibid., sec. 227.

70 Plato, *Republic*, 419–421c.

71 Ralph Waldo Emerson, "Self-Reliance," in *Essays*, first pub. 1841 (London: Dent; New York: Dutton, 1906), 37.

72 Nietzsche, *Beyond Good and Evil*, sec. 40.

73 Cf. W.H. Walsh, *Metaphysics* (London: Hutchinson, 1963), 34–8.

74 Nietzsche, *Beyond Good and Evil*, sec. 226.

75 Ibid., sec. 260.

76 Ibid., secs. 260–2.

77 Ibid., sec. 61.

78 Helmut Thielicke, *Nihilism*, first pub. 1951, trans. John W. Doberstein (New York: Harper and Row, 1961), 164–6.

79 Morgan, *What Nietzsche Means*, 324.

80 Nietzsche, *Beyond Good and Evil*, sec. 260.

81 Ibid., Pts. VII and IX. Cf. Morgan, *What Nietzsche Means*, chap. 5.

SIX: TWO RECENT STUDIES AND AN OVERVIEW

1 George Soulé, *The Ideas of the Great Economists*, first pub. 1952 (New York: New American Library, 1955), 135.

2 Cf., for example, Thorstein Veblen, "The Socialist Economics of Karl Marx and His Followers" (1906–7), in *The Place of Science in Modern Civilization and Other Essays* (New York: B.W. Huebsch, 1919), 409–56.

3 David Riesman, *Thorstein Veblen: A Critical Interpretation* (New York: Charles Scribner's Sons, 1953), 26.

4 Ibid., chap. 5.

5 The expression is Ernest Manheim's. Cf. Riesman, *Thorstein Veblen*, 26.

6 J.A. Hobson, *Veblen* (New York: John Wiley and Sons, 1937), 12.

7 Soulé, *The Ideas of the Great Economists*, 137.

8 Veblen, *The Theory of the Leisure Class*, first pub. 1899 (New York: New American Library, n.d.), chap. 14.

9 Veblen, *The Theory of the Leisure Class*, 235.

10 Thorstein Veblen, *The Instinct of Workmanship* (New York: Macmillan, 1914), 25–8. Cf. Riesman, *Thorstein Veblen*, 56.

11 Hobson, *Veblen*, 66.

12 Ibid., 9.

13 Riesman, *Thorstein Veblen*, 19, 54.

14 Ibid., 53.

15 Ibid., 19.

16 Ibid., 52.

17 Ibid., 174.

18 Ibid., 74.

19 Ibid., 56.

20 Ibid.

21 Ibid., 57.

22 Ibid., 74.

23 Veblen, *The Theory of the Leisure Class*, chap. 12.

24 Riesman, *Thorstein Veblen*, 66.

25 Thorstein Veblen, "Christian Morals and the Competitive System," in *Essays in Our Changing Order*, ed. Leon Ardzrooni (New York: Viking Press, 1934), 200–18. This article originally appeared in *International Journal of Ethics*, 20 (1910).

26 John P. Diggins, *The Bard of Savagery: Thorstein Veblen and Modern Social Theory* (New York: Seabury, 1978), 136.

27 Ibid., 135–6.

28 Ibid., 135.

29 Cf. Veblen, *The Instinct of Workmanship*, 25.

30 David W. Noble, "The Theology of Thorstein Veblen," in Carlton C. Qualey, ed., *Thorstein Veblen: The Carleton College Veblen Seminar Essays* (New York: Columbia University Press), 72–105.

31 Cf., for example, Walter R. Rauschenbusch, *Christianity and the Social Crisis* (New York: Macmillan 1907); Shailer Mathews, *The Gospel and the Modern Man* (New York: Macmillan, 1912).

32 Theodor Adorno, "Veblen's Attack on Culture," *Studies in Philosophy and Social Science*, 9 (1941), 389–413. Cf. Diggins, *The Bard of Savagery*, 80–1.

33 Hobson, *Veblen*, 36–7.

34 Riesman, *Thorstein Veblen*, 51.

35 Veblen, *The Instinct of Workmanship*, 25.

36 Ibid., 27.

37 Plato, *Theaetetus*, 155d.

38 Riesman, *Thorstein Veblen*, 175–6.

39 Plato, *Republic* 362e–363a.

40 Allan Bloom, *The Closing of the American Mind* (New York: Simon and Schuster, 1987).

41 William A. Galston, "Socratic Reason and Lockean Rights: The Place of the University in a Liberal Democracy," *Interpretation*, 16 (1988), 101.

42 Ibid.

43 Ibid.

44 Ibid., 102.

45 Ibid.

46 Ibid., 103. The numbers refer to pages in Bloom, *The Closing of the American Mind*.

47 Bloom, *The Closing of the American Mind*, 239.

48 Ibid., 60. The passage is cited and discussed in Harry V. Jaffa, "Humanizing Certitudes and Impoverishing Doubts: A Critique of *The Closing of the American Mind* by Allan Bloom," *Interpretation*, 16 (1988), 115–16.

49 Fred Matthews, "The Attack on 'Historicism': Allan Bloom's Indictment of Contemporary American Historical Scholarship," *American Historical Review* 95 (1990), 441.

50 Ibid.

51 Ibid., 442–4.

52 Cf. Alfred Adler, *Understanding Human Nature*, trans. W. Béran Wolfe (New York: Greenberg, 1927), especially Book II, chap. 1–2.

53 Henri Ellenberger, *The Discovery of the Unconscious* (New York: Basic Books, 1970), 525.

54 Sigmund Freud, *Civilization and Its Discontents*, first pub. 1930, trans. James Strachey (New York: W.W. Norton, 1962), 91.

55 Plato, *Republic*, 520e–521a.

56 Ibid., 521b.

SEVEN: CONTEMPORARY APPLICATIONS

1 Cf. Harold A. Innis, *The Bias of Communication* (Toronto: University of Toronto Press, 1951); Marshall McLuhan, *Understanding Media: The Extensions of Man* (New York: New American Library, 1964).

2 Arthur Asa Berger, *Television as an Instrument of Terror: Essays on Media, Popular Culture, and Everyday Life* (New Brunswick, NJ: Transaction Books, 1981), 89.

3 McLuhan, *Understanding Media*, 24–7, 273–4.

4 Ibid., 268–9.

5 Ibid., 286–7.

6 Berger, *Television as an Instrument of Terror*, 110.

7 Ibid., 15.

8 Jerry Mander, *Four Arguments for the Elimination of Television* (New York: Quill, 1978).

9 Ibid., 51.

10 Ibid., 113.

11 Ibid., 155.

12 Ibid., 261.

13 C. Wright Mills, *The Power Elite* (New York: Oxford University Press, 1956), 10.

14 Ibid., 71.

15 Ibid., 356.

16 A parallel analysis of the situation of the journalist is offered in Jay Newman, *The Journalist in Plato's Cave* (Rutherford, NJ: Fairleigh Dickinson University Press, 1989), chap. 3. See also Jay Newman, *Religion vs. Television: Competitors in Cultural Context* (Westport, Conn.: Praeger, 1996), especially chap. 4.

17 Mander, *Four Arguments*, 356.

18 Joyce Nelson, *Sultans of Sleaze: Public Relations and the Media* (Toronto: Between the Lines, 1989), 17–18.

19 Ibid., 19.

20 Edward L. Bernays, *Crystallizing Public Opinion* (New York: Boni and Liveright, 1923), 12.

21 Cf. Karen Halttunen, *Confidence Men and Painted Women: A Study of Middle-class Culture in America, 1830–1870* (New Haven, Conn.: Yale University Press, 1982), 204–10.

22 H. Frazier Moore and Bertrand R. Canfield, *Public Relations: Principles, Cases, and Problems*, first pub. 1952, 7th ed. (Homewood, Ill.: Richard D. Irwin, 1977), 4.

23 Ibid., 14.

24 Ibid.

25 Ibid.

26 Ibid., 15.

27 Irwin Ross, *The Image Merchants: The Fabulous World of Public Relations* (Garden City, NY: Doubleday, 1959), 15.

28 Leonard L. Knott, *The PR in Profit: A Guide to Successful Public Relations in Canada* (Toronto: McClelland and Stewart, 1955), 11.

29 Moore and Canfield, *Public Relations*, 5–6.

30 Ibid., 4–5.

31 Knott, *The PR in Profit*, 20.

32 Laurence Evans, *The Communication Gap: The Ethics and Machinery of Public Relations and Information* (London: Charles Knight, 1973), 15.

33 Bernays, *Crystallizing Public Opinion*, 12.

34 Ibid., 122.

35 Ibid., 212.

36 H. Gordon Lewis, *How to Handle Your Own Public Relations* (Chicago: Nelson-Hall, 1976), 2–3.

37 Ibid., 3.

38 Ibid., 9.

39 Bernays, *Crystallizing Public Opinion*, 173.

40 Ibid., 215.

41 Ibid., 218.

42 Ibid., 86.

43 Oliver Thomson, *Mass Persuasion in History: An Historical Analysis of the Development of Propaganda Techniques* (Edinburgh: Paul Harris, 1977), 6.

44 Evans, *The Communication Gap*, 3.

45 Ross, *The Image Merchants*, 32–3.

46 Kim B. Rotzoll, James E. Haefner, and Charles H. Sandage, *Advertising in Contemporary Society: Perspectives Toward Understanding* (Cincinnati, Ohio: South-Western, 1986), 15–23.

47 Ibid., 137.

48 Ibid., 147.

49 Ibid., 141.

50 Ibid.

51 Plato, *Seventh Letter*, 326b–351e.

52 Vance Packard, *The Hidden Persuaders* (New York: David McKay, 1957), 265.

53 Thomson, *Mass Persuasion in History*, 131.

54 Baruch (Benedict) Spinoza, *A Theologico-Political Treatise* (*Tractatus Theologico-Politicus*) (1670), trans. R.H.M. Elwes, first pub. 1883 (New York: Dover, 1951), 216.

55 Ibid., 205–7.

56 Ibid., chap. 20.

57 Plato, *Republic*, 519d.

58 Ibid., 520c.

59 Ibid., 365d–e.

60 Michel Despland, *The Education of Desire: Plato and the Philosophy of Religion* (Toronto: University of Toronto Press, 1985), 221.

61 Nicolas Berdyaev, *The Fate of Man in the Modern World*, first pub. 1935, trans. Donald A. Lowrie (Ann Arbor: University of Michigan Press, 1963), 114.

62 Cf. Jay Newman, *Fanatics and Hypocrites* (Buffalo, NY: Prometheus Books, 1986), 128–37.

63 Cf. Jay Newman, *On Religious Freedom* (Ottawa: University of Ottawa Press, 1991), 113–23.

64 Cf. Newman, *Fanatics and Hypocrites*, 128–37.

65 Ibid., chap. 2, especially pp. 42–8.

66 Cf. Jay Newman, "The Faith of Pragmatists," *Sophia*, 13 (1974), 1–15.

67 Immanuel Kant, *Critique of Practical Reason* (1788), trans. Lewis White Beck (Indianapolis: Bobbs-Merrill, 1956), 155.

68 Charles Hartshorne, *The Divine Relativity: A Social Conception of God* (New Haven, Conn.: Yale University Press, 1948), 156.

69 Ibid., 148.

70 Cf. Aristotle, *Nicomachean Ethics*, 1109b–1115a.

71 Ernst Cassirer, *The Logic of the Humanities*, trans. Clarence Smith Howe (New Haven, Conn.: Yale University Press, 1961), 215.

INDEX